AMERICA'S FOUNDING
· SON ·

AMERICA'S FOUNDING SON

JOHN QUINCY ADAMS,
from President to Political Maverick

BOB CRAWFORD

Illustrations by Garrett Morlan

zando
NEW YORK

Interior illustrations by Garrett Morlan

zandoprojects.com

First Edition: March 2026

Text design by Neuwirth & Associates, Inc.
Cover design by Christopher Brian King
Cover illustration by Patrick Leger

Library of Congress Control Number: 2025946485

978-1-63893-260-4 (hardcover)
978-1-63893-496-7 (BNSE)
978-1-63893-522-3 (BAMSE)
978-1-6389-326-1 (ebook)

10 9 8 7 6 5 4 3 2 1
Manufactured in the United States of America
LBK

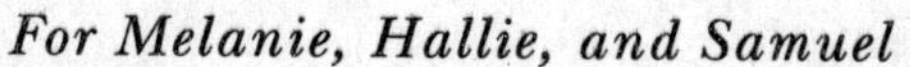

For Melanie, Hallie, and Samuel

CONTENTS

"My good and worthy son . . . All my hopes are in him, both for my family and country."

—JOHN ADAMS

• • •

"This is a cause I am entering at the last stage of my life and with the certainty that I cannot advance in it far; my career must close, leaving the cause at the threshold. To open the way for others is all that I can do. The cause is good and great."

—JOHN QUINCY ADAMS

• • •

"If our fellow citizens *will*, notwithstanding all the expositions that have been given, take to their arms that *Babylonish Harlot*, whose gates, politically and morally speaking, are the ways to hell, and whose embrace will be eventual death, why be the sin and its consequences upon them!"

—BENJAMIN LUNDY

AUTHOR'S NOTE

Sitting at his desk, the aged congressman was caged in by his colleagues' sneers and stares. Enough with his moralizing diatribes. A rule to silence him was no longer good enough. Nothing less than censure—maybe even expulsion—would do. The rules of the House of Representatives had been weaponized against its own members.

But this congressman, this elder statesman, knew their tactics would not work. He knew how to expose their disdain for constitutional government and their antidemocratic thirst for power. Because he knew the Constitution better than they did. He knew the First Amendment was the mustard seed of democracy. Heck, he had spent almost his entire life protecting, upholding, serving, and defending it.

His enemies' views about American governance were not only misguided—they were amoral, the antithesis of the nation's founding principles. The very principles—set down in the founding documents—that his accusers once held sacred.

After multiple attempts to silence the elder statesman failed, Congress charged him with "treason," accusing him of not being a "true American."

The question *Who are the "true Americans"?* threatened the dissolution of the Union. For almost a decade, deep polarization sparked action and reaction on every issue facing the electorate: a declining vision of America, tariffs, an economy on the brink, and, of course, race.

Activists gathered in the streets, town halls, and places of worship. They held rallies, made speeches, and circulated petitions demanding equality and freedom. At every turn, they were met by rowdy, angry mobs led by men of great wealth and power who used threats and violence to preserve the status quo.

The year was 1842.

The aged congressman from Massachusetts was the seventy-five-year-old former president of the United States, John Quincy Adams. Never before—or since—had a former president served in Congress after his term. Now here he was, a former president turned congressman, sitting before the House, on trial for censure. That fact alone is remarkable. But it is the *why* of it all that makes it relevant to us today. John Quincy Adams was on trial for defending the First Amendment right to free speech—and the right of all Americans to be heard, to petition the government for a redress of grievances.

Why did I want to tell the story of John Quincy Adams? Since 2016, I have cohosted a history podcast called *The Road to Now* alongside my good friend Dr. Ben Sawyer. The mission of our program is to try to understand: *How did we get here?*

I'm also not your typical historian. I'm the bassist for the band the Avett Brothers. For the last twenty-plus years, I've studied American history while seeing it up close, traveling up and down interstate highways, freeways, and back roads of this country.

And so when I look around at the current challenges facing America—upheaval, the struggle for racial and gender equality, the pandemic, January 6, inflation, the second election of Donald Trump, tariffs—they all led me to reflect on the years between the Missouri Compromise and the Civil War, and how Adams's story relates to our own time. I've come to understand this critical moment thanks to the great historians, who for more than a century have brought rigor to the study of John Quincy Adams and his era—many of whom I quote in the pages that follow. I've also had access to a wealth of source materials from the period, including John Quincy Adams's personal diaries. While some period language has been adjusted for grammar and clarity, the sentiments ring remarkably true today.

Some say that history repeats; others credit Mark Twain with the phrase *history does not repeat, it rhymes.* I can't say for sure whether history repeats or rhymes, but I do notice echoes from the past in our present. That's because history is driven by people—and people haven't changed since 1776. Truth be told, people haven't changed since Adam and Eve, or however you signify the beginning of time (or should I say, history?). Spend a little time reading about the 1830s and 1840s, and you'll encounter figures who feel eerily familiar. They dressed differently and used different slang, but in a very real sense, we are them and they are us.

John Quincy Adams

INTRODUCTION

Washington, DC, January 1842

From an elevated rostrum on the flat side of the semicircular chamber, beneath a red draped canopy, the Speaker of the House, a Kentuckian named John White, presided over the proceedings as politicians, foreign dignitaries, and members of Washington society watched from the gallery.

The muse of history, Clio, soared above it all, her foot perched on the edge of a winged car, emblazoned with the likeness of the father of the country, George Washington, blowing a horn. The wheel of the chariot: a clock, a wheel of time marking the seemingly endless hours as the consequential events unfolded below it.

John Quincy Adams stood before the bar of the House, accused of high crimes and treason for presenting a petition from forty-six citizens of Haverhill, Massachusetts, who would prefer to dissolve the Union rather than continue to take on the burdensome, peculiar practice of the Southern states, slavery.

Going all the way back to the first session of Congress in 1789, there was nothing unusual about a congressman presenting petitions and memorials before the House on behalf of his constituents. The practice is enshrined in the First Amendment to the Constitution:

Congress shall make no law respecting an establishment of religion or prohibiting the free exercise thereof; or abridging the freedom of speech, or the press; or the right of the people to peaceably assemble, and to petition the government for a redress of grievances.

Before the days of congressional offices, websites, and constituent services, presenting a petition was the only way people lobbied their representatives. But by the middle of the 1830s, Southern congressmen—or as John Quincy Adams referred to them, the slavocracy—grew weary of the flood of antislavery petitions flowing into Congress. These antislavery petitions typically came from Northern states and were sent by a small but pesky group of activists known as abolitionists. Many abolitionists were Christian, and often they were women, who had come to believe that slavery was a sin against God. These petitions so threatened Southern congressmen that, with the help of their Northern allies, they passed a rule in the House of Representatives known as the gag rule. The gag rule stated that

All petitions, memorials, resolutions, propositions, or papers, relating in any way, or to any extent whatsoever, to the subject of slavery or the abolition of slavery, shall, without being either printed or referred, be laid on the table and that no further action whatever shall be taken.

Adams believed slavery was morally reprehensible, but he did not believe the Constitution gave Congress the power to do anything about it in the states where it existed. He also disagreed with the tactics radical abolitionists used to try to bring an end to the practice. He believed the reforms championed by antislavery societies popping up across the North were impractical and unrealistic. "The captious disputations of moral and political casuistry, about non-resistance, defensive war, the rights of women, political action, no Government, the social condition of the colored race, the encouragement given to the slaves to escape from their masters, and exaggerated representations of the miseries of the condition, have eminently concurred not only to counteract their influence upon the main object of their association, but to make them unpopular and even odious, not only in the South, but in all parts of the Union."

However, Adams revered the First Amendment as the cornerstone of the American republic. The gag rule usurped a citizen's freedom of speech—a right endowed to all Americans, abolitionist and enslaver alike. Adams reasoned if freedom of speech could be so easily dismissed in the People's House, then freedom of religion, freedom of the press, and the freedom to peaceably assemble were also in jeopardy.

In the years following May 1836 when the first gag rule was enacted, Adams openly and actively worked to subvert it. He attacked the gag rule by employing an array of procedural tricks, manipulations, and sleights of hand to outsmart, outthink, and outdo his opponents. I like to say that he practiced the art of verbal jujitsu. Year after year, in the face of hisses from the chamber, Adams offered antislavery petition after antislavery petition. But the Haverhill petition was different than the others. It was an escalation in rhetoric coming from the North.

Therefore, it should not have surprised any of his congressional colleagues on Monday, January 25, 1842, when Adams read that petition from forty-six citizens of Haverhill, Massachusetts, who preferred to dissolve the Union rather than let slavery continue. "Because," the petition read, "no union can be agreeable or permanent which does not present the prospects of reciprocal benefits," and "Because a vast proportion of the resources of one section of the Union is annually drained to sustain the views and course of another section without any adequate return." In other words, a house divided against itself cannot stand.

Ignoring calls of "Order, order!" Adams read on. The sound of long and loud gasps hung in the air as Southern congressmen feigned shock and outrage. The pearl-clutching was a ploy. Over the past decade, the slavocracy had issued their own threats of disunion when the occasional challenge to slavery came before the House. For Adams, this was not a slavery issue. It was about freedom of speech. He was no stranger to trials of any kind, and it was not the first time he'd been called before the bar for censure. It had occurred once, a few years before, in 1837. At that time, he'd so enraged his Southern colleagues that they walked out of the chamber and threatened never to return.

Adams had many a Southern nemesis, but for all the fiery wrath that could come from the tongue of antagonists like South Carolina's James Henry Hammond and Waddy Thompson, or Virginia's Henry Wise, nothing cut him as deep as the rejection of the American people themselves. In 1828, after he lost reelection to Andrew Jackson, he confessed to his diary, "The Sun of my political life sets in the deepest gloom—But that of my Country shines unclouded."

In the winter of 1842, Adams had a far gloomier view of American political life. For two weeks over the end of January and into early February, he faced a new Southern prosecutor in the form of Kentucky Congressman Thomas Marshall, a nephew of the late chief justice John Francis Marshall. Adams's actions, the younger Marshall told the assembly, "merit expulsion," but he deemed it "an act of grace and mercy, when they only inflict upon him their severest censure for conduct so utterly unworthy of his past relations to the State, and his present position. This they hereby do for the maintenance of their own purity and dignity; for the rest, they turn him over to his own conscience and the indignation of all true *American* citizens."

The indignation of all true *American* citizens? Who are the *true Americans*? This was as much a partisan attack line in 1842 as it is today—a question meant to divide us, to slice us and dice us into smaller and smaller subgroups, which makes us easier to manipulate. The indignation of all *true Americans*? Did Marshall suggest that John Quincy Adams, a son of John and Abigail Adams, was not a *true American*?

John Quincy Adams might be the truest American. He lived his life in service of his country. Born in 1767, in Braintree, Massachusetts, John Quincy was the second child, and elder son, of John and Abigail. A month shy of his eighth birthday, young John Quincy felt the vibrations of the cannon blast, as his mother took him by the hand, and the two climbed a nearby overlook to watch the Battle of Bunker Hill from the relative safety of Quincy, Massachusetts.

When his father was appointed special envoy to Paris in 1778, he carried eleven-year-old John Quincy with him across the dangerous waters of the Atlantic. Thus began a seven-year journey in which Adams spent his adolescence being educated in the best schools Europe had to offer.

While John Adams was negotiating military support from the French and economic support from the Dutch, and ultimately peace with Great Britain, his son was learning new languages, tasting exotic cuisines, attending the opera with Thomas Jefferson. In 1781, John Quincy spent a year as translator and personal secretary for Francis Dana, the newly appointed US emissary to St. Petersburg.

Upon his return to the United States in 1785 to attend Harvard, the young Adams was already well on the path to an extraordinary life of public service. The founding son's talent for diplomacy even caught the eye of George Washington.

As a struggling young lawyer, Adams published a series of anonymous essays in support of President Washington and his administration's policies. In 1794, in recognition of the young man's understanding of geopolitics and fluency in French and Dutch, Washington appointed John Quincy minister to the Hague. Washington saw in the young man someone with all the abilities to be a great public servant for the new nation, as well as someone who could help renegotiate the repayment of Dutch loans. During his father's administration, John Quincy was appointed to the same post in Prussia.

In 1797, John Quincy married Louisa Catherine Johnson. The two met while Adams was traveling through London on a diplomatic mission. Louisa's father was from Maryland but served as American consul in London. Because Louisa's mother was English, John Quincy's parents were not thrilled about the arrangement. In their minds, how would it look for a future president to have a foreign-born wife?

After his father's loss to Thomas Jefferson in 1800, the elder Adams recalled his son from his diplomatic post in Berlin to spare him the embarrassment of being fired by his successor. John Quincy returned home to Massachusetts and entered the political fray. He won election to the Massachusetts state senate and in 1803 was appointed to the United States Senate by Massachusetts Federalist Party elders.

A streak of independence that would cut both ways for the rest of his life quickly got him in trouble. Adams refused to toe the party line. When he supported Thomas Jefferson on the issue of the Embargo Act, Adams earned the reputation of being a political maverick and stoked the ire of the Federalist Party. Though his days in the Senate were numbered, his career was just getting started.

President James Madison appointed Adams as the first US minister to Russia and the head of the commission to negotiate the Treaty of Ghent, a peace agreement ending the War of 1812. The group included Henry Clay of Kentucky and began a relationship that would forever tie the two men together in the history books—some might say in infamy.

By the time of James Monroe's election in 1816, John Quincy Adams had long established his diplomatic bona fides. Monroe appointed Adams secretary of state, a position in which John Quincy Adams excelled. As America's top diplomat, he focused on realizing the dream of a democratic nation that would one day stretch from coast to coast. He negotiated the Adams-Onís Treaty, which ceded Florida to the United States and assumed Spain's claims to Oregon Country. But Adams's greatest diplomatic achievement does not bear his name. He was the main architect of the Monroe Doctrine, which declared to Great Britain and Europe that the United States would no longer tolerate colonization or interference of any kind in the American hemisphere.

The presidency of James Monroe has been branded the Era of Good Feelings, a period of momentary calm from the partisan strife of the Adams, Jefferson, and Madison years. Sometimes, however, good branding is, well, just branding. In February 1819, New York Representative James Tallmadge Jr. introduced an amendment to the admission of Missouri to the Union that would bar the introduction of slaves to the state. Missouri Territory had long been occupied by Southerners who emigrated with their human property. The Tallmadge Amendment called forth memories of sectional wounds from the Constitutional Convention that had never healed.

The Three-Fifths Compromise awarded Southern states extra representation for the people they had enslaved, counting each a fraction of a person and therefore increasing the political power of those who claimed ownership of them. William H. Freehling points out the South's extra representation in Congress was just enough to seal Thomas Jefferson's victory over John Quincy's father in the election of 1800 and ensured a dynastic supremacy of slaveholding presidents from Virginia for thirty-two of the nation's first thirty-six years.

James Tallmadge ripped off the Band-Aid of compromise to reveal the scar of the original sin of slavery. John Quincy watched the congressional debates over the Missouri controversy from his office at the State Department. Publicly, he kept his own counsel. Privately, to his diary, he confessed the evil at the root of slavery. While he supported the Missouri Compromise that Speaker of the House Henry Clay shepherded through Congress, John Quincy Adams could not help but see civil war on the horizon.

This is where our story begins. This is the story of how John Quincy Adams, privately and publicly, struggled with the issue of slavery. From diary confessions about the need for an "Angel upon Earth" to arise and smite the slave power, "one man . . . with a Genius capable of comprehending, a heart capable of supporting and an utterance capable of communicating those eternal truths . . . to lay bare in all its nakedness that outrage upon the goodness of God, human Slavery," to the realization, a decade later, that it was he who had been called to that duty.

Since he was a teenager, Adams had been saddled with the burden of public service by his parents. By 1824, with the nation on the verge of a generational shift, winds of change blew away the shroud of inevitability that *he* would be the president of the nation his parents had dedicated their lives to founding. Of the five previous secretaries of state, three became president. But by the time it was Adams's turn, the national mood had shifted. America, fresh out of years of economic recession, found itself in the grip of a populist revolution. By the end of a contentious election that turned most of the members of James Monroe's cabinet against one another, Adams won the presidency, not by the acclimation of his fellow citizens but by the activation of a constitutional fail-safe vote in the House of Representatives. This left him tainted for the rest of his life with the accusation of being part of a corrupt bargain in a stolen election.

In office, Adams put forward an ambitious, forward-looking agenda of government-funded infrastructure, scientific research, a naval academy, and universities. President Adams knew these proposals would be unpopular to much of the country, so in his first annual message he warned Congress not to be "palsied by the will of their constituents." This had a similar effect as calling a sizable portion of the country "a basket of deplorables." John Quincy Adams did not have the common touch like the war hero Andrew Jackson, who easily defeated Adams in 1828.

In between his unsuccessful presidential term and his later career as America's constitutional avenging angel, John Quincy Adams experienced the trials of Job. Two of his three adult sons died, one in a suspected suicide, another of alcoholism. He and Louisa had also previously lost a daughter in infancy while he was serving as minister to Russia during the Madison administration. Following the deaths of her sons, Louisa grew weary of her husband's need for the political battlefield and became increasingly confined to her bedchamber with mysterious illnesses. Time and again, John Quincy persevered by throwing himself into his work.

Which more and more meant working alongside, at times begrudgingly, a group of radical antislavery activists known as abolitionists. Adams was a truth teller and had no trouble condemning abolitionists for their shortsighted agenda, lack of coherent strategy, or downright foolishness. Yet, it was thanks to Adams's efforts, usually at great personal expense, that abolitionists could claim an occasional victory in the 1830s and '40s. It got to the point where antislavery societies around the country issued resolutions to honor Adams one day and scathingly denunciate him the next.

The ice-cold Adams did form a special, almost tender, bond with two men who represented different generations of abolitionists, Benjamin Lundy and Theodore Weld. Lundy, a Quaker by faith and saddler by trade, became convicted in his heart against slavery at the age of twenty-six after witnessing the brutality of the slave coffle marching down the main thoroughfare in Wheeling, Virginia (now West Virginia). In 1819, Lundy traveled to Missouri as debate raged over whether the territory would come into the Union as a free state or a slave state. Failure in Missouri led him to publish an antislavery newspaper called *The Genius of Universal Emancipation* and make multiple trips on foot to Canada and across Mexico, all in service of a promise he made to God to "break one link in the chain of Slavery." It was during his trips to Mexico that Lundy gathered intelligence which he believed pointed to a conspiracy between Texans and Southerners in Congress for the United States to annex the independent Republic of Texas. The acquisition would give the United States enough new territory to carve out multiple slave states whose representation would forever tip federal power in favor of the slavocracy. Adams would use Lundy's intel in his harangues against Texas annexation and slavery on the floor of Congress. These speeches put the Southern annexationists and Martin Van Buren's administration on their back foot and denied annexation of the slave state for another seven years, a feat Adams would not have achieved without Lundy's help.

Connecticut native Theodore Weld came from a long line of congregational ministers. But like many young men of his period, Weld became swept up in the fervor of the Second Great Awakening, a reform-focused religious movement that burned like a wildfire across the Northern states during the first half of the nineteenth century. Devotees rejected the Calvinistic orthodoxy of their forebearers and embraced a more benevolent revivalism that inspired the next generation of abolitionists with the belief that social reform had the power to bring about the kingdom of God on Earth.

Weld was a charismatic and celebrated orator. In that capacity he worked as an agent for the American Anti-Slavery Society and was an architect of the petition campaign in which Adams found himself deeply involved. In the early 1840s, Weld came to Washington to work for a small abolition caucus that had formed on the hill. Weld worked closely alongside Adams during his censure trial. Adams found in Theodore Weld and Benjamin Lundy friendships he had rarely known at any other period in his life. These partnerships were born out of a politically and culturally transformational moment in American history.

The founding generation were all but gone from the scene and with them the republican ideals that formed the basis for the Declaration of Independence. After the revolution, some states had aspired to live up to the idea that "All men are created equal and are endowed by their creator with inalienable rights." In Massachusetts, New York, and New Jersey, to name a few, a postrevolutionary emancipation movement took hold and freedom—though not equality—for some Blacks was written into those state constitutions. For a time, manumission societies had prevailed even in the Southern states of Virginia, North Carolina, and Tennessee, inspiring abolitionists of Benjamin Lundy's generation to focus their energies on the upper South.

With the Missouri question, a great threat loomed. Southern politicians, most notably from South Carolina, where wealthy plantation owners were already cash-strapped by a financial panic, were suspicious of protective tariffs that benefited Northern manufacturers. If it was allowed to persist, Northern antislavery rhetoric would agitate what Adams called their "living machinery" to insurrection. The days of the Southerner who acknowledged the ugliness of slavery like Washington and Jefferson were over. No longer was the practice a necessary evil; it was just necessary. Over the decades of the 1830s and 1840s, Southern intellectuals and theologians would construct an economic and theological philosophy upon which slavery could become a permanent feature of American democracy. Southerners in Congress became convinced that any restriction on slavery would be its undoing. To endure, it must be expanded. And the best opportunity to spread slavery lay south of the Mexican border.

Economic and domestic turmoil further complicated the slavery issue and contributed to simultaneous populist movements. Andrew Jackson's 1828 rise was powered by the common man, a mass of newly enfranchised farmers and tradesmen seeking to seize their own destiny by settling their families on the thousands of empty acres that lay beyond the mountains and the Mississippi.

Once elected, Jackson brandished executive power more forcefully than his predecessors. He fired hundreds of federal employees and installed loyalists in their place. He declared war on the nation's financial structure, the Bank of the United States, calling it a "corrupting monster" that favored merchants and speculators over farmers and laborers. He also threatened to call out the military against a group in South Carolina, which included his sitting vice president, when they sought to "nullify" federal law and refused to collect the tariff at the port of Charleston. Jackson's attack on the nation's banking system and its ultimate breakup contributed to cycles of economic panic in the coming decades and doomed the president's handpicked successor, Martin Van Buren. His penchant for executive overreach inspired the rise of a formidable opposition party, the Whigs, whose coalition included a cast of odd bedfellows.

John Quincy Adams stood in the center of these chaotic times. His struggles over the gag rule and his congressional trial were the opening salvo in the battle for racial justice and freedom of speech. Theodore Weld wrote that it was "the first victory over the slaveholders in a body ever yet achieved since the foundation of the *government.*" Weld may have been a little premature in his prediction of the demise of slavery, but he was correct in his assessment that it was John Quincy Adams who struck the first blow against slave power. This was one of many necessary events that would occur on the very long and bloody road to emancipation.

The skirmishes of the turbulent decades that followed the Missouri Compromise in 1820 were the prequel to the bloody Civil War. What were mostly threats in the 1840s begat unrelenting violence in the 1850s, as when a Southern member of the House of Representatives caned a Massachusetts senator almost to death at his desk, or when a proslavery California congressman shot an immigrant Irish waiter in cold blood at the Willard Hotel.

Perhaps the most incredible thing about Adams's amazing life is that he wrote it all down. As a young man, John Quincy had dreams of being a poet and literary writer. Fate had other plans for the founding son, but that did not stop him from possibly being the most prolific American writer of the nineteenth century. John Quincy Adams recorded the events of nearly every day of his life from the age of twelve until his death at eighty. The diary runs roughly fourteen thousand pages in length. It is a tick-tock, day-by-day, play-by-play account of America's tortured adolescence and a gift to historians.

Adams's real-time analysis of America's transition from republic to an enslaver oligarchy is crucial to our understanding of the period. What is most striking is the prophetic precision with which he predicted how it would all play out in the decades after his passing.

The O.G. political maverick, John Quincy Adams, failed as a president in part because he refused to wield the power political parties use to inspire loyalty and build winning coalitions.

Not only did Adams refuse to fill the roles of government patronage with loyal appointees, but he also did not fire anyone who was working with the opposition if they were good at their job. Former New York City Mayor Philip Hone said upon Adams's death in 1848, "His desire to avoid party influence lost him all the favor of all the parties."

This is the story of how a man with the pedigree of being John Adams's son, and after his own career as a Washington insider, brought the power of thousands of grassroots antislavery activists to bear on the People's House, making straight the path for the next generation—Lincoln's generation—to fulfill the promises embedded in the Declaration of Independence. This is not a cradle-to-grave biography of John Quincy Adams. It is the story of an American politician blessed with a deep insight into the foundational principles of the nation in which he was raised and uncanny foresight into the issue at the center of the American conscience: slavery.

· ACT ONE ·

· 1 ·

THE SLAVE DRIVERS, AS USUAL, BLUSTER AND BULLY . . .

The darkness in the cabin made distinguishing faces a challenge, but that did not stop one man from making conversation with John Quincy Adams. The gentleman, who did not give his name, went on and on about a "plan for sending a Colony of Free People of Colour to Africa." He handed John Quincy a pamphlet and claimed that there were proceedings in Washington on the subject and that he had applied to join the mission.

John Quincy Adams had long struggled with the issue of slavery. Like his parents, he did not believe in owning enslaved people. However, Adams accepted slavery as a reality in America, a political expedience to yield to Southern sentiment for the sake of preserving harmony in the Union. Privately, he found it repulsive. He *preferred* not to think about it at all. The day would come when it was all he would think about.

It had been a hot and breezeless mid-September morning in 1817. John Quincy, Louisa, and their party were en route to Washington, where Adams would accept the appointment of secretary of state in the presidential administration of James Monroe. As their steamship disembarked from New Haven, Connecticut, bound for New York, the couple were packed elbow to elbow alongside close to 150 people. Many were New Yorkers returning from Yale commencement ceremonies. The captain drew lots for the ship's sixty berths. Adams drew three and gave one to his wife and two other traveling companions. The captain offered his own berth to Adams, explaining that he would be too busy to use it. He recognized the son of a United States president and founding father.

Much had changed in the United States since 1809, when President Madison appointed John Quincy minister plenipotentiary to Russia. Another war with Great Britain had come and gone from American shores, leaving behind the burned-out remains of a sacked Capitol and a charred President's House. Teddy Roosevelt would not coin the term *White House* until 1901. However, the United States came out of the war bigger, stronger, and more self-assured. Andrew Jackson's victory at the Battle of New Orleans put an exclamation point on what many considered a second war for independence.

A westward migration commenced. Settlers, many from New England and Northern states, poured into the lands of the old Northwest Ordinance. After the Revolutionary War, the United States gained control of all the lands west of the Appalachian Mountains to the Mississippi River. The Northwest Territory—encompassing present-day Ohio, Indiana, Illinois, Michigan, Wisconsin, and part of Minnesota—was declared free soil under Article 6 of the 1787 Northwest Ordinance, which prohibited slavery and involuntary servitude. This was after Thomas Jefferson's 1784 proposal to ban slavery in all western territories failed by a single vote. But by 1817, the Ordinance's restrictions were proving to not be absolute. Proslavery migrants streamed into Illinois, igniting political tensions that exposed the limits of federal authority and the fragility of antislavery policy in the western lands. The same held true for neighboring Missouri Territory where there were no restrictions at all on slavery in the land acquired by Jefferson in the Louisiana Purchase.

• • •

John Quincy and Louisa arrived in Washington on the afternoon of Saturday, September 20, 1817. It is possible enslaved persons greeted them at the home of Louisa's sister, Carolina, and her new husband, Nathaniel Frye. Unlike the Adamses, Louisa's side of the family had no such aversion to enslaved labor.

Within hours, the acting secretary of state, Richard Rush, came by to welcome the man who was about to take his place. Rush was an old family friend. His father, Dr. Benjamin Rush, served alongside John Adams in the Continental Congress and was a signatory to the Declaration of Independence. In a few weeks, Richard would assume the role of minister to Great Britain. For now, Rush was helping John Quincy get reacclimated to Washington. Much had changed since he left his seat in the Senate almost a decade ago.

Greeted by the strong odor of wet plaster and fresh paint, Adams stepped into the President's House and mused that these necessary improvements were the result of the "British visit in 1814"—a reference to when the British put the torch to the President's House, the Capitol building, and half of the city of Washington during the War of 1812. President Monroe had just moved in, but he was making plans to retreat to his Virginia farm. The old Revolutionary War veteran had concerns that the foul-smelling construction materials may be harmful to his health. The three men had only a general conversation regarding the state of relations between the United States, Great Britain, Spain, and France. Adams spent the remainder of the weekend with family.

Monday morning, John Quincy Adams walked to his office at the Department of State, which then occupied a brick building on Seventeenth Street.

When he arrived, District of Columbia justice of the peace Robert Brent was waiting and administered the oath of office.

Adams sat down at his desk and got right to work. Before him sat piles of unopened mail, much of it high-level correspondence that had been waiting months for his arrival. For every memorandum he sifted through and filed and every letter he replied to, there was a fresh note to take its place. It was an endless river of responsibility, most of which fell on the shoulders of one man. His predecessor, the current president, was neither detail oriented nor organized.

For the first several weeks of his tenure, Adams toiled for hours at his desk. He set up systems for indexing diplomatic and consular correspondence and another for notes received from foreign ministers. During his term in office, Adams reorganized department financial accounts, set up a register of department correspondence, and established a State Department library. All this work was in addition to the massive responsibility of leading high-stakes negotiations with Great Britain, France, and Spain. Regardless of whether it was dealing with Great Britain over issues related to policing the international slave trade in the Atlantic, or reimbursements to Southerners for slave property seized during the War of 1812, the slavery issue was ever present.

On March 12, 1819, the subject of the American Colonization Society (ACS) came up during a cabinet meeting. The proceedings that mysterious fellow traveler discussed aboard the steamship two years earlier had borne fruit in the form of a congressional committee and an act of Congress for a small appropriation of $100,000. The money had been earmarked to buy territory in Africa to emigrate enslaved men and women captured on the high seas in violation of the international slave trade. President Monroe and some of the other Southern members of his cabinet, such as Treasury Secretary and ACS Vice President William H. Crawford from Georgia, wanted a more liberal interpretation of the act to open the proposed colony to all freed Blacks in the United States.

The organization had Southern supporters and friends in high places. The House Speaker, Henry Clay, was one of the society's organizers and would later serve as its president in the 1830s. Thomas Jefferson thought colonization an important first step towards emancipation, while others, such as President Monroe, saw it as a bulwark against slave insurrection.

Adams found the idea of shipping freed Blacks out of the United States impractical. Doubtful colonization could emancipate enough enslaved persons to make a difference, Adams questioned the motives of those involved. He thought the society's members were either weak-minded humanitarians, political opportunists playing both sides of the slavery issue, or slaveholders who believed colonization would increase the value of their own slaves.

President Monroe had personal reasons to support the plan. As the governor of Virginia in 1800, he was a target of the Gabriel Prosser insurrection plot. Monroe had long looked for "suitable measures" to be taken to prevent another such incident. He told his cabinet that shortly after the American Revolution, the Virginia citizens who emancipated their slaves "had introduced a class of very dangerous people, the free blacks, who lived by pilfering, and corrupted the Slaves; and produced such pernicious consequences . . ." Monroe wanted to remove all free Blacks from the state of Virginia. Why stop there? Why not rid the country of all its free people of color?

The American Colonization Society would gain many adherents throughout the country over the next couple of decades. Even Abraham Lincoln supported the organization for a while. For some, the ACS was the obvious, maybe even easy, answer to the slavery question. But those in James Monroe's cabinet and around the country were about to find out, with slavery, there were no obvious or easy answers.

In February 1819, freshman Congressman James Tallmadge Jr. proposed an amendment to the Missouri statehood bill to restrict slavery. Modeled on New York State's recent gradual emancipation bill, which Tallmadge helped craft, the first amendment barred any future slaves from entering the state. The second freed Missouri-born slaves at the age of twenty-five.

For years, Southerners had brought their enslaved property into Missouri Territory. The prevailing opinion had always been that Congress would admit Missouri to the Union as a slave state. Now, as if from out of nowhere, James Tallmadge placed a big fat question mark on the end of Missouri statehood and laid bare a sectional riff that dated all the way back to the Constitutional Convention.

Secretary of State John Quincy Adams kept his opinions to himself. He followed the debates on the issue closely but was not a member of Congress and therefore would not get to vote on Missouri statehood or the Tallmadge amendments.

Adams understood slavery as the fruit of the poisonous tree perpetuated by the Three-Fifths Compromise. The compromise, agreed to during the Constitutional Convention in 1787, sought to balance political power and financial responsibilities between the states of the North and the states of the South. Southern states agreed to pay higher taxes in return for counting three-fifths of their enslaved population for representation in Congress.

In the election of 1800, the apportionment of three-fifths of slaves to the white population in the House of Representatives gave the South just enough leverage in the Electoral College to swing the election. Consequently, the age of John Adams became the age of Thomas Jefferson. A dynasty of Virginia-born, slave-holding presidents, four of the first six, appointed Supreme Court justices and cabinet officials who helped to shape the policy and image of the young nation. Southern domination extended beyond the Virginia dynasty; think of Andrew Jackson's appointment of Roger Taney to replace John Marshall on the Supreme Court. John Tyler's administration's annexation of Texas. James K. Polk's war against Mexico. The Three-Fifths Compromise had given the South outsize influence in the federal government. Soon there would be a name for this powerful syndicate—the slavocracy.

For decades, Northern congressmen blamed Southern political hegemony on the Three-Fifths Compromise. As the prospect of Missouri statehood became inevitable, Northerners realized a new slave state with two slave-state senators and one slave-state congressman would further tip the balance of federal power in favor of Southern interests. Some in the North realized they had to do something to stop the institution of slavery from spilling into the vast undeveloped American territory.

All this was going down during a generational shift. The founding generation with their lofty ideals about republican compromise were ceding the stage to their sons who were high on the democratizing power of the common man.

By 1819, the nation had reached a modicum of equilibrium. There were eleven free states and eleven slave states. Whenever Missouri entered the Union, it would be the first state settled on land west of the Mississippi River. In Missouri Territory, roughly 15 percent of the population were enslaved. What kind of precedent would it set if Congress refused the territory admission on the condition that Missouri became a free state? Did the federal government have the right to dictate such things to a territory? To a state? Besides, with the Northern territory of Maine on a path to admission as a free state, it would seem reasonable to keep sectional balance. For Southerners, admitting Missouri to the Union as anything other than a slave state was nonnegotiable. Tallmadge's amendments were a line in the sand. Whatever happened in Missouri would set a precedent for how the rest of the Louisiana Territory, much of it in the North and the West, would be settled.

Southerners needed the institution of slavery to flourish beyond their own plantations if they were going to continue to have a say in the future direction of America. Southern congressmen argued that by attacking slavery, the amendments were a threat to their economic livelihood.

Supporters of the amendments, like New York Senator Rufus King, admitted the issue at hand was not about emancipation; it was about power and which section of the country held it: "I have no business with Slavery as a social system over blacks . . . I oppose slavery because it bears upon whites great political interests."

After the United States passed a ban on the international slave trade in 1808, it looked as though domestic slavery might also be on a slow road to extinction. The road took a sharp turn after the Napoleonic Wars, when instability in global markets benefited states like Alabama and Mississippi whose climate was well-suited for growing cotton. Plantations flourished with the invention of Eli Whitney's cotton gin, a machine that separated the seeds from the fibers of cotton. Big Cotton needed more hands in the field so it could continue churning out the most valuable crop in the Atlantic world. The hands in demand were bound by chains.

The Missouri question dulled the bipartisan sheen of what had become known as the Era of Good Feelings, a phrase coined by a Boston newspaper on the eve of President James Monroe's visit to the city in July of 1817. What made the visit historic was that it represented a rapprochement between Monroe's Democratic-Republican Party and the Federalists who tossed John Quincy out of the Senate almost a decade before.

At his inauguration, Monroe declared, "Equally gratifying is it to witness the increased harmony of opinion which pervades our Union. Discord does not belong to our system." A swing through the North by a Southern president ripped a page right out of George Washington's playbook. Americans recognized this and had an appreciation for Monroe as the last president from the founding generation. As nostalgic and sentimental as that may have been, the Era of Good Feelings was nothing more than good branding. For James Monroe, appointing the son of the Federalist John Adams to the post—at the time considered the presidential stepping stone—was very on-brand. John Quincy's experience, and his service to the Virginia dynasty, made him an obvious candidate for secretary of state.

The truth is there were plenty of bad vibes going around Monroe's cabinet. The Missouri question only added to the tension. To make matters worse, several cabinet members were already positioning themselves for the knife fight of a succession battle that lay ahead. It was a battle Secretary of State John Quincy Adams detested but could not avoid.

Adams tried to stay above the fray in a cabinet full of drama, packed with slaveholders, and in which half of the cabinet believed that they should be the next president. The secretary of state might as well have been a cast member in a spin-off of television's *Real Housewives* franchise. "These Cabinet Councils open upon me a new Scene and new views of the political world. Here is a play of Passions, Opinions and characters different in many respects from those in which I have been accustomed heretofore to move."

Adams showed little tolerance for the heel of the cabinet, Secretary of the Treasury William H. Crawford. Crawford, an overweight, pink-cheeked, old-school Jeffersonian republican, determined to succeed Monroe at almost any cost. Minister to France and secretary of war under James Madison, in 1816, Crawford lost his first bid for the presidency in the congressional caucus. Monroe won sixty-five votes to Crawford's fifty-four votes. Throughout his tenure in the administration, Crawford actively worked behind the scenes to thwart his boss's agenda.

After a cabinet meeting on January 6, 1818, Adams evaluated his fellow cabinet member: "If I understand the character of my

Colleagues, Crawford's point d'honneur is to differ from me." He noted that Attorney General William Wirt and Secretary of the Navy Benjamin Crowninshield "will always be of the President's opinion." Adams got along well enough with both men, especially Wirt. But it was war secretary John C. Calhoun whom Adams respected the most.

Today, the South Carolinian is remembered as the intellectual heavyweight behind the states' rights ideology that helped lead to the Civil War. But during his time in the Monroe administration, Calhoun was a nationalist like Adams who believed in a strong federal government. Of course, Adams and Calhoun did not agree on every issue, but the two were intellectual equals who shared an open dialogue and mutual respect. Part of the reason the men got along so well was that Calhoun was no stranger to Northern attitudes. He attended Yale and won a seat in Congress at the age of twenty-eight.

A serious man, rail thin, Calhoun had dark hollow eyes that looked like holes in his head, yet people who knew him claimed that they blazed with intensity. I believe a picture of middle-aged John C. Calhoun on your front door in October would be a suitable addition to any exterior Halloween design aesthetic.

Adams used less ghoulish terms to describe his friend and associate. "Calhoun thinks for himself, independently of all the rest, with sound judgment, quick discrimination, and keen observation. He supports his opinions too with powerful eloquence."

Unfortunately, sound judgment, quick discrimination, and keen observation were not phrases used to describe the man at the top. William Wirt said of Monroe that his mind was neither as "rapid nor rich" as that of Thomas Jefferson or James Madison. Adams confided to his diary, "There is slowness, want of decision and a Spirit of procrastination in the President which perhaps arises more from his situation than his personal character." Adams's biographer James Traub described President James

John C. Calhoun

Monroe as "the last, and the least, of the great Tidewater aristocracy to serve as chief executive." That might sound harsh, but it is true. Monroe certainly was not as revered as Washington—no one ever could be. Still, apart from Washington, James Monroe was the only other veteran of the American Revolution to serve as president. He still wore the clothes to prove it. As late as the 1820s, Monroe still dressed the part of Revolutionary War veteran from the previous century. While most senators and congressmen around Washington would be seen donning long pants, Monroe wore breeches, long hose, and buckled shoes, and on special occasions even his old military uniform.

Adams's description of Monroe's procrastination is proper considering the controversy over the Tallmadge amendments and the growing crisis over Missouri statehood. Monroe refused to discuss the issue with his cabinet until it landed on his desk but quietly worked behind the scenes to ensure the issue did not blow up in his face or lead the nation to civil war.

On February 16, 1819, the House of Representatives voted the Tallmadge Amendment into the Missouri statehood bill. Congress voted on the two parts of the amendment separately. The first part of the amendment—to restrict slavery in Missouri—passed the House 87–76. The second part of the amendment, to emancipate slaves born after Missouri's admission at age twenty-five, also passed by a slim margin. The results were sectional, with the North voting for the amendments and the South voting against.

Almost two weeks later, the Senate blocked both parts of the amendment. Five free-state senators crossed sectional lines to oppose the measure. Among them was Illinois Senator Jesse Burgess Thomas. Senator Thomas was a proslavery former Marylander who owned five Black "apprentices." He was determined to forge a compromise that would placate his Northern constituents as well as Southerners hoping to diffuse slavery across the West.

The House and Senate left Washington after the vote—and the nation was left with an incredibly divisive cliff-hanger. The Fifteenth Congress closed shop, and the Sixteenth Congress would not meet until December. When it did, it would be sans James Tallmadge Jr., whose term expired on March 4. Tallmadge served only one congressional term, but he managed to rip the Band-Aid off the still-blistering sore of slavery and expose the infected mess that had been rotting beneath since the Constitutional Convention.

The dark cloud of Missouri draped over the country. With Congress no longer in session, the contentious issue of slavery's expansion took on a life of its own in newspapers, state legislatures, and town halls across the country. Virginia Senator James Barbour intoned "that the little speck we . . . saw [last session] was to be swelled into the importance that it has now assumed, and that upon its decision depended on the duration of the Union."

John Quincy did not comment about it in his diary until July 5, 1819. Adams had attended an Independence Day gathering with Treasury Secretary Crawford. At the celebration dinner, Adams, who noticed there had been only twenty-one toasts, offered a mundane toast welcoming Alabama, the new twenty-second state, into the Union. Crawford, not to be outdone by his chief cabinet rival, offered his own: "The admission of new States on the principles of the federal Constitution, that they should be *Republican*." Adams pointed out in his diary that Crawford's toast "glanced" at Missouri's failure to gain statehood.

The events of the evening, and perhaps a little Madeira, freed up Adams's mind and pen to reveal how he really felt about the Missouri Crisis. "The attempt to introduce the restriction introduced a violent agitation among the Members from the Slave-holding States," he wrote. "The Slave drivers, as usual, whenever this topic is brought up, bluster and bully, talk of the white Slaves of the Eastern States, and the dissolution of the Union, and

Oceans of blood; And the Northern men, as usual pocket all this Hectoring; sit down in quiet, and submit to the Slave-scourging Republicanism of the Planters."

Adams brought it back to his nemesis. "Crawford who sees how this affair will ultimately go, and who relies on the support of the Slave Drivers, is determined to shew them that he is on their side."

2

TO BREAK ONE LINK IN THE CHAIN OF SLAVERY

In 1819, John Quincy Adams may not have been ready to become slavery's avenging angel, but antislavery activists had been around since before the American Revolution. They represented a small slice of the population, most of whom opposed slavery on religious grounds. The movement existed in pockets around the country, but it was strongest in Northern states like New York, where politicians such as James Tallmadge passed state emancipation laws, or Massachusetts, where John Adams helped abolish slavery in the state constitution. While half-hearted efforts to curtail slavery, like the American Colonization Society, existed, a mass movement for universal emancipation did not emerge until the Missouri Crisis galvanized those who viewed the institution as immoral and unworthy of the ideals of the Declaration of Independence. One such person was a Quaker saddlemaker who lived in Saint Clairsville, Ohio, named Benjamin Lundy.

Benjamin Lundy was born to Joseph and Elizabeth Shotwell Lundy, on a farm in Sussex County, New Jersey, on January 4, 1789. Lundy received little formal education. He attended school only until his mother's death when he was five. Two years later, Joseph Lundy married Mary Titus, and Benjamin returned to school briefly to learn how to write and then again briefly to learn arithmetic when he was sixteen.

What he lacked in education, Lundy made up for in determination. "When my father hired men to work on his farm, I laboured with them, much too hard for my physical frame, in order to convince them, that though a mere boy, I could do the work of the largest and strongest man," he wrote. "By this means, I partially lost my hearing, and otherwise injured my health. In this, I was alone to blame, as my father often cautioned me against it." Lundy dealt with infirmities and bad hearing for the rest of his life. However, a fragile constitution and small frame could not hamper his work ethic.

The Lundy family were members of their local religious Society of Friends meeting, established by Benjamin's great-grandfather. Every week, the boy sat quietly for hours in a one-room meetinghouse nestled in the foothills of rural western New Jersey. There he contemplated Quaker doctrine on the importance of denying oneself the pleasures of the physical world and was encouraged to dedicate his energies to serving the poor, marginalized, and sick. Quakers believe within each of us there is an "inner light" of God, and that it is our calling to be responsive to human suffering, wherever we find it, without regard for a person's race or wealth.

Young Lundy likely heard stories about saintly Quaker abolitionists such as John Woolman, Anthony Benezet, and the radically theatrical Benjamin Lay. Born in 1677, Benjamin Lay was the author of *All Slave-Keepers That Keep the Innocent in Bondage.* Printed in Philadelphia in 1737 by Lay's good friend Benjamin Franklin, *All Slave-Keepers* was one of the first antislavery tracts written in Colonial North America.

Benjamin Rush, close friend of the Adamses, signer of the Declaration of Independence, and doctor of the American Revolution, recorded a description of Lay in a collection of biographical anecdotes: "His size, which was not much above four feet, his dress, which was always the same, consisting of light-coloured plain clothes, a white hat, and half boots; his milk-white beard, which hung upon his breast; and, above all, his peculiar principles and conduct, rendered him to many, an object of admiration, and to all, the subject of conversation."

Benjamin Lay–inspired conversation was often precipitated by one of his scandalous antislavery-inspired outbursts, perhaps the most famous of which has become known as the Bladder of Blood. It's 1738, at the annual Quaker business meeting in Burlington, New Jersey. Try to imagine how quiet and boring your typical eighteenth-century Quaker business meeting might be. It would be akin to a boring Zoom meeting that most definitely could have been an email—but at church.

As the meeting got underway, Lay stood up and shouted, "Oh, all you negro masters, who are contentedly holding your fellow-creatures in a state of slavery during life, well knowing the cruel sufferings those innocent captives undergo . . . especially you, who profess to do unto all men as ye would they should do unto you . . . you might as well throw off the plain coat as I do."

The stunned congregation watched as Lay threw off his cloak, revealing a military uniform. Unhinged, he continued the diatribe. "It would be as justifiable in the sight of the Almighty, who beholds and respects all nations and colors of men with an equal regard, if you should thrust a sword through their hearts, as I do through this . . ."

Lay unsheathed a sword and began repeatedly stabbing himself in the stomach. What happened next was a scene out of Stephen King's *Carrie*. Breathless gasps and shouts filled the small room as plainly dressed Quaker women sitting in the pews were splattered and covered in blood—which happened to be pokeberry juice Lay had stored in a fake bladder under his shirt.

Lay had punked the congregation.

The men seized Lay, drove him from the building, and forced him onto the ground on the front steps outside the hall. Dramatic to the very last, Lay remained lying on the steps for the rest of the rain-soaked afternoon so the parishioners would be forced to step over him as they exited the meeting. Benjamin Lundy came of age shaped by the legacy of Quaker activists like Benjamin Lay.

At nineteen, Lundy thought it might be better for his constitution if he set out on his own. He headed west, following the old post road, making stops in Berks County, Pennsylvania, and the Quaker enclave of Mount Pleasant, Ohio, before accepting an apprenticeship with a saddlemaker at the crossroads town of Wheeling, Virginia (now West Virginia).

Ben behaved like many college-aged men when they leave home. He did some partying and fell in with a group of ne'er-do-well, "worldly minded people." He hung out with a rough crowd that had no regard for his "future welfare." Oddly enough, during this period of debauchery, Lundy's ill health, at least temporarily, improved.

After a walk on the wild side, Benjamin Lundy returned to his Quaker roots. He "had some concern for the future," so he resolved to check his "unreasonable propensities, before it should be too late." Translation: Check yourself before you wreck yourself.

Resolved to do better, Lundy closely observed the simplistic Quaker style of dress and speech and continued attending Society of Friends meetings. Lundy also formed a bond with another young Quaker, Benjamin Stanton, the uncle of Edwin Stanton, who would grow up to become James Buchanan's attorney general and Abraham Lincoln's secretary of war. Stanton had moved to Wheeling from Mount Pleasant to study medicine. Wheeling was a wild "unchurched" town. The two men learned to lean on each other and their Quaker faith.

Situated on the Ohio River, Wheeling was a gathering point for slave drivers as they awaited a passage down South. Lundy witnessed slave coffles parading down the main thoroughfare toward awaiting ships on the Ohio River. The enslaved were being "sold down the river," from the Ohio all the way to the Mississippi, until they reached their destination—the new plantations of the South. Lundy's heart broke: "I heard the wail of the captive; I felt his pang of distress; and the iron entered my soul." Lundy could not get the image out of his mind of men bound hand and foot, chained together; stumbling over each other, lashed by the whip. In that moment he made a vow to God to "break at least one link of that ponderous chain of oppression."

After four years in Wheeling, Lundy moved a few miles west to the antislavery stronghold of Mount Pleasant in Ohio. There, Benjamin Stanton's brother-in-law hired him as a journeyman saddlemaker. After two years as an apprentice, Lundy went into business for himself.

Lundy's father encouraged him to come home and open a saddle shop in New Jersey. Benjamin returned to the family farm for a visit but explained to his father that prospects were better in Ohio. And indeed they were. Benjamin Lundy had fallen in love with a Quaker woman from Mount Pleasant named Esther Lewis.

In February 1815, he and Esther were married. The newlyweds settled ten miles west of Mount Pleasant, in the town of Saint Clairsville, where Lundy opened a saddle and harness shop. Business was good, and within four years Lundy saved $3,000. "I had then a loving wife and two beautiful little daughters, that it was real happiness to possess and to cherish; I was at peace with my neighbours, and knew not that I had an enemy."

But even with such personal success, Lundy was restless. Something gnawed at him. At night he tossed and turned. He could hear the cries of the men in the slave coffles, the crunch and clang of their chains dragging through the dirt. The poor, wretched victims of men stealers. The world was drenched in sin, and like Benjamin Lay before him, Benjamin Lundy felt duty-bound to take a stand and do something about it.

On January 4, 1816, his twenty-seventh birthday, Benjamin Lundy acted. He assembled a coterie of friends at his home and formed the Union Humane Society. A big thinker, Lundy wanted to build a national organization that could envelop all existing antislavery organizations. Here was a man who had no experience, no training, no financial resources, but was determined with an infinite supply of grit and a deeply ingrained sense of purpose.

Over the past two decades, the antislavery movement had suffered from a lack of interest. Many activists reconsidered the potential consequences of the emancipation of thousands of enslaved persons after Toussaint Louverture led an uprising of enslaved people in Saint-Domingue, present-day Haiti, in 1791. Black rebels burned plantations and slaughtered their white European overseers. The revolution ended slavery and paved the way for Haitian independence. Reports of massacred whites in Haiti struck terror in the hearts of American slave owners. Many Southerners asked the question: Could it happen here? The answer was yes.

In 1800, authorities in Virginia foiled an insurrection plot hatched by an enslaved man named Gabriel Prosser. Inspired by the revolution in Saint-Domingue, the Gabriel Prosser plot rattled members of the Virginia House of Delegates so much they sent out a plea to Governor James Monroe to please find somewhere to colonize Blacks considered "obnoxious to the laws or dangerous to the peace of society."

Another reason some previously amenable to ending slavery cooled on the idea had to do with money. When the Act Prohibiting the Importation of Slaves was enacted in 1808, the domestic slave trade flourished. Many Southerners who had decried the ugliness of the institution now saw the value of their enslaved increase exponentially.

Fear and profit blunted the development of a coherent, unified antislavery movement. Existing associations, such as the Quaker-affiliated American Convention for Promoting the

Abolition of Slavery and Improving the Condition of the African Race, did not have the teeth to make real and lasting change. The organization met in Philadelphia once every two years to discuss the issue and lacked the ability to implement a real plan to solve it. However, there were individual antislavery activists of note such as the elderly John Kenrick in New England, the Reverend George Bourne in Virginia, and Charles Osborn in Tennessee. These men worked alongside local manumission societies to spread antislavery doctrine throughout the upper South.

The goal of the Union Humane Society was to establish a network of activists who could make change happen. Within months, membership grew to nearly five hundred with eight associated groups springing up around Ohio. One of the ways Lundy got the word out about the new organization was through an appeal he sent to a reform newspaper, Charles Osborn's *Philanthropist.* Osborn printed Lundy's appeal and was so taken by Lundy's passion for the cause that he asked Lundy if he would help him edit the paper.

The offer was a vote of confidence by a deeply respected member of the movement. Lundy wrote, "The thought that I could do such a thing had not then even occurred to me. But on his repeating the request, I consented to try;—and from that moment, whenever I have thought that something ought to be done, my maxim has been, though doubtful of my ability—'try.'" The more Benjamin Lundy tried his hand at writing antislavery articles, the more confident he grew and the more he impressed Osborn. Within months Osborn offered Lundy the opportunity to become the *Philanthropist*'s co-editor. Lundy believed the offer to be divinely inspired. But it was a difficult decision. His saddle business was thriving, and he had the well-being of his wife and two young daughters to think about.

After considerable prayer and deep meditation, Benjamin Lundy decided to liquidate his entire shop's inventory and, along with a few employees, travel to the Missouri Territory where much-needed supplies were hard to come by. Lundy kissed Esther and his young daughters, Susan and Elizabeth, goodbye and set out down the Ohio River.

In Missouri, Benjamin Lundy interacted daily with enslaved people and their enslavers. He realized the institution of slavery was thriving. Diffusing slaves across the Missouri Territory only seemed to promote the buying and selling of more enslaved labor. As Lundy engaged with the growing community of Southern emigrants, he realized that they had zero interest in ever giving up the peculiar practice. Lundy believed that Southerners were determined to expand slavery into each new state and territory. Slavery was not on the road to extinction. It was just getting started.

Benjamin Lundy's journey to Missouri and back took about six months. When he returned to Mount Pleasant, he learned an impatient Charles Osborn had sold the *Philanthropist* to Elisha Bates, a transplant from Yorktown, Virginia, who had no interest in having a co-editor. But the bigger news was the debate in Congress over James Tallmadge's amendments and slavery in Missouri.

Controversy over the Missouri statehood bill in Washington had sparked renewed interest in the antislavery movement. Down in Jonesborough, Tennessee, a man named Elihu Embree started the *Tennessee Manumission Intelligencer*. Information about the antislavery movement was in demand.

But then a terrible financial panic struck the nation. Americans now faced the threat of financial ruin at the same time the social fabric of the nation was beginning to fray.

3

WE ARE ON THE EVE OF A GREAT CRISIS, OF WHICH SCARCELY ANY ONE IS YET AWARE

Between 1819 and 1822, the nation found itself in the grips of the worst economic depression it had ever faced up to that point. The result of a series of cascading factors at home and abroad that converged to crush the American economy. After Napoleon's 1815 defeat at the Battle of Waterloo, British-made goods flooded American markets, overwhelming the protective tariff of 1816 and pressuring American manufacturers that had been booming since the War of 1812. Turmoil in the manufacturing sector was matched by exponential price increases in agricultural exports due to European crop failures, and a skyrocketing British demand for American cotton that sparked land speculation in the American South.

In 1817, Congress chartered the Second Bank of the United States. The Bank of the United States (BUS) acted as a check on state banks that, since the war, had flooded the market with banknotes, creating a speculative bubble. At the same time, political unrest in Mexico and Peru restricted supplies of gold and silver, which led to a shortage of specie. The shrinking money supply placed downward pressure on commodity prices. As European agricultural markets recovered, Britain increased imports of East Indian cotton. American cotton prices plummeted.

In 1820, John C. Calhoun told Adams, "There has been within these two years an immense revolution of Fortunes in every part of the Union: enormous numbers of persons utterly ruined; Multitudes in deep distress." From spinning jenny operators in the North to plantation owners in the South, Americans felt the pain of the financial crisis.

Benjamin Lundy arrived back home to Ohio with little money to show for his six-month western escapade. But Lundy couldn't care less about his financial situation. The threat of the expansion of slavery into new territory breathed new life into the antislavery movement and invigorated members of the Union Humane Society.

His work with the Union Humane Society was no longer good enough. Lundy needed to be closer to the action. He borrowed $300, kissed his wife and daughters goodbye, and once again set off down the Ohio River. Lundy steered a small boat while three indentured apprentices stitched saddle skirts and bridles. When the men stepped onshore at Herculaneum, Missouri, a new village on the Mississippi between Saint Louis and Sainte Genevieve, they found themselves at ground zero of the Missouri question.

Lundy struggled. The financial crisis had cut the demand for saddles. One of his servants ran away. Lundy and the other two men opened a shop and tried to press on. For whatever demand there might have been for saddles in an economic depression, Lundy had little interest in selling them. All around him, people were taking up sides on the Missouri question. As hostilities reached a boiling point, Benjamin Lundy withdrew deeper into abolitionist work. Lundy honed his antislavery ideas in letters to the press. Saving Missouri from slavery was unlikely, but the work he did there made him a seasoned activist.

Missourians had little interest in Lundy's opinion and seethed as they read what Northern congressmen and senators were saying in the debates taking place far off in Washington. The future was on the line. A growing sense of unease spread throughout the country as the thorny questions raised by James Tallmadge's amendments and the resulting congressional deadlock on the issue was all anyone was talking about.

John Quincy Adams could see the big picture. He understood that the Missouri Crisis had awakened divisions burrowed deep within the American psyche. "There are several Subjects upon which the public mind in this Country is taking a turn which alarms me greatly for the continuance of this Union—The Bank; the Currency; the internal improvement Question; The extension, repression of Slavery . . . , it seems to me we are on the eve of a great crisis of which scarcely any one is yet aware." Translation: America was having a nervous breakdown.

Southerners would rather secede than live in a nation run by Northerners. They viewed the Missouri Crisis as a direct assault on states' rights and personal liberty. Northern congressmen's attempt to restrict slavery to the states where it already existed was nothing more than a federal power grab, part of a broader Northern strategy for consolidation. This included chartering of the Second National Bank of the United States, the John Marshall–led Supreme Court decision in *McCulloch v. Maryland* (which ruled the Bank of the United States constitutional and denied states the power to tax the bank), and Henry Clay's American System, which proposed federal infrastructure investment in roads, bridges, and canals.

For Briscoe G. Baldwin, a member of the Virginia House of Delegates, Missouri was a point of no return. "If we should unfortunately fail in support of our principle, the certain effect will be to make all the territory west of the Mississippi, and 36°30' a Yankee country, governed by the sniveling, sanctimonious doctrines in politics and religion which, as a Virginian, I early learned to abhor."

In January 1820, Adams, convinced the Union was in peril, took his concerns directly to President Monroe. "A prospect thus dark and unpropitious abroad, is far more gloomy and threatening when we turn our eyes homeward. The Bank, the national currency, the stagnation of commerce, the depression of manufactures, the restless turbulence, and jealousies and insubordination of the State Legislatures, the Missouri Slave Question, the deficiencies of the revenue to be supplied; the rankling passions and ambitious projects of individuals, mingling with every thing, presented a prospect of the future, which I freely acknowledged was to me appalling."

After he concluded with his hot take, Adams pressed the president for his thoughts. Monroe's response was muted. Adams recorded in his diary that the president "apprehended no great danger from that. He believed a compromise would be found and agreed to, which would be satisfactory to all parties." Adams left the meeting perplexed. He considered three possibilities: "There is an underplot in operation . . . of which I had no suspicion," the president did not understand the gravity of the situation, or he was just playing it cool.

On January 3, 1820, the Senate Judiciary Committee introduced a bill for Missouri's admission to the Union without the Tallmadge Amendment. On February 16, the Senate voted 23–21 to admit Maine as a free state and Missouri as a slave state. Senator Jesse Burgess Thomas proposed banning slavery in the Louisiana Purchase territory north of latitude 36°30', except for Missouri. The following day, the Senate passed the Maine and Missouri bill with this provision by a vote of 24–10. President Monroe secretly lobbied for the bill's passage in the House, using his "Good

Feelings" political capital and enlisting help from his son-in-law, Senator James Barbour.

American history gives credit for the passage of the Missouri Compromise to Speaker of the House Henry Clay. In this case, Clay's apparent ability to forge compromise is more accurately the way he used deft political instincts and exploited the parliamentary power of his office to shepherd the legislation through the House of Representatives.

At six foot one with fiery red hair, Henry Clay fashioned the image of the "star of the West." His childhood had been marred by the turmoil of the Revolution—his family home in Hanover County, Virginia, was ransacked by British Lieutenant Colonel Banastre Tarleton and his troops. Yet Clay's destiny was steered by advantageous family connections that secured him a coveted clerkship under Judge George Wythe. There, he furthered his legal education under the guidance of Virginia's attorney general, Robert Brooke.

Clay could not find adequate work due to a glut of Virginia lawyers, so he headed west to Kentucky. The Bluegrass State was the perfect launching pad for a man of twenty to launch a career in law and politics. He was elected to the state legislature in 1803, and a few years later, Clay filled in and served two unexpired terms in the United States Senate before being elected to the House of Representatives in 1810. Henry Clay was then elected Speaker of the House of Representatives, the youngest man who had ever held the position.

Adams and Clay had a complicated relationship. James Madison appointed both men as commissioners to the Treaty of Ghent—where the men shared an apartment during their time across the pond. (Cue composer Neal Hefti's *The Odd Couple* theme music.) Adams and Clay were different in every way. Adams paid no attention to style; he wore the plain clothes of a New England Puritan. He was notorious for being a curmudgeon who preferred his own company and adhered to a strict personal schedule; up before the sun writing in his diary, reading classical literature, and answering correspondence.

Clay, on the other hand, dressed in the latest fashion, which on many occasions was a perfectly tailored black coat and crisp white cravat. He had a reputation as a carouser who was known to stay up into the early morning hours gambling. James Traub writes that, in Ghent, "Adams would find himself waking up just as Clay was going to sleep."

To continue the *Odd Couple* homage, "Can two ambitious diplomats share an apartment without driving each other crazy?" The answer is barely.

Tensions from Ghent carried over into the Monroe administration. When Monroe chose John Quincy for secretary of state, Clay took it personally and became the administration's arch critic. Clay's steel-blue eyes fixed upon being the first president from the West, and the stepping stone of secretary of state was a must. Clay declined Monroe's offer of war secretary. That position went to Southerner John C. Calhoun. Thus, there was not a Westerner in the Monroe cabinet, which Clay took as an insult to himself and the region.

In his diary on March 9, 1821, Adams wrote of Clay, "Clay is an eloquent man, with very popular manners and great political management . . . his school has been the world, and in that he is proficient. His morals, public and private, are loose but he has all the virtues of an indispensable and popular man . . . Clay's temper is impetuous, and his ambition is impatient. He has long since marked me as the principal rival in his way." Rivalry aside, Adams and Clay shared similar domestic priorities. They were nationalists who believed the federal government should fund the construction of roads, canals, and bridges. What Clay called his American System, today we call infrastructure. The two men also agreed that the Missouri Crisis had put the nation in peril. One

Adams and Clay, the O.G. Odd Couple

Sunday afternoon during the height of the crisis, Adams and Clay walked home together after church service in the Capitol. Clay confessed to Adams, "he had not a doubt that within five years from this time the Union would be divided into three distinct confederacies," North, South, and West.

A week later, Adams received a visit from a New Jersey congressman who shared a letter from a neighbor who asked "whether a civil War would not be preferable to the extension of Slavery beyond the Mississippi." Adams commented in his diary, "This is a question between the rights of human nature and the Constitution of the United States."

When the bill arrived in the House, Clay took control over its fate. The House and the Senate proposed separate bills regarding Missouri. The Senate's bill incorporated the 36°30' compromise, while the House passed a bill opposing slavery. The two bills were sent to a conference committee stacked with Clay-appointed moderates. Clay proposed separating the bill into its individual parts, which assured passage by the whole Congress.

After the final vote, John Randolph, a proslavery Virginian opposed to the compromise, tried to kill the bill by issuing a motion to reconsider. Clay deferred the motion until the following morning. The next morning, when Randolph rose again to offer the motion, Clay ruled him out of order and moved on to the routine hearing of petitions. Later, when Randolph again attempted to offer the motion, Clay told him the bill had already been signed and was now in Senate hands. In other words, "too late." Randolph lost it! He moved that the body of the House overruled the Speaker, but before the motion could be voted on, the Senate had enacted the bill. Clay's game of keep-away ensured passage of the Missouri Compromise and, for now, preserved the Union.

• • •

Secretary of State John Quincy Adams had no vote. If he did, he would have voted in favor of the compromise. For Adams, the South would give up being enslavers by force alone, which made the practice a political necessity, no matter how dehumanizing.

As a senator, Adams opposed a bill to prohibit the importation of slaves into Louisiana Territory. He also argued against prohibiting the importation of slaves into the United States before the international slave trade ban was set to go into effect in 1808.

As secretary of state, Adams presented the British with indemnification of property claims made by Southern slaveholders and put the full weight of the State Department behind the extradition of escaped slaves from Canada. Adams biographer Samuel Flagg Bemis points out that in his role as a diplomat, Adams never "allowed a foreign government to exploit any personal squeamishness he had about the domestic institution of his country."

But the political and public debate over the Missouri Crisis signaled a turning point in the way John Quincy Adams thought about the issue of slavery. His diary entries over the winter of 1820 reveal that he could no longer deny that his father's generation made serious mistakes in dealing with slavery.

Adams believed the Three-Fifths Compromise found in Article I, Section 2 of the Constitution was a poison pill that would assuredly lead to the nation's destruction. He confided to himself, "The fault is in the Constitution of the United States, which has sanctioned a dishonourable compromise with Slavery." Adams knew the Missouri Compromise was not a solution. It was a Band-Aid.

John Quincy blamed free-state representatives for caving to their Southern counterparts. "It is a contemplation not very creditable to human nature, that the cement of common interest produced by Slavery is stronger and more solid than that of unmingled freedom. In this instance the Slave-States have clung together in one unbroken phalanx, and have been victorious by the means of accomplices and deserters, from the ranks of Freedom."

The enslavers were better at making their side of the argument. "The Slave men have indeed a deeper immediate stake in the issue than the partizans of freedom; their passions and interests are more profoundly agitated, and they have stronger impulses to active energy than their antagonists, whose only individual interest in this cause arises from its bearing on the balance of political power between North and South."

There was one voice on the side of freedom, though, who could match wits with the most dogged, fire-eating, slave-holding Southerner: New York Senator Rufus King. King was a member of the Constitutional Convention and in the room the day the Three-Fifths Compromise was born. He hated it then and hated it still. King blamed the compromise for being at least partly responsible for the undoing of the Federalist Party—the party Adams was unceremoniously marched out of when he was a senator.

Adams watched King lay into his Southern counterparts from the Senate gallery.

"The great Slave-holders in the house gnawed their lips and clenched their fists as they heard him." Adams then walked over to the House of Representatives where R. C. Anderson from Kentucky was "speaking upon the same subject, but on the other side of the question—He speaks with fluency, as do almost all the members of Congress."

Adams observed it was the eloquence with which American politicians debate issues in Congress that distinguished them from their British counterparts in Parliament. There, two or three particularly gifted orators deliver each side of the argument and the body votes before they adjourn for the day. "Here a single question is sometimes debated for three weeks, and Members make speeches three days long."

John Quincy spent months discussing the issue with various congressmen and government officials in his office. He took in speeches on both sides of the issue in the Senate and the House. Reading his diary, you get a glimpse of a man processing all of it—America's founding son reconciling the nation's founding documents with the harsh reality of the slave system and the threat it now posed to the survival of the Union.

Adams attended a party at the home of John C. Calhoun, where King's Senate speeches were the focus of conversation. "Slave-holders," Adams said, "cannot hear [the speeches] without being seized with cramps." Calhoun was one slaveholder with whom Adams spoke freely on the subject. John Quincy believed Calhoun had a superior intellect to others in Washington and always found him to be genuine in his thoughts and actions. Though they disagreed often, they were real with each other. On a cold, late February afternoon, Calhoun and Adams got on to the subject of the "Slave question" during a meeting in Calhoun's War Department office.

Calhoun told Adams that he did not think the Missouri Crisis "would produce a dissolution of the Union, but if it should the South would be from necessity compelled to form an Alliance Offensive and Defensive with Great-Britain." Adams, stunned by the comment, replied, "That would be returning to the Colonial State." I imagine him thinking: *We fought an eight-year-long and bloody revolution to free ourselves from those guys. Then, a few years ago, they came back and burned down the President's House and the Capitol. The repairs were only recently completed. There are still big chunks of white caulk outside the building. And you are suggesting the South would jump back in the king's arms over slavery? What is wrong with you?*

Calhoun essentially replied, *Yes, pretty much.* Adams pressed his colleague, asking him, "If by the effect of this alliance offensive and defensive, the population of the North should be cut off from its natural outlet upon the Ocean, it would fall back upon its rocks bound hand and foot to starve, or whether it would not retain its powers of locomotion, to move Southward by Land." Translation: *Just so I understand you—if the North is cut off from the ocean by the British navy and cut off from the South by the British army, do you expect us to just roll over?* Calhoun replied that the South "would find it necessary to make their communities all military." At this point, you can imagine John Quincy trying to appear nonchalant as he picks his jaw up off the floor. Adams did not press the conversation any further.

Adams realized that if the Union were to dissolve over Slavery, the result would be "the destructive progress of emancipation, which like all great religious and political reformations is terrible in its means though happy and glorious in its end."

It is important that we take a beat here to adjust our twenty-first-century norms to those of the nineteenth century. Slavery disgusted Adams. It must end. But Adams could not foresee an interracial society. There are several examples throughout his life of Adams thinking in a manner that today would be considered racist. In the 1820s, apart from some abolitionists like Benjamin Lundy and a few others, most of those who were strongly antislavery still could not conceive of a society like the one in which we are currently living.

Adams continued in his diary that night, "Slavery is the great and foul stain upon the North-American Union; and it is a contemplation worthy of the most exalted soul, whether its total abolition is or is not practicable—If practicable, by what means it may be effected, and if a choice of means be within the scope of the object, what means would accomplish it, at the smallest cost of human sufferance."

Then Adams, like a lightning bolt, snatched a glimpse of the future: "A dissolution, at least temporary of the Union as now constituted, would be certainly necessary, and the dissolution must be upon a point involving the question of Slavery and no other. The

Union might then be reorganized, on the fundamental principle of emancipation. This object is vast in its compass—awful in its prospects, sublime and beautiful in its issue. A life devoted to it would be nobly spent or sacrificed." John Quincy had no idea that, a decade later, he would fully dedicate the rest of his life to such a noble cause.

4

FOR THE PRESENT THE CONTEST IS LAID TO SLEEP

President Monroe assembled his cabinet shortly after Congress passed the Missouri bill. Having previously avoided on-the-record discussions about Missouri, he now demanded the administration speak with one voice.

Monroe posed two questions to the cabinet and ordered that their written answers be archived in the Department of State:

1. Did Congress have a constitutional right to prohibit slavery in the territories?
2. Did Section 8 of the Missouri bill—which banned slavery north of the 36°30' latitude—apply only to territories, or would it extend to future states?

On the first question, all agreed: Congress *could* prohibit slavery in the territories. But Southern cabinet members—Calhoun, Crawford, and Wirt—insisted there was not "express power to that effect given in the Constitution." Adams was beside himself, writing in his diary that "these Gentlemen in the simplicity of their hearts had come to a conclusion in direct opposition to their premises; without being aware or conscious of inconsistency."

On the second question, Adams found himself at odds with the rest of the cabinet. The Missouri bill interdicted slavery in a territory north of 36°30', but when that territory became a state, could the state constitution open itself up to slavery? According to the slavery-supporting members of the cabinet, the Article IV, Section 3 constitutional powers to "make all needful Rules and Regulations" for a territory was limited to land only—not the people who live on the land in the territory. Congress could prohibit slavery, but once that territory became a state, the state legislature had the power to pass whatever laws they wished.

Adams argued, "The additional words authorising needful rules and regulations respecting it, must have reference to persons connected with it, or could have no meaning at all." The meaning of *needful*, Adams explained, was whatever the Constitution of the United States needed it to be to fulfill the compact set out in the preamble. Adams continued, "What can be more needful to the establishment of Justice, than the interdiction of Slavery where it does not exist." Adams's blood was boiling. I imagine his face growing red and the massive veins in the corners of his bald forehead about to burst.

Crawford told Adams that once a territory became a state, regardless of the conditions under which they were admitted, slavery could be sanctioned by a simple vote of the legislature. Adams snapped back that "the Declaration of Independence not only asserts the natural equality of all men, and their unalienable right to Liberty; but that the only *just* powers of government are derived from the consent of the governed." He added, "A power for one part of the people to make slaves of the other can never be derived from the consent, and is therefore not a just power." Crawford told Adams he was starting to sound like Rufus King. Adams agreed.

Adams noted that the president had signed a bill restricting slavery in the state of Illinois. There was a precedent that gave the federal government the power to restrict slavery in a state, adding, "Why should the question be made now, which was not made then?"

Adams referred to the Northwest Ordinance from 1787. Crawford maintained the compact "was a nullity, not binding upon the Legislatures of those States." The Georgian's assertion sickened Adams to his soul, but he held his tongue, knowing that to respond would have kindled in the executive branch the same simmering debates over slavery that Missouri had unleashed on the country.

The discussion now turned to implied powers granted by Congress under the Constitution. Adams argued, "Congress had a right to say that no State undertaking to establish [slavery] de novo should be admitted into the Union . . . it would put herself out of the pale of the Union, and forfeit all the rights and privileges of the connection." President Monroe agreed that Congress had implied powers at its disposal, reminding his cabinet that Congress approved relief aid to Caracas after Venezuela suffered a deadly 1812 earthquake. Congress was given that authority under an implied power.

Adams asked to be given a "dispensation" from answering the second question because his opinion differed from everyone else in the cabinet, and if required to give it, it would be only fair that he explain his reasoning behind it. Calhoun, not wanting a permanent and public record of the argument, suggested the president change the second question to whether the cabinet members agreed the "8th Section of the Bill was consistent with the Constitution." The slavery-leaning cabinet members, including President Monroe, agreed that it was applicable only to the territorial state and Adams would be saved from publicly splitting from the other cabinet members.

As the meeting broke up and the cabinet members parted ways, Adams took a long look at Crawford. John Quincy had recently received a letter from Jonathan Jennings, the governor of Indiana, telling him Crawford had been supporting, and maybe even personally engaging in forming a party whose goal was to establish slavery in the state. The governor had reason to believe there was a similar movement afoot in Illinois and Ohio. Crawford's presidential ambitions were an open secret, but the lengths to which he would go to grow his support disturbed Adams to no end.

After the meeting, Calhoun and Adams walked home together. Calhoun let Adams know that the "principles" Adams "avowed were just and noble; but that in the Southern Country, whenever they were mentioned, they were always understood as applying only to white men." Calhoun added if he "were to keep a white servant in his house, his character and reputation would be irretrievably ruined." Adams suggested that slavery had warped perceptions of labor and servitude. Calhoun told Adams it wasn't all labor, just menial labor, "the proper work of Slaves." Remarking that "No white person could descend to that—And it was the best guarantee to equality among the whites. It . . . did not even admit of inequalities, by which one white man could domineer over another." Likely shocked at his colleague's words, Adams told Calhoun that he did not see things "in the same light."

To the solitude of his diary Adams confessed, "It is in truth all perverted sentiment—mistaking labour for Slavery, and dominion for Freedom—The discussion of this Missouri question has betrayed the secret of their Souls—In the abstract they admit that Slavery is an evil . . . but when probed to the quick upon it they show at the bottom of their Souls, pride and vain-glory in their very condition of masterdom."

Adams continued, "It is among the evils of Slavery that it taints the very sources of moral principle—It establishes false estimates of virtue and vice. . . . It perverts human reason, and reduces men endowed with logical powers to maintain that Slavery is sanctioned by the Christian religion—That Slaves are happy and contented in their condition."

Adams poured out his soul into his diary, finally hitting upon the crux of the matter. "The impression produced upon my mind by the progress of this discussion is that the bargain between Freedom and Slavery contained in the Constitution of the United States is morally and politically vicious—inconsistent with the principles upon which alone our revolution can be justified. . . . The consequence has been that this Slave-representation has governed the Union."

Our founding son, John Quincy Adams, came to the same horrible conclusion his Northern and Southern brethren would face forty years later. "I have favoured this Missouri compromise, believing it to be all that could be effected under the present Constitution, and from extreme unwillingness to put the Union at hazard. But perhaps it would have been a wiser as well as a bolder course to have persisted in the restriction upon Missouri, till it should have terminated in a Convention of the States to revise and amend the Constitution. This would have produced a new Union of thirteen or fourteen States, unpolluted with Slavery, with a great and glorious object to effect; namely rallying to their Standard the other States, by the universal emancipation of their Slaves."

It was a confession for now and a prediction of what was to come. "If the Union must be dissolved, Slavery is precisely the question upon which it ought to break. For the present however this contest is now laid asleep."

At this moment in 1820, John Quincy Adams seemed to have the ability to see the past, present, and future all at the same time. Well, some of the future. Adams did not see himself as the man who would awaken the nation to reckon with slavery once and for all or be destroyed by what Jefferson referred to as the "wolf" the nation "had by the ears." Before he made such a realization, Adams would face two bruising elections, a failed one-term presidency, and more heartbreak than a father is meant to endure.

Three days later, President Monroe signed the Missouri Compromise into law. The two new states of Maine and Missouri would restore momentary balance and a fragile peace to the Union.

• 5 •

TO AROUSE AND AWAKEN THE AMERICAN PEOPLE TO A SENSE OF THE INCONSISTENCY, THE HYPOCRISY, AND THE INIQUITY . . .

With passage of the Missouri Compromise, restrictionists shifted their focus to electing antislavery delegates to Missouri's state constitutional convention.

From Herculaneum, Missouri, Lundy prosecuted the case against slavery from every side of the argument. He organized antislavery groups as he had in Mount Pleasant; he published articles in the Missouri and Illinois newspapers. Lundy rebutted the argument made by locals that slavery would increase land values and attract white settlers by pointing out that Northern land values were greater than those in the Southern states. He argued against the idea of diffusion, made popular by Jefferson, that spreading slavery across a wider geographical area would "make them individually happier and proportionally facilitate the accomplishment of their emancipation," a theory now widely embraced by the defenders of slavery.

Lundy's effort to change hearts and minds was futile. The notion that even one restrictionist delegate could be elected to the constitutional convention was foolish. Lundy knew in his heart only political power would defeat slave power.

In Missouri, proslavery forces outnumbered antislavery advocates seven to one. Lundy's outspokenness earned him hostility and death threats. He was accused of being a blue light and Hartford Convention Man, nicknames given to a group of New England antiwar Federalists who hatched a plot to secede from the Union over the War of 1812. He was also accused of being a Tory, the name given to supporters of the king during the Revolutionary War.

Not one antislavery delegate was elected to the Missouri constitutional convention. A slate of proslavery delegates voted for a state constitution that not only condoned slavery, but prohibited free Blacks from other states from entering Missouri, in direct conflict with the United States Constitution.

Away from his wife for almost two years and down to his last $13.50, it was time for Lundy go home. He set out from Saint Louis on foot. In the cold of winter, he walked nearly six hundred miles to Ohio. "My bed, at night, was the floor, or the ground . . . my knapsack was a substitute for a pillow." Along the way Lundy had resigned himself to moving his family to Illinois where, thanks to Crawford and his allies, the Northwest Ordinance was in jeopardy.

Although Lundy and the antislavery activists were unable to convince the United States Congress to refuse Missouri's admission to the Union as a slave state, or to elect an antislavery representative to the Missouri constitutional convention, their efforts in Missouri were not in vain. He returned more determined than ever to use what God gave him to warn the American people of the true horrors of slavery. The best way to get the word out? Publish a newspaper.

On a brisk Sunday morning in November, eight hundred fifty miles east of Saint Louis, John Quincy Adams was attending a Unitarian church service when he received a note that the president had called his cabinet department heads to a meeting at the President's House at one o'clock.

"I then called upon Calhoun," Adams wrote, and found him concerned about what he had read about the Missouri state constitution. Legislators inserted a clause that raised alarm throughout the Capitol. The article in question declared it "the duty of the Legislature to pass Laws prohibiting free Negroes and persons of colour from coming into the State; which is directly repugnant to the Article in the Constitution of the United States which provides that the Citizens of each State shall be entitled to all privileges and immunities of Citizens in the several States."

Calhoun feared the only outcome was for the federal government to declare the article in the Missouri Constitution to be null and void, which would provoke calls for secession in Missouri and throughout the South. Calhoun feared nullification. Nullification is a theory advanced by Thomas Jefferson and James Madison in 1798 that a state had a right to nullify a federal law it believed was unconstitutional.

Massachusetts Congressman Dr. William Eustis, Adams's home congressional representative, paid him a visit. The two New Englanders were of one mind on the subject. Eustis told Adams, "The clause in their Constitution [is] directly repugnant to the Article in the Constitution of the United States." He had no doubt about that, nor did Adams. But what was to be done?

Adams believed the only course of action was to "Pass a Resolution declaring the State to be admitted, from and after the time when they shall have expunged from their Constitution the Article repugnant to the Constitution of the United States." Eustis unsuccessfully offered the resolution on the House floor.

In another conversation with Pennsylvania Congressman Henry Baldwin, Adams said that the article in the Missouri Constitution was "repugnant to the rights reserved to every Citizen of the Union in the Constitution of the United States." He said that if he was a member of a state legislature, he would propose a law that threatened that if Missouri deprived "the coloured Citizens of the State say of Massachusetts of their rights as Citizens of the United States within the State of Missouri . . . the white Citizens of the State of Missouri should be held as aliens within the Commonwealth of Massachusetts, not entitled to claim or enjoy within the same any right or privilege of a Citizen of the United States."

Adams tiptoed up to the nullification line himself. If Missouri had such disregard for the United States Constitution, he would pass a law denying the "delivery of any fugitive Slave, upon the claim of his master. All which I would do not to violate, but to redeem from violation the Constitution."

Baldwin noticed the secretary of state growing agitated. I imagine the lines in Adams's forehead coming together to form a chasm, his face turning a deep, dark red.

Adams did not stop there. "That article was in itself a dissolution of the Union. If acquiesced in, it would change the terms of the federal compact—Change its terms by robbing thousands of Citizens of their rights—And what Citizens, the poor, the unfortunate, the helpless, Already cursed by the mere colour of their skin, already doomed by their complection to drudge in the lowest offices of Society, . . . excluded from the benefits of a liberal education; from the bed, from the table, and from all the social comforts of domestic life this barbarous Article deprives them of the little remnant of right yet left them—their rights as citizens and as men."

The words that flew from his mouth had previously been consigned to the private confessions of his diary. Now they were leaping from the page into the air. Baldwin just sat there, listening.

The son of the cantankerous John Adams did not hold back, publicly exposing himself as America's number one prophet of doom. "If the dissolution of the Union must come let it come from no other cause but this. If Slavery be the destined Sword in the hand of the destroying angel which is to sever the ties of this Union, the same sword will cut in sunder the bonds of Slavery itself. A dissolution of the Union for the cause of Slavery would be followed by a servile war in the Slave-holding States, combined with a War between the two severed portions of the Union. It seems to me that its result must be the extirpation of Slavery from this whole Continent, and calamitous and desolating as this course of Events in its progress must be, so glorious would be its final issue that as God shall judge me I dare not say that it is not to be desired."

The fire and fury of Adams's tirade only made the silence at its conclusion more awkward. Adams's words still hung in the air when Baldwin nonchalantly replied, "He entertained different opinions . . . of this class of our population. I think they are far more mischievous than useful. Of all the petty crimes committed in the part of the Country where I reside, nine tenths are by free people of colour. I believe it is the same throughout the Country, though there may be an exception in the Eastern States. All the States make laws for the exclusion of paupers and vagabonds, and persons whose residence within the State would become a nuisance. For my part, I am willing to admit Missouri, in any form in which it has been proposed with the condition or without it."

Adams expected Baldwin's NIMBY, Archie Bunker–esque response. Samuel Flagg Bemis points out that Baldwin's response "was a weak rejoinder, by a man whom nobody now remembers."

After much debate in Congress, Henry Clay managed to put the matter to rest by getting a resolution passed that admitted Missouri into the Union on the condition that the state would agree to never pass a law that restricted the rights of a citizen from another state. In 1820, very few, if any, congressmen had an appetite for a war between the states and were happy to make loud speeches but vote for compromise.

Adams knew the peace was temporary. "There must be at some time a conflict upon this very question between Slave and free representation; but this is not the time; nor was this the proper occasion, for contesting it." Adams would spend the remainder of his time as secretary of state prioritizing diplomacy over emancipation.

Abraham Lincoln said of his times, "In this and like communities, public sentiment is everything. With public sentiment, nothing can fail; without it nothing can succeed. Consequently he who molds public sentiment goes deeper than he who enacts statutes or pronounces decisions."

A few antislavery newspapers began springing up in the North and upper South. Lundy feared there was no need for another antislavery newspaper in Ohio. He reasoned the best way for him to break at least one link in the ponderous chain of slavery was to go to a region of the country where there was a need: the West. Illinois was a place where proslavery forces, fresh off their victory in Missouri, smelled opportunity.

On the long journey back to Ohio, news reached Lundy that Elihu Embree had died in Tennessee on December 6, 1820. He was just thirty-eight years old. With the *Emancipator* suddenly silent, Lundy saw an opportunity to start his own newspaper.

When Lundy arrived back home to Saint Clairsville, he moved his family to Mount Pleasant. In June 1821, Elisha Bates published the prospectus for Benjamin Lundy's *The Genius of Universal Emancipation* in the pages of the *Philanthropist.* The newspaper's name was taken from John Philpot Curran's 1794 defense of the Irish radical Archibald Hamilton Rowan against the charge of sedition. The newspaper's motto was, "Let Justice be done, though the heavens should fall."

Lundy announced his intention "to arouse and awaken the American people to a sense of the inconsistency, the hypocrisy, and the iniquity of which many of them are chargeable." He promised to make his paper "an active instrument in the attempt to abolish that cruel and disgraceful system in the American Republic."

Starting a newspaper was a gutsy move for a guy who did not know the first thing about printing a newspaper, or even own a printing press. At the start, Lundy had only six subscribers and was broke. "I had begun the work without a dollar of funds, trusting for success to the sacredness of the cause; nor was I disappointed. In four months from the commencement, my subscription list had become quite large."

Elisha Bates published the first edition of *The Genius* in Mount Pleasant. The next six issues were published nearby in Steubenville, Ohio, by James Wilson. Lundy was known to make the forty-mile round trip on foot carrying his papers on his back. As *The Genius of Universal Emancipation* added subscribers around the country, the word began to spread about a young abolitionist named Benjamin Lundy.

Thomas Embree invited Lundy to move to Tennessee to resume printing his late son's *Emancipator.* The Tennessee Manumission Society owned the press and was losing money with their investment sitting there silent.

Lundy was intrigued by the idea of spreading the antislavery message in the South where he believed it needed to be heard the most. He still had faith that the cause of emancipation depended on the benevolence of slaveholders. Once they learned the horrendous truth about slavery, once they learned that free labor was not only more humane but more profitable, once their hearts were made soft by the mercy of God, they would emancipate voluntarily. Benjamin Lundy was convinced they need only to be educated.

But he had no intention of reviving the *Emancipator*. *The Genius of Universal Emancipation* was his baby. It was the newspaper he was determined to publish. The Tennessee Manumission Society agreed to Lundy's demands.

In 1822, Benjamin Lundy traveled four hundred miles on foot and by water to Greeneville, Tennessee. He was accompanied by Isaiah Osborn, the son of the noted abolitionist Charles Osborn, who served both as Lundy's printer and printing instructor.

In the wake of the Missouri question, Southern slave owners had come to view the abolitionist movement, emboldened by the speeches of politicians like Rufus King and James Tallmadge and the actions of activists like Benjamin Lundy, as a threat they needed to take seriously. Southerners were beginning to get a little paranoid that all this emancipation talk coming from the North might start giving communities of free Blacks and slaves ideas. In Charleston, South Carolina, slave owners' deepest anxieties became a reality.

In 1822, Charleston was the largest and fastest growing free Black community in the South. By one estimate, Blacks outnumbered whites 63,615 to 18,768. The city boasted several Black tradesmen and a powerful African Methodist Episcopal church. Denmark Vesey, a freed Black man, was among its prominent members.

Historians believe Denmark Vesey was likely born in Saint Thomas or Guinea, Africa. He became the property of Captain Joseph Vesey and worked in the sugarcane fields of Saint-Domingue as a boy. In 1783, Denmark moved to Charleston with Captain Vesey and trained as a carpenter. He became a skilled tradesman, a strong man, and married an enslaved woman, fathering at least three children.

Everything changed for Vesey in 1799 when he won over $1,500 in the East Bay Lottery. Denmark was able to purchase his own freedom, but not that of his wife—possibly wives—and apparently many children. He opened a carpentry shop on Bull Street and established himself as a successful businessperson and an influential member of the AME church. Vesey had gained a reputation for being bitter about the conditions of the Black man. He was angry that his wives and children remained enslaved and that he was powerless to free them. A Black man told investigators, "If a slave stepped into the street to allow a white to pass," Vesey "would rebuke him, and observe that all men were born equal." The AME church had also been under scrutiny by the local authorities for violating a state and local law prohibiting enslaved and free Blacks from holding religious services without the supervision of whites. The incident led to the jailing of some of the church's ministers. Incarceration seems tame compared to what happened next.

In the summer of 1822, Denmark Vesey was accused of being the leader of a plot to foment an insurrection among the enslaved population. A few men leaked word of the plot to their owners. One informant told his master that the insurrection was set to begin on an upcoming Sunday at midnight when slaves from nearby plantations typically flooded the city to sell their owners' produce.

Another account accused the plotters of wanting to assemble. "Nine thousand slaves and free blacks from Charleston and its hinterlands who would seize the city arsenal, exterminate the white male population, and ravage the white women, before escaping by ship to the black republic of Haiti." Authorities arrested over one hundred Blacks and executed thirty-five, including Vesey. Those who warned their masters about the plot were repaid with their freedom.

Hysteria swept across the South. The specter of Haiti and Gabriel Prosser had come to South Carolina. At the heart of

Southern paranoia were witness reports that Denmark Vesey was known to read the antislavery speeches made by Rufus King during the Missouri controversy to enslaved locals in his shop and at church. One co-conspirator confessed, "If it had not been for the cunning of that old villain Vesey, I should not now be in my present situation. He employed every stratagem to induce me to join him. He was in the habit of reading to me all the passages in the newspapers that related to Santo Domingo, and apparently every pamphlet he could lay his hands on, that had any connection with slavery. He one day brought me a speech which he told me had been delivered in Congress by a Mr. King on the subject of slavery; He told me this Mr. King was the black man's friend, that Mr. King had declared that he would continue to speak, write, and publish pamphlets against slavery as long as he lived, until the Southern States consented to emancipate their slaves, for that slavery was a disgrace to the country."

Many free and enslaved Blacks were murdered in the aftermath of the Vesey conspiracy. The AME church was burned to the ground, though it was rebuilt later. In 1834, Black churches were outlawed. But the ban could not stop the congregation from meeting secretly. After the Civil War, the congregation reorganized and adopted the name Emanuel, which means "God with us."

In our own time, Mother Emanuel African Methodist Episcopal Church has been a place of violence committed upon Charleston's Black community. On the night of June 17, 2015, a young white man named Dylann Roof opened fire inside the church during Bible study, killing nine parishioners. Roof chose the church to commit his act of violence because of its historical significance. Whatever his malevolent intentions, the incident prompted the removal of the Confederate flag from atop the South Carolina state capitol building.

• • •

The citizens of South Carolina were shocked as they read details of the Denmark Vesey conspiracy in the newspaper. Slaveholders connected the dots from Northern rhetoric over the Missouri question to the Charleston insurrection plot. People throughout the country were beginning to realize things would never be the same again after Missouri.

To remove the threat of future insurrections, the South Carolina legislature passed the Negro Seaman Act. The act codified the imprisonment of free Black sailors from any vessel either foreign or from the North coming into the port of Charleston until the vessel departed. The purpose of the law was to prevent visiting Black sailors from giving the local enslaved population any ideas about plotting another insurrection.

The law was put to the test when a Jamaican-born free Black British subject, Henry Elkison, was imprisoned while his ship sat in Charleston harbor. British consul Stratford Canning challenged the law and petitioned Supreme Court justice William Johnson, himself a native of South Carolina, for a writ of habeas corpus. Elkison argued that the United States had treaties with foreign nations that granted him the privilege to live and work freely during his stay in the city. Lawyers for the state of South Carolina argued that the Constitution gave the federal government delegated powers to make laws and pass treaties. The state, however, retained certain reserved powers, such as the power to protect itself from an insurrection. Johnson denied Elkison's appeal on a technicality. A federal judge only had the power to issue a writ under federal law, and the Seaman's Act was a state law. But Johnson could see where arguments between state and federal power could lead: "Where is this to land us? Is it not asserting the right in each state to throw off the federal Constitution at its will and pleasure?"

Adams was apoplectic. The Negro Seaman Act conflicted with federal law—full stop. The Constitution placed foreign policy squarely in the executive branch. The arrest of British sailors, Black or white, defied the executive branch's ability to enforce treaties between nations. It was a dangerous precedent for any administration to allow a state to make foreign policy. It also complicated negotiations with his British counterparts over the United States signing onto an agreement on how to enforce the ban on the international slave trade. Adams tried to balance American sovereignty and tensions with Southerners against his personal disdain for the international and domestic slave trade.

It was unconstitutional, but that didn't matter to the South Carolina legislature or even the governor. They were determined to clamp down on the movement of free Blacks inside the city. The last thing they wanted was for a gainfully employed free Black sailor to influence another uprising.

The secretary of state let South Carolina know that their state law was in defiance of federal law. South Carolina refused to amend its laws for anyone, including the president of the United States. It was a situation not unlike the provision in Missouri's state constitution, but this time there would be no compromise. South Carolina was putting nullification into practice.

The South was pulling out its hair over the Vesey episode. South Carolina had come to the realization that if you are going to enslave someone, you need to expect that, at some point, they may murder you and your family in your sleep. Particularly if they are a domestic slave and live in the room next door. *Paranoid* is not a strong enough word to describe how enslavers were feeling in the early 1820s. But the folks who traded in the enslaved had no intention of letting go. As tensions rose throughout the nation, the South looked everywhere but inward to lay blame for its problems.

They blamed Northern politicians like Rufus King who gave antislavery speeches during debate over the Missouri question. They blamed educated free Blacks like Denmark Vesey, angry that their freedom did not include the freedom of their spouses and children. They blamed Black preachers who preached the gospel of freedom. However, more and more, Southerners focused their angst on abolitionists like Benjamin Lundy who in the pages of the *Genius* called out enslavers as man stealers.

It's been said there is no such thing as bad publicity. Lundy was starting to feel the heat in Tennessee, but increasing criticism seemed to coincide with a boom in subscription numbers. Proslavery men accused Lundy of stirring slaves to commit "acts of fire and blood, in a fruitless struggle for liberty." They also accused Lundy of being a tool of Great Britain, the nation's arch enemy.

The War of 1812 and the 1814 burning of Washington remained fresh in the minds of American citizens. Newspapers circulated stories that the British cabinet was subsidizing the *Genius.* Those same correspondents charged that the abolitionist movement in America was a British plot to regain control of its former colonies. The conspiracy also included the claim that the British were also in control of the other great American bogeyman, the Bank of the United States. This was ironic considering that, not long before, John C. Calhoun had told Adams that in the case of a civil war over slavery, the South would seek the support of Great Britian in its own defense. Politics, am I right?

Anxiety makes people more susceptible to conspiratorial thinking. All this was believable to Southern slave owners. The British abolition movement had been gaining momentum in England since the time of the Revolution. It's a little ironic that the nation who introduced the practice to the colonies would soon squelch it out of existence.

In 1807, Britain outlawed the purchase of slaves directly from the African continent. A year later, a similar ban passed in the

United States went into effect. Enforcement of this ban was what Adams had spent the last year negotiating with Great Britain. But in the 1820s, a wave of abolitionist sentiment was being pushed forward by a reform movement that swept across England and its colonies, and it influenced abolitionist thinking in the United States.

In the summer of 1823, Lundy published William Wilberforce's antislavery speeches before Parliament in the *Genius*. While attending the American Convention for Promoting the Abolition of Slavery in Philadelphia that fall, he became acquainted with the works of other important British abolitionists like Thomas Clarkson and James Cropper and published their speeches and pamphlets as well.

Founded in 1794, the American Convention for Promoting the Abolition of Slavery was a loosely affiliated collection of state and local organizations that met biannually. Benjamin Lundy may have cut his teeth in the West and the South, but the convention in Philadelphia opened his eyes to the writing of several British activists as well as to the organization's ineffectiveness.

Lundy hoped the convention would help him gain support and subscribers for the *Genius*. He served on the committee on arrangements to help draft the convention's agenda. The committee recommended the convention draft a memorial to Congress and state legislatures asking for the abolition of slavery in the District of Columbia, a memorial to Congress against the domestic slave trade, and another supporting that an enslaved person was competent to testify in court (something denied women at the time as well). The committee also suggested the investigation of Haiti as a location for Negro emigration and a request for aid from churches in the antislavery cause.

The convention rejected all of the committee's proposals apart from investigating Haiti as a suitable destination for emigration. The time for an organized pressure campaign conducted under the aegis of an antislavery organization would not come under this old and toothless convention.

After the rejection of the committee's proposals, Lundy asked the convention to sponsor an antislavery newspaper in the hopes that they would agree and that it would be the *Genius.* The convention formed another committee to discuss Lundy's motion, but after consideration, the motion was rejected. As a token of their appreciation for his enthusiasm, the convention agreed to buy ten subscriptions of the *Genius* and appointed Lundy to the acting committee to discuss the next convention.

At the convention, Benjamin Lundy saw an American antislavery movement that was unorganized, uninspired, and without direction. The big takeaway for him was that he would not put a dent in the institution of slavery if he remained in eastern Tennessee. It was time to move east and base his operation in a city with a free Black population willing to support the *Genius.* In the spring of 1824, Benjamin Lundy once again kissed his wife and children goodbye and set out on foot for Baltimore.

6

WAS THERE EVER WITNESSED SUCH A BAREFACED CORRUPTION IN ANY COUNTRY BEFORE?

Two hundred years ago, American elections were not the beauty contests they are today. There were no bloated campaign organizations consisting of a top-down hierarchy of political operatives. Candidates did not have a campaign calendar marked up with rallies and fundraisers. There were no Super PACs or 24/7 news cycles for candidates to win or push back against.

By 1824, one of the two original political parties, the Federalists, had long since disintegrated, leaving only the Democratic-Republican Party. Since every candidate was technically a member of the same party, this period became known as the Era of Good Feelings. Despite the name, there was plenty of factionalism and discord. The four-way race to replace Monroe devolved into an all-out brawl.

In the words of James Traub, "In John Quincy Adams's day, the presidency was almost a thing that you succeeded to by right." In 1824, of all the not-so-declared candidates, John Quincy Adams had earned his right to the highest office in the land. He was concluding two terms as secretary of state, which, as previously noted, was at the time considered the presidential stepping stone.

Adams's CV certainly included all the experience you could want in a presidential candidate: decades of public service at every level of the diplomatic core, a term in the United States

Senate, a lawyer who argued before the Supreme Court, and a Harvard professor of rhetoric. But Adams had bespoke qualities that made him particularly suited to the office as well. Let's face it, John Quincy had been groomed for the gig by the circumstance of being born into colonies in revolt. He himself was a living witness to the battle that lit the fuse, and his father was one of the most important revolutionaries.

The time the younger Adams spent in France with an up-close view of early American diplomacy, as well as his intimate relationship with men like Benjamin Franklin and Thomas Jefferson, were experiences second to none. As was the immense pressure placed upon him and his brothers by their parents, John and Abigail.

In a letter written to him when he was twenty-six, his father admonished, "If you do not rise to the head not only of your Profession but of your Country it will be owing to your own *Laziness Slovenliness and Obstinacy.*" That's a lot of pressure to place on your children, and it affected John Quincy his entire life.

If Adams wanted to succeed James Monroe to the presidency, he was going to have to face off against a crowded field that included other members from the "Good Feelings" cabinet, including Adams's nemesis, treasury secretary William Crawford; his ally in the cabinet, war secretary John C. Calhoun; and Henry Clay. But the most potentially potent challenger was Andrew Jackson, a US senator and the hero of the Battle of New Orleans.

Andrew Jackson and John Quincy Adams were both born in 1767. Both came of age during the American Revolution. But each man experienced a radically different war. While Adams was in Paris going to the Opera with Thomas Jefferson, Jackson was experiencing the horrors of war.

Andrew Jackson was born in a border region between North and South Carolina that ran along the Catawba River known as the Waxhaw Settlements. His parents were Irish immigrants who, like so many others, came to America poor and toiled in the rugged Carolina backcountry in hopes of building a cabin and farming their own small piece of land. Andrew Jackson's father died while his mother was pregnant with him. Andrew's mother would work hard for the rest of her life to care for him and his older brothers.

The American Revolution in the South was a civil war. Jackson's Scotch-Irish community who had suffered under the British in their native country took up arms against former Scottish highlanders who declared their Tory loyalties. In an incident that shaped the rest of his life, young Andrew Jackson, who served as a courier for the local militia, was captured by a British soldier. When the young Jackson refused to shine his captor's boots, the soldier raised his sword and struck him over the head. The depredations by the British against his family did not end there. Jackson's brother was a prisoner in a British prison camp where the conditions were so bad he died two days after his release. His mother, Elizabeth Jackson, served as a nurse for other prisoners before coming down with cholera and dying. By war's end, Jackson was an orphan. He would carry a physical scar from the soldier's beating and a deep-seated hatred of the British to his grave.

After the war, Jackson worked odd jobs before he earned a law degree, moved west to Tennessee, and established himself as a wealthy landowner with a short temper. He loved horse racing and every now and again found himself involved in a duel.

In one duel, Jackson killed a man. In another, he took a bullet to the shoulder—something else, besides his hatred of the British, that he carried to the grave.

The field of battle is where Jackson distinguished himself as the greatest American war hero since Washington. His victory in the War of 1812 against the British at New Orleans is the stuff of

Andrew Jackson

legend. The battle took place about two weeks after John Quincy Adams and Henry Clay signed the Christmas Eve treaty at Ghent, but news traveled slowly in those days.

On Sunday, January 8, 1815, Jackson and a ragtag army of four thousand farmers, frontiersmen, Native Americans, and free Blacks faced off against a disciplined and much larger British force. After four days of fighting, only thirteen Americans lost their lives and thirty-nine were wounded, compared to almost three hundred British casualties, including two British generals, and another twelve hundred soldiers wounded.

Jackson remarked, "It appears that the unerring hand of providence shielded my men from the Powers of Balls, bombs, & Rocketts, when every Ball & Bomb from our guns carried with them the mission of death." In an instant, Jackson became a national hero. But the Hero of New Orleans was soon to become a national security nightmare for the Monroe administration.

In the years after 1815, the American southern border with then Spanish Florida was the scene of violence between the Seminole Indians and American troops often under the command of General Andrew Jackson. In December 1817, President Monroe sent a vague note to Jackson asking him to extinguish the Seminole threat. Monroe let Jackson know that now was not a time for "repose" and "Until our course is carried through triumphantly . . . you ought not to withdraw your active support from it." Monroe did not explicitly tell Jackson to invade Florida, put to death two British subjects—Robert Ambrister and Alexander Arbuthnot—and take Pensacola by force. But he didn't tell him not to.

The members of Monroe's cabinet, particularly John C. Calhoun, were personally offended by Jackson's actions—but not John Quincy Adams. "I have thought that the whole conduct of General Jackson was justifiable under his orders; although he certainly had none to take any Spanish Fort—My principle is that every thing he did was *defensive*—That as such it was neither War against Spain, nor violation of the Constitution—The developement [*sic*] of this principle in its application, first to the facts, then to the Laws of Nations and lastly to the Constitution; and the defence of it against the objections of the President, and of all the other members of the Cabinet present." In the end, Jackson returned Pensacola to the Spanish. The whole affair made Adams's negotiations with Spain over Florida considerably easier.

Congress believed the Monroe administration, through Jackson, had usurped its war powers. A congressional committee was established to investigate the matter and threatened Old Hickory with a censure. Speaker of the House and presidential aspirant Henry Clay, the old star of the West, held a deep-seated mistrust of Jackson, the rising star of the West. Clay had curated for himself the image of being the first Western president of the United States—now it looked like he had some competition.

Clay denounced Jackson. To let Jackson escape justice would be "a triumph of the principle of insubordination—a triumph of the military over the civil authority—a triumph over the powers of this house—a triumph over the constitution of the land. And I pray most devoutly to Heaven that it may not prove, in its ultimate effects and consequences, a triumph over the liberties of the people." Jackson returned the insult to Clay. To a friend Jackson wrote, "You will see him skinned, here & I hope you will roast him in the west." Jackson knew how to hold a grudge.

Jackson recognized and appreciated John Quincy's support during the Seminole War affair. John Quincy Adams thought that Jackson would make a great vice president. He so admired Jackson that, in 1824, he and Louisa threw a party in his honor on the anniversary of the Battle of New Orleans. The celebration was not initially her idea, but Louisa quickly got on board.

It was the largest party ever thrown in Washington at that time. The Adamses had five hundred invitations printed up. Louisa spent days running all over Washington hand-delivering them. The guest list included every member of the House and Senate. If you were living in the district and did not receive an invitation, you were having some serious FOMO, because everybody was there. In addition to wooing Jackson, the event was an opportunity for Louisa to show that if her husband was elected, she would be the most exciting First Lady to occupy the President's House since Dolley Madison.

The preparations entirely upended the family's life. John Quincy was kicked out of his office. The second floor turned into a ballroom. Louisa had extra pillars installed on the first floor for support. Garlands were used to disguise them. Louisa herself helped construct laurel wreaths that were hung on the walls of the house.

When General Jackson arrived at nine o'clock, Louisa took him by the arm and led him around the house introducing him to guests. The general raised a glass and drank to his hostess's health. Already overwhelmed and exhausted by the evening's excitement, when Louisa finally had a chance to sit down in the ballroom, an oil lamp fell on her head. Apparently, it was not a party ender, Louisa wrote in her diary: "This gave rise to a good joke and it was said that I was already anointed with the sacred oil and that it was certainly ominous." Louisa changed her dress and rejoined the celebration, which went on until one thirty in the morning. Even John Quincy joined the crowd and danced until the end. The party was a tremendous hit, but it did nothing to dissuade Jackson from the presidency.

And why should it have? From the moment Jackson's name was put forward as a candidate in the *Nashville Gazette*, his candidacy took off like a bullet fired in one of his many duels. Jackson received the endorsement of meetings throughout the West in cities like Louisville and Pittsburgh.

In the custom of the day, Jackson denied he was in the running. "I have no desire, nor do I expect ever to be called to fill the Presidential chair, but should this be the case, contrary to my wishes or expectations, I am determined it shall be without any exertion on my part." Jackson's Tennessee supporters sent him to the United States Senate in 1823 to make his presence known.

Jackson's candidacy might have been a problem for Adams, but it was a campaign killer for John C. Calhoun. Calhoun's Southern support was bound to Jackson, so he got out of the race and allowed his name to be put forward for the vice presidency.

Henry Clay had his own beef with Andrew Jackson. Of course, they were Western rivals. But Clay also thought of Jackson as a Napoleonic figure: a military man with a short fuse and a long memory, who liked to hold a grudge. America had not chosen a military man since General George Washington, and in Clay's opinion, Andrew Jackson was no George Washington.

On the other hand, Adams believed William Crawford was *his* greatest obstacle to succeeding Monroe. He was disgusted by the way Crawford used the Treasury Department to further his own political career. More than any other department, the treasury sat atop a bonanza of patronage. Federal land offices, customs surveyors, appraisers, and revenue collectors in every port all needed to be staffed and were under the command of William Crawford.

Crawford was not ashamed to use political leverage to get what he wanted. It was Crawford who involved himself in the movement to rewrite the Illinois state constitution to make it a slave state as a means of gaining Southern support. Adams believed Crawford had been secretly working behind the scenes against the Monroe administration and considered the treasury secretary "a worm preying upon the vitals of the Administration within its own body."

Adams was unaware just how strained relations were between Crawford and Monroe. During a meeting in the waning months of the administration, Monroe and Crawford got into an argument over the appointment of certain customs officials. When the president refused to yield to Crawford's recommendations, the treasury secretary "raised his Cane, as in the attitude to strike, and said 'you damned infernal old Scoundrel.'" Monroe, known to have a bit of a hot temper himself, and no stranger to the culture of dueling, sensed that he was in danger and grabbed a pair of fire tongs. Crawford quickly composed himself, apologized, and left the President's House. It was the final meeting between the two men. Monroe did not publicize the scuffle because he did not want any bad vibes souring the Good Feelings brand.

Crawford suffered a paralytic stroke a year before the election. He recovered slowly over the next year, but he was unable to speak very well. He would never regain himself fully. But the candidate's health crisis did not stop a Republican congressional caucus from nominating the sixty-four-year-old in February of 1824. All those years of machinations and patronage gave Crawford a firm base of loyal supporters—enough support, particularly in the important state of Virginia, to split the Southern vote and deny any candidate a majority of electoral votes.

Around the country, a weakened caucus system showed that everyday Americans were in no mood to have their leaders chosen by professional politicians. This may have made sense in the early years of the republic, but as the nation continued its westward drift, a new democratic force consisting of laborers from the North and East and farmers from the West and South demanded to have their voices heard.

As the election of 1824 came into focus, Andrew Jackson had a clear edge. He had the image of a war hero. Jackson promised to wrestle federal government control from New England and East Coast elites and put it in the hands of the people. Whether it was true or not, he had cultivated the image of a common man who pulled himself up by his bootstraps. Jackson parlayed a career of lawyering and land speculation in Tennessee into a vast plantation called the Hermitage. Over one hundred enslaved persons did the planting and harvesting that made Andrew Jackson a very wealthy man.

To men like John Quincy Adams and Henry Clay, a man like Andrew Jackson living in the President's House would be a disaster. Jackson made the transition from war hero to politician by trying to seem all things to all factions. While serving in the Senate, Jackson did not behave like a populist icon. He was moderate on the policy issues driving the election. Jackson voted for the same protective tariff Henry Clay supported and the Bank of the United States, two issues he would later famously oppose. Jackson favored domestic spending when it came to internal improvements that supported the military, but opposed spending on infrastructure, like the Cumberland Road bill, which Monroe vetoed.

The election of 1824 did not come down to the issues of the candidates; it was a vibes election. Andrew Jackson gave people good vibes, and John Quincy Adams, although a loyal and noble servant to the nation, was anything but a man of the people. Adams was a relic of the American past. Jackson represented the future: a westward-facing nation where democracy would take the power away from the elites and place it in the hands of the hardworking common man. In the eyes of supporters, the revolutionary republican ideals by which John Quincy Adams was reared had become the establishment, a bloated bureaucracy hell-bent on usurping the power of the people.

Adams wanted to be president but refused to lift a finger to make it happen. He refused to canvass for votes and promised himself he would not indulge "sectional antipathies" in his run for high office. Louisa was over it. She had no confidence in the American people's ability to come to the correct decision. "He has little, in fact nothing to gain [from becoming president] and should he lose the election which is most likely from present appearances the disgrace will not fall upon him but heavily on that *very enlightened* Country and people who couldn't discriminate between sterling worth and base intrigue." And while he stuck to his refusal to participate in outward politicking, there are instances where Adams perhaps bent his own rules.

As the election drew near, Adams began to receive frequent visitors representing various states and factions of the Democratic-Republican Party. One was George McDuffie from South Carolina. McDuffie was on his way home to meet with members of his state's legislature. Now that Calhoun was out of the running, the state's support drifted between Adams and Crawford. McDuffie wanted to know Adams's opinion on the recent tariff bill.

In the 1820s, we did not have an income tax. The federal government used tariffs to raise revenue. Tariffs protected American manufacturers from being undersold by foreign goods. In New England, manufacturing was *the* economic driver. In factories in cities like Lowell, Massachusetts, tens of thousands of spindles cranked out the latest style of coats, shoes, and the like. At the same time, industries in New York and Pennsylvania produced the iron that built the railroads that had begun to tie the nation together like never before. Northern-based industry attracted wealth and a demand for Southern cotton, which in turn drove the demand for slave labor. The Tariff of 1824 was one of the cornerstones of Henry Clay's American System. Clay and other politicians from the North and West intended to use tariffs to protect domestic manufacturers from the competition of British imports. Southerners viewed the tariff to be as much of a threat to their survival as slave insurrections. McDuffie and his fellow South Carolinians believed the tariffs would raise duties on European imports and provoke retaliatory tariffs on cotton exports, which would lower the price of cotton for Northern manufacturers.

John Quincy told McDuffie he supported the bill. "The two parties had contested every inch of the ground between them with great ardour and ability. . . . With the result it was reasonable to expect that both parties would be satisfied." Adams volunteered that there was one more issue he wanted to make sure the folks down in South Carolina understood. "It was upon the Slave question generally and the Missouri Restriction particularly—My opinion had been against the proposed restriction in Missouri, as contravening, both the Constitution, and the Louisiana Treaty. This was the first Missouri question—The second was upon an Article introduced into the Constitution of the State of Missouri, which I thought contrary to the Constitution of the United States." Adams clarified for McDuffie his belief that the Tallmadge Amendment was unconstitutional. Just as it was also unconstitutional for Missouri to deny free Blacks their constitutional rights. Adams also let McDuffie know that he was frustrated with the South Carolina legislature for passing the Negro Seaman Act. It was a violation of international treaties. Adams reminded his guest that Supreme Court justice William Johnson, himself a native of South Carolina, agreed the law was unconstitutional. Regardless of his feelings on the tariff or the Negro Seaman Act, Adams wanted South Carolinians to know he, if elected, was not going to take their slaves away.

That summer, Adams kept up a steady routine of waking around five or six and going for a swim in the Potomac. Watching the morning sun rise over the shimmering water brought him a little peace of mind and a break from the steady stream of visitors coming by the house every day. Adams really needed this daily moment of zen. When he returned home and picked up the morning papers, he found them "pouring forth continual streams of Slander upon my character and reputation, public and private—No falsehood is too broad, and no insinuation too base for them. . . . The result is a great waste of time . . . to the necessary neglect of public business, and detriment to the public service. . . . To pass through it with a pure heart, and a firm Spirit, is my duty and my prayer." As August turned to September, Adams took his last skinny dip in the Potomac. He confessed to his diary that it might be his last ever. The end of what he called "the bathing season" meant it was time for him to head North.

When Adams arrived in Quincy, Massachusetts, he found his father's health had declined since his last visit. The ex-president was a revelation of what age and time does to us all. The old patriot struggled to walk and was no longer able to read or write. But he still had an active mind for politics and would comment on the news of the day with "sound discernment" as it was read to him. John Quincy commented, "The most remarkable circumstance of his present state, is the total prostration of his physical powers, leaving his mental faculties scarcely impaired at-all."

Pondering his own fate, John Quincy walked through the family graveyard, visiting his older sister, Nabby, who had died from breast cancer in 1813. Adams also stopped at the grave of his great-great-great-grandfather Henry Adams, who came over from England nearly two centuries before. "Pass another century, and we shall all be moldering in the same dust or resolved into the same elements. Who then of our posterity shall visit this yard? And what shall he read engraved upon the Stones? This is known only to the Creator of all. The record may be longer—may it be of as blameless lives."

If Adams lost the election, he believed it would be a personal rejection of him by the nation he had devoted himself to serve his whole life. "To suffer without feeling, is not in human nature, and when I consider that to me alone of all the Candidates before the Nation, failure of success, would be equivalent to a vote of censure by the Nation upon my past service, I cannot dissemble to myself, that I have more at stake upon the result than any other individual in the Union. . . . If I am able to bear success, I must be tempered to endure defeat . . . I look to wisdom and strength from above."

John Quincy left for Washington on September 24. "I took leave of my father, with a heavy and foreboding heart. Told him I should see him again next year." Adams headed south to face the voice of the people.

During his travels, John Quincy met with the esteemed French hero of the American Revolution, Lafayette, and his son, George Washington Lafayette, in Philadelphia. President Monroe had extended an invitation for Lafayette to tour the United States. Adams joined Lafayette and his entourage for a commemorative event at Independence Hall, where John Quincy's father had signed the Declaration of Independence nearly fifty years earlier. Over the course of thirteen months, Lafayette would visit all twenty-four states. His visit occurred during a complex period as memories of the founding era were being overshadowed by an emerging and unpredictable populism.

The election of 1824 was held between October 26 and December 2. John C. Calhoun easily locked up the votes needed to become vice president. In the presidential race, Andrew Jackson emerged as the leading candidate. However, the four-way race divided the votes significantly, preventing any single candidate from obtaining a majority of votes or electors. According to the Twelfth Amendment, the top three candidates advanced to an election in the House of Representatives.

For the second time in America's brief history, the House of Representatives would decide who would become the next president. If that sounds like a complicated and contentious way to decide an election, it is. Not to mention the House of Representatives circa 1824 was not exactly like what we see these days on C-SPAN. It was a rough and rowdy place where tobacco spit landed on straw-covered floors.

The House scheduled the vote to decide the election for early February. Henry Clay was eliminated because he got the fewest votes. But Clay was not the type of guy to sit on the sidelines. Clay lost the election but became a kingmaker in the process. Everyone wanted and needed his support. Clay preferred Adams. But Clay also could not just come out and say that he supported Adams. That would appear unseemly.

Really, who else could Clay support? He hated Jackson and everybody knew Crawford was in no condition to serve, even though he won the electoral votes of Virginia, Georgia, and Delaware, as well as a few votes from New York, go figure.

Clay and Adams both wanted a strong, centralized government. They wanted a central bank. They wanted the federal government to fund national infrastructure projects to bind the East to the growing West. And they wanted tariffs to protect Northern manufacturers from foreign products. They were also worried about what Jackson might do if elected. Would he be pro-Union? Would he declare himself king and tear up the Constitution? No one knew.

And you really cannot overstate the degree to which Henry Clay despised Andrew Jackson. He once said, "I cannot believe that killing 2,500 Englishmen at New Orleans qualifies for the various difficult and complicated duties of the chief magistracy." Clay told friends he should "consider the elevation of the Hero, as the greatest calamity, which could befall the Country."

In December, after Louisiana announced the results of their vote, and everyone knew the election would be decided in the House of Representatives, Adams began receiving visits from certain friends of Clay who spoke in vague terms about Clay supporting Adams, "if he could thereby serve himself." Adams knew this meant that if he promised Clay's friends that Clay would have a prominent role in the Adams administration, it might "induce them" to vote for Adams instead of Jackson, who they were pledged to vote for.

At a party held in honor of Lafayette on New Year's Day, 1825, Clay told Adams he looked forward to meeting with him privately to have a "confidential conversation upon public affairs." Clay and Adams would meet twice to discuss the election. After their second meeting, Adams wrote, "He spoke to me with the utmost freedom of men and things—Intimated doubts and prepossessions concerning individual friends of mine, to all which I listened with due consideration." No one would say aloud what everyone knew Clay wanted, secretary of state in the Adams administration. Clay wanted to stand on the presidential stepping stone. To support Adams would force the Kentucky delegation to go against the vote of their state legislature. In a phrase that has become popular in our own time, they would become "faithless electors."

As any political operative from any decade or century will tell you, it is impossible to keep a secret in Washington. As word of Clay's support for Adams leaked, Jackson's supporters grew hostile. In the days before the vote was set to take place, Adams feared there might not be a peaceful transition of power. "I received this morning an anonymous Letter from Philadelphia, threatening organized opposition, and civil war, if Jackson is not chosen. . . . This blustering has an air of desperation—But we must meet it."

Dawn broke, cold and snowy, on the morning of February 9. The House was set to decide the presidency. A long line of people, dressed in their finest clothes, braved the weather, camping outside the Capitol for hours. Many traveled days to get a front-row seat for the political spectacle about to unfold.

Even though this was one of the most intense moments of John Quincy Adams's life, he avoided the commotion surrounding the vote. Adams did what he did every other day. He woke up, wrote in his diary, and went to the office.

No one could predict exactly how the vote would go. The last time something like this happened was in 1800 when it took thirty-six rounds of balloting to determine Thomas Jefferson would be the third president. Thanks a lot, Aaron Burr. Worst veep ever.

While the buildup to the 1824 election was long and arduous, the vote itself was simple. There were twenty-four states at the time. The delegation from each state would cast a single vote for either Andrew Jackson, John Quincy Adams, or William Crawford. Even though no one really saw Crawford as a threat.

It all came down to a two-way race between Jackson and Adams. One of them needed to capture an absolute majority of thirteen votes to win. Behind the scenes, Henry Clay was whipping delegations into the Adams camp . . . encouraging state delegates who had supported him to now vote for Adams.

Legend has it that the vote came down to the aged General Stephen Van Rensselaer from New York, the brother-in-law of the late Alexander Hamilton. Van Rensselaer was under pressure from Martin Van Buren to vote for Crawford, but Henry Clay and Daniel Webster pulled him aside and told him that the election was in his hands and that if he did not vote for Adams, chaos would follow that would threaten his vast wealth and property. Van Rensselaer, anxious and unsure about what to do, did what he always did when he found himself in a moment of doubt. He put his head down on his desk, closed his eyes, and prayed to God for a sign. When he opened his eyes, he looked down and saw a ticket on the floor with the name John Quincy Adams on it. He picked it up and dropped it into the ballot box.

Thanks to Henry Clay, Adams won thirteen states in the first round of voting. A slim majority, but enough to win. An old friend and former colleague, Alexander Hill Everett, ran to Adams's home on F Street with the news. He won! He would become the

Feeling the pressure, Stephen Van Rensselaer prays for a sign from God as he casts his vote in the 1824 election

first son of a president to become commander in chief. Adams wrote, "May the blessing of God rest upon the events of this day."

Later that night, President Monroe held a celebration in honor of President-Elect Adams. All of Washington was there. As the story goes, the crowd parted as Jackson, with a woman on his arm, approached Adams. Nobody knew what he might say or do. This was a man with a history of gunning down his rivals, a bullet still lodged in his shoulder. When Jackson got to Adams, he said, "I give you my left hand, for the right, as you see, is devoted to the fair. I hope you are very well, Sir."

The gentility did not last. Just days after winning the House vote and becoming president, Adams nominated Clay, not Jackson, to be his secretary of state. Jackson was outraged. Clay's selection proved that he and Adams had in fact hatched a corrupt bargain.

Andrew Jackson's hatred of Henry Clay would last for the rest of his life. Jackson wrote to a friend, "The *Judas* of the west has closed the contract and will receive the thirty pieces of silver. Was there ever witnessed such a bare faced corruption in any country before?"

Adams offered Jackson the War Department, but Jackson had no intention of taking the position. *He* was the rightful president. How could he work with the usurper, Adams?

Stoked by fire and fury, Jackson supporters geared up for his next presidential run in 1828. Meanwhile, in Congress and in the press, Jackson's supporters were laying the groundwork to make John Quincy Adams a one-term president. Just like his father.

7

I WOULD NOT EXCHANGE CIRCUMSTANCES WITH ANY PERSON ON EARTH

Adams wanted to ensure his cabinet reflected the nation. Having lost the popular vote and being only the second president elected by a vote in the House of Representatives, he was determined to be a president for the whole Union. Of course there was the controversial choice of the Westerner Henry Clay of Kentucky for secretary of state. Adams also retained Marylander William Wirt as attorney general from the Monroe administration and added James Barbour of Virginia, a slaveholder, as secretary of war.

Barbour was one of those Southerners who'd had it with abolitionists. In October of 1825, he gave a speech in which he called out by name and condemned Benjamin Lundy and *The Genius of Universal Emancipation* as the "croakings of the distempered, who seek to establish a character for philanthropy at the expense of others." According to Barbour, Lundy best keep his mouth shut and leave talk of slavery to the slaveholders. And furthermore, keep Congress out of it.

In Baltimore, Benjamin Lundy established ties with the local free Black and antislavery communities. He focused both on establishing an antislavery foothold in the political world and helping free Blacks immigrate to Haiti. Free Blacks were suspicious of the idea of Haitian emigration and the American Colonization Society.

Where the goal of the ACS was the removal of all Blacks from the United States, which Benjamin Lundy did support for some time, he saw Haitian emigration as an opportunity for freed men and women to build a prosperous society that would prove finally that Blacks were capable of self-government.

Haiti's president, Jean Pierre Boyer, had been optimistic that an influx of Black Americans would help stabilize the political situation. He sent a special agent, Jonathan Granville, to the United States to aid in the process. When Granville arrived in Baltimore, he met with a community of free Blacks and convinced them to "use all honourable means to procure a speedy and effectual emigration of the free people of colour" to Haiti. To entice Blacks to relocate, the Haitian government offered generous financial incentives. Granville recruited more than six hundred emigrants while on his four-month tour through New York, Philadelphia, and Baltimore.

Just when the initiative appeared to gain momentum, rumors, likely started by supporters of the ACS, began to circulate. The ACS looked upon Haitian emigration as a rival operation, not to mention a danger to the United States. Southerners did not need to be reminded that Black Haitians gained their independence by slaughtering their European oppressors. In addition, claims were being made that the emigrants in Haiti experienced similar challenges to those who settled the West African colony of Liberia. Settlers there suffered from a lack of resources, disease, and violence committed on them by local tribes. In the pages of the *Genius*, Lundy attributed these rumors to proslavery activists who were trying to debase the project. To rebut the accusations, he published testimonials he claimed came from happy Haitian emigrants.

Then came the death blow. The Haitian government announced that after June 15, 1825, it would no longer offer financial support to American emigrants. According to the Haitian government, many of the new arrivals quickly became disenchanted with life on the island and immediately applied for permits to return to the States.

Ever the optimist, Lundy pressed on. He agreed to accompany a group of freedmen to Haiti in hopes of meeting with government officials and seeing conditions on the ground himself. Why was the Haiti plan so important to him? Lundy viewed Haiti as an opportunity to put communitarian philosophy into action.

Lundy had an idea while operating a free produce store in Baltimore. He hoped to purchase a piece of land that could support a sizable number of freemen and their families who would farm the land. In return, Lundy would sell the cotton and other products they produced in Northern cities like Philadelphia, where the Quaker-led Free Produce movement provided goods to those who wanted products not made or grown by enslaved hands.

On his way to Haiti, Benjamin once again left Esther alone to care for their three young children. But this time Esther was pregnant and frail, suffering a rheumatic illness. She didn't want him to go but finally assented. He promised her this time it would be different. He would be gone only eight weeks.

Lundy was on a mission from God. Any hardship his family experienced in his absence bore no comparison to what those who are enslaved suffered under the lash.

Lundy set out for Haiti in the fall of 1825, accompanied by a small group of recently freed Blacks from North Carolina. It had been reported by Haitian officials that out of the six thousand emigrants who received financial incentives to emigrate, one-third had requested a permit to return to the United States. However, Lundy met quite a few settlers as he toured the countryside who he said worked diligently and lived contentedly in their new homes. Regardless of the attitude of the Haitian government, Benjamin Lundy was still committed to the project. So he sought the support of a local philanthropic society for help. This kept him in Haiti longer than he had planned. Longer than he promised Esther he would be gone.

His ship home from Haiti arrived with the devastating news that Esther died while giving birth to twins. Lundy's ship was kept in quarantine when it entered the port of Baltimore. "I persuaded the captain, however, to go on shore with me at night, that I might see my little orphan children. We rowed a small boat several miles to the shore. I hastened to my dwelling, but found it deserted."

Lundy ran through the moonlit, cobblestone streets of Baltimore. He burst through the door of his house. It was dark, empty, and silent. He woke his neighbors, but no one knew what had become of his children. Heartbroken, Lundy and the captain returned to the quarantined ship, arriving before daybreak. When the authorities allowed Lundy to return to shore, he learned that a group of friends had taken his children into their homes the night his wife died. Lundy's sister would later write, "He thought of the five infant minds, of which he was now the sole sustainer and guide . . . and his heart almost fainted within him."

With the death of Esther, Benjamin Lundy threw himself deeper than ever into antislavery work, placing his commitment to the cause over caring for his children. He sent his three older children to live with his father and stepmother in New Jersey. He hired a nurse and secured a place for the newborn twins at a boardinghouse. When they turned three, they went to live with his sister-in-law and her husband in Ohio. The couple had tragically lost their children and were excited to raise them.

Baltimore was unique in that it had a thriving free Black population but was also a hub for the slave trade. It is not surprising that Lundy's *Genius of Universal Emancipation* took aim at the city's most notorious slave trafficker, Austin Woolfolk. Lundy claimed Woolfolk was the head of the largest slave-selling enterprise in the state and possibly the entire country. According to historian Calvin Schermerhorn, "If Lundy's reporting is accurate, the Woolfolk enterprise was actually responsible for 87 percent of the Baltimore slave trade during the sample period."

Woolfolk stood six feet one with an athletic frame. As a teenager, he served in a Tennessee militia regiment under his father, Major William Woolfolk. Father and son both served under General Andrew Jackson at the Battle of New Orleans.

After the war, looking to get rich and make a name for himself, Austin moved to the notorious seaport city of Baltimore, which one Boston newspaper tagged as being "made up of adventurers from other parts of this country, of foreigners, fugitives from justices, the outcasts of society and the disgrace of it."

Woolfolk began dealing in slaves and established a network of personal connections including with his relatives who extended from Baltimore all the way down to New Orleans. His newspaper ad catchphrase was "CASH FOR NEGROES." Woolfolk's agents scoured the region looking for slaves to purchase. The enslaved individuals Woolfolk acquired were kept at his pen on Pratt and Cove Streets. When he had enough people and a buyer, he would either march them to Georgia or ship them south from Fells Point.

In 1826, Woolfolk shipped between thirty-one and thirty-three enslaved persons to New Orleans aboard the *Decatur.* At sea there was a mutiny led by a twenty-four-year-old captive from West River, Maryland, named William Bowser. Bowser helped throw the captain and first mate overboard as the other captives took control of the vessel. Having no navigator among them, the *Decatur* drifted aimlessly until it was spotted off the Georgia coast by a whaling ship on its return voyage from the Pacific. When the crew of the whaler pulled alongside the *Decatur* to request supplies, they realized there had been a rebellion and seized control of the ship.

Bowser was tried in a US circuit court in New York City, the whalers' home port. He was guilty of the murder of the captain and the first mate and sentenced to hang. A New York newspaper reported that Austin Woolfolk was present at the hanging. As he was led to the gallows, Bowser made a speech in which he forgave Woolfolk for the wrong he had done to him. In response, Woolfolk allegedly shouted an "angry profanity" just as the floor dropped and the rope did its dirty job.

In the pages of the *Genius*, Lundy accused Woolfolk of being the one to blame for the deaths of the captain, first mate, and Bowser. Woolfolk denied being present for Bowser's execution and had had enough of Lundy's attacks on him, his business, and the institution of slavery.

In early January 1827, Woolfolk cornered Lundy while he was on Charles Street on his way to the post office. Bigger, stronger, and younger than his foe, the enslaver accused the reporter of libel. Lundy tried to ignore Woolfolk and stated he only printed the truth. Woolfolk followed Lundy, verbally chastising him. Lundy continued to ignore his pursuer, when, according to Lundy, Woolfolk "stripped off his coat, gave it to one of the by-standers, and took hold of [his] collar." Before he could comprehend what was going on, Woolfolk threw Lundy to the ground and began pummeling him. Lundy testified, "He choked me until my breath was nearly gone, and stamped me in the head and face, with the fury of a very demon." As a result of the incident, Lundy spent the next few days in bed on doctor's orders.

Woolfolk was charged with assault. The case landed before Judge Nicholas Brice, who scolded Lundy for attacking Woolfolk in the press. Brice believed Lundy should be the one on trial. Poor Austin Woolfolk was an honest and respectable businessman; he did not deserve to have that kind of filth written about him in the newspaper. Woolfolk was guilty of assault but was only fined $1 plus court costs. Judge Brice recommended he file a libel suit against Lundy.

Neither a public beating nor verbal chastisement in a court of law made Lundy any less determined in the cause for which he had sacrificed everything. His beloved Esther was dead. His children scattered. Even with Lundy on the verge of financial ruin, the judge wanted to press charges against him!

Undeterred, Lundy picked up the work that had been started when the Woolfolk fiasco fell upon him. He and an associate, Daniel Raymond, "drafted" a memorial to Congress asking for an end to the institution of slavery in the District of Columbia.

The First Amendment to the Constitution enshrined the right of citizens to petition the government for a redress of grievances. In the 1820s, citizens sent petitions to their congressional representatives. There were no lobbyists. Citizens did not have organizations like the NRA or MoveOn to mobilize pressure campaigns. Petitions were often a personal request like asking for the remittance of someone's Revolutionary War pension. However, it was not unusual for antislavery petitions to make their way to the floor of the House of Representatives. In fact, it happened during the very first Congress.

In February of 1790, a petition arrived in the House of Representatives from the Pennsylvania Abolition Society. It was the Second Session of the First Congress. The petition requested that Congress "entreat your serious attention to the subject of slavery . . . to countenance the restoration of liberty to those unhappy men, who alone, in this land of freedom are degraded into perpetual bondage . . . that you will devise means for removing this inconsistency from the character of the American people." The petition was signed, "Benj. Franklin, *President.*" The eighty-four-year-old Franklin would be dead in two months. His reputation had taken a hit in recent years in part due to his friendship with France, now in the throes of revolution, and his support for abolition.

The petition set off a ferocious debate over what the Constitution, and the Bible, for that matter, did and did not express about slavery. Georgia Congressman James Jackson asked if raising this antislavery "business" was a good move. Would it not light up the flame of civil discord? For the people of the Southern states would resist the tyranny as soon as another. The petition inspired no action of consequence; however, the event shows Congress was no stranger to antislavery petitions. It also shows that if Benjamin Franklin, albeit past his prime but still revered, could not stoke action on slavery, could an ordinary citizen like Benjamin Lundy?

More than a thousand people signed Benjamin Lundy's memorial. When Lundy sent the memorial to Representative John Barney, it triggered a series of events that changed the course of the abolition movement in the United States. Adams, sitting in the President's House, had no idea the role Lundy, his memorial, and his right to send it would play in his life once he left office.

But we are getting ahead of ourselves.

Barney presented the memorial on the floor of the House on February 12, 1827. "Of sundry citizens of Baltimore, in the State of Maryland, praying that a law may be passed providing that all children hereafter born of parents held to slavery within the District of Columbia, shall be free at a certain age, and moved that it be printed."

That Lundy requested "all children hereafter born of parents held in slavery" sounds a lot like James Tallmadge's Missouri amendment—the one John Quincy wrote that caused Southern politicians to seize with cramps.

However, Lundy petitioned for emancipation only within the District of Columbia. Congress had decided during its first session that it had no constitutional authority to interfere with slavery in the states. The District of Columbia was under federal jurisdiction (a fact that does not seem fair to many Washington, DC, residents to this day—check out their "Taxation without Representation" license plates).

No sooner did Barney put a period on the end of his final sentence than Congressman George McDuffie leapt to his feet and challenged the memorial. McDuffie began by saying it is the job of Congress to represent the people of the District. "They are under as perfect a despotism as ever existed in the Provinces of Rome. . . . They have no voice in the election of those who legislate for them." Hence the license plate motto and all the bumper stickers. McDuffie asks, who are we (Congress) to tell them who they can or cannot hold in bondage?

McDuffie said if the people of the District of Columbia wished to abolish slavery, they would submit their own petition, and he would support them. But the people of Maryland have no authority to deny slaveholders in DC "of their property, by means which they have no agency in creating or promoting." For that reason, McDuffie said he did not support even printing the memorial.

Virginia Congressman Alfred H. Powell agreed with McDuffie, adding that printing the petition would "disseminate a partial and intemperate view of the subject of slavery, a measure very likely to do harm, and from which no possible good could arise."

Barney told his colleagues that he understood dealing with the slave question was "premature, impolitic, and injudicious . . . to the present generation." And that he only offered the petition because his constituents had a constitutional right to submit it. The request to print was denied and petition laid upon the table.

In 1827, there were few congressmen willing to go to the mat for abolitionist petitions after all the bitterness stirred up in the battle over the Missouri question. The exception was Charles Miner, a congressman from Pennsylvania who had supported both Adamses' presidencies. Miner was a colorful character whose CV includes frontiersman, printer, historian, and songwriter. Just like Benjamin Franklin, in the early 1800s, Miner published a newspaper with his brother in Luzerne County. The paper printed Charles's column, "From the Desk of Poor Robert's Almanack," which sounds a lot like Benjamin Franklin's *Poor Richard's Almanac.* Miner is credited with the phrase *ax to grind.* There is evidence Franklin coined the phrase. But that is a debate for another day.

For now, let us focus on Miner's two terms in Congress, which overlapped with John Quincy Adams's presidency. Unlike Adams, who wanted nothing to do with the slavery issue throughout his stay in the President's House, Miner was all in against slavery. And his actions in Congress caught the attention of Benjamin Lundy.

Miner at best imitated the homespun wisdom of Benjamin Franklin; at worst, he stole it. However, he was definitely an innovator in Congress. I admit it. I have spent many hours of my life watching C-SPAN. Occasionally, I've noticed representatives use visual aids in their floor speeches. For example, maybe a rep is standing next to a chart that shows the ballooning deficit. Miner had a friend "produce engravings depicting the capital's slave trade" and used them during his floor speeches blasting the institution. Miner even went as far as to conduct his own congressional investigation, visiting the city's slave pens and interviewing enslaved people about their lives and treatment. Ultimately, Miner served only two terms. Congress would not see the likes of a Charles Miner again for another decade.

Lundy used the pages of the *Genius* to highlight Miner's antislavery petitions and floor speeches. Lundy also convinced the American Convention for Promoting the Abolition of Slavery to adopt his resolution to "prepare an address to the several

Abolition and Manumission Societies in the United States, requesting them to have memorials signed by as many of the citizens of their vicinity as practicable, and forwarded to Congress, praying for the abolition of slavery in the District of Columbia."

For Lundy, a man who had already done a lot of traveling in his life, a good deal of it on foot, 1828 would be a banner year. According to the great historian of nineteenth-century abolitionism Richard Newman, in the year 1828, Benjamin Lundy "traveled over 4,000 miles and visited an estimated 7,000 antislavery activists among 120 abolition groups in eight states." Lundy toured the Northern and New England states in support of the petition campaigns of Miner and the American Convention. He held lectures on the Free Produce movement and encouraged the formation of antislavery societies. As always, he was selling subscriptions to *The Genius of Universal Emancipation.*

The cities of the North had yet to become the bastions of antislavery sentiment they would be in the 1830s, but Lundy met some who would play an integral role in the years to come, like philanthropist Arthur Tappan. Within five years, Tappan would be like George Soros or the Koch brothers of today and open his checkbook to the abolitionist movement. But unfortunately for Lundy, not yet.

Many reform groups in New England focused on issues like temperance, lotteries, and Sabbath-breaking, but they were not ready to go all in on the antislavery cause. In Boston, Lundy lodged at the home of William Collier, a Baptist preacher and backer of the *National Philanthropist,* one of the emerging reform journals of the time. There, Lundy addressed a gathering of clergy members and received praise for his work on the *Genius,* but they were hesitant to go any further. Present among them was a friend of John Quincy Adams, William Ellery Channing. Channing shared much the same attitude Adams had at the time. Too much antislavery agitation would at the very least rankle the

South, at worst cause a civil war. Once again, Lundy came away empty-handed.

But Benjamin Lundy's stay in Boston was not a waste of time. It was at Collier's Milk Street boardinghouse where Benjamin Lundy first met young William Lloyd Garrison.

From Newburyport, Massachusetts, Garrison had recently moved to Boston in search of printing work and cofounded the *National Philanthropist.* Garrison had been aware of Lundy from copies of the *Genius* he picked up "as an exchange in his own newspaper office."

To Garrison, the Benjamin Lundy standing in front of him looked nothing like the Superman of abolitionism, single-handedly capable of taking on slaveholders and their allies with his printing machine. The much older, slender-framed, hard-of-hearing Lundy, whom Austin Woolfolk had tossed around the streets of Baltimore like a rag doll, was not as physically impressive as the words he wrote.

The two men bonded over long talks in which Lundy articulated the antislavery cause in ways that captivated Garrison. In Garrison's eyes, Lundy had found a cause to which he had sacrificed everything: wealth, family, physical safety. Yet, Lundy had a satisfied mind. The older man told the younger, "I would not exchange circumstances with any person on earth." Lundy converted Garrison. Garrison would convert thousands.

8

PALSIED BY THE WILL OF OUR CONSTITUENTS

On the morning of March 4, 1825, Vice President–Elect John C. Calhoun arrived at the Senate chamber. Having secured his election months before the House of Representatives resolved the presidential quandary, he was content to serve with either Jackson or Adams, an ironic twist given the history of recent events. In 1818, while Calhoun was war secretary, Andrew Jackson undertook an unauthorized invasion of Spanish Florida, executing two British citizens working with the Seminole and Red Stick Indians. This set off an international incident, raising the specter of war with Spain and Great Britain. Adams recorded in his diary that Calhoun was "personally offended" by Jackson's defiance of his authority as head of the War Department. Monroe and Adams defended Jackson, while Calhoun felt Jackson was unhinged. However, over the past year, perhaps due to Jackson's rising popularity, the South Carolinian warmed toward him, and the two began corresponding. Calhoun expressed their shared governing philosophy, stating, "I have a thorough conviction, that the noble maxim of yours, to do right and fear not is the very basis, not only of Republicanism, but of all political virtue; and, that he who acts on it, must in the end prevail." None the wiser to his previous condemnations, Jackson accepted the war secretary's compliments. Calhoun had undergone a political metamorphosis.

The suffering of his fellow South Carolinians during the recent financial panic, their paranoia about slave insurrections, and the fear that the 1824 Tariff had left the South under the federal government's boot heel convinced Calhoun to change his views or risk being left behind by the electorate. Clay's appointment as secretary of state was the final straw. Adams's vice president was now firmly in the Jackson camp.

Fate is a funny thing. On inauguration day, Andrew Jackson was still a senator from the state of Tennessee. As the oldest member of the Senate, weeks away from his fifty-eighth birthday, fellow senators selected him to administer the oath of office to Calhoun. Jackson and Calhoun stood face-to-face and stared deeply into each other's eyes, having no idea what the future held for them.

At 11:30 a.m., several militia companies and a throng of citizens arrived outside John Quincy Adams's F Street home in Washington, DC. Trumpets blared. Cannons boomed. President Monroe joined the procession in a carriage awaiting his successor. Louisa lay sick in her bed upstairs. The night before, she had had a violent fever. Louisa had long suffered from physical and mental illnesses. John Quincy bid his ill wife farewell, put on his plain black coat, and headed to his inauguration alone.

When the parade arrived at the Capitol, the president and president-elect were greeted by the Marine Corps. A band played as the entourage was escorted inside. In the Senate chamber, the body was in session following Calhoun's swearing-in to office. The crowd made their way over to the House of Representatives. According to reporters, the cavernous hall was packed with over a thousand handsomely dressed ladies, their gentleman escorts, and foreign dignitaries.

Unlike today, in the nineteenth century the president-elect gave his inauguration speech prior to taking the oath of office. At 12:20 p.m., Adams ascended the Speaker's rostrum and plunged into a forty-minute, difficult-to-hear, extremely ambitious forward-looking agenda. His detailed plans for the nation did not include gradual emancipation or the abolition of slavery in the District of Columbia. Adams pledged the focus of his administration would be on making national "improvements." Today, we call it infrastructure. He wanted the federal government to invest in a massive network of roads, canals, and bridges that would bind the Union together. Adams pledged investments in institutions like a naval academy, a national university, and what he called lighthouses of the skies, telescopes for scientific research. At the conclusion of his address, the galleries erupted in a rousing applause that lasted for several minutes. It was to be the last burst of adulation Adams would receive from his fellow citizens for years to come.

Joined by Chief Justice John Marshall, John Quincy Adams placed his left hand on a "Volume of the Laws," raised his right hand, and promised "faithfully to execute the Office of President of the United States." The founding son had become the nation's sixth president. A newspaper reporter observed that in the chaos of the celebration that followed, one of the first men to shake the new president's hand was none other than Andrew Jackson. "General Jackson we were pleased to observe, was among the earliest of those who took the hand of the President; and their looks and deportment toward each other were a rebuke to that littleness of party spirit, which can see no merit in a rival, and feel no joy in the honour of a competitor." Accounts of blessed bipartisanship belied the brutal campaign already afoot by Jackson's supporters to kill the infant Adams administration in its crib.

Over the next month, Adams was all set to lay out his administration's agenda in his first message to Congress. But when he shared a draft of his speech with his cabinet, they blanched at the ambition they heard coming from the chief executive.

The idea of a strong federal government stoked fears of tyranny. Freedom meant freedom *from* government. Many ascribed to the idea that government is best which governs least. Lawmakers believed the Constitution would not allow the government to fund John Quincy's infrastructure projects. Adams ignored the advice of his cabinet and threw all his energy and political capital into the American System anyway. On top of that, many Americans considered Adams an illegitimate president. Congress elected him, not the people.

John Quincy refused to compromise his beliefs and his political ambitions. His worldly experience and privileged upbringing made him detached from the typical American. The new president lacked the feel-your-pain empathy needed to bond him to his fellow citizens. Sure, he was quick to show off his Harvard education, quoting Cicero and Tacitus at will. But presidents back then did not give a State of the Union address and then hit the road to sell it to the American people. Instead, they wrote a speech, sent it to Congress, and people read it in the newspapers.. Adams delivered his first annual message to congress on December 6, 1825. In it he wrote, "While foreign nations are advancing with gigantic strides in the career of public improvement, were we to slumber in indolence or fold up our arms and proclaim to the world that we are palsied by the will of our constituents, would it not be to . . . doom ourselves to perpetual inferiority?"

You may not understand exactly what "palsied by the will of our constituents" means. But Adams might as well have called a vast swath of Americans "a basket of deplorables." In the early 1800s, America was still mostly an agrarian society. Many of its citizens were planters, farmers, and mechanics with no formal education. And Adams essentially said that they were the reason America couldn't compete with Europe.

Was it a gaffe? Maybe Adams could have been a little more nuanced. Adams was just pointing out that Europe was making investments in universities and scientific research, and they were seeing real advancements as a result. Adams believed lawmakers should not let public opinion hold the United States back from leading the world. It was the kind of thinking that made the twentieth century the American century, but in 1825, Americans were in no mood.

With the next election in his sights, Andrew Jackson weaponized Adams's own words. "When I view . . . the declaration that it would be criminal for the agents of our government to be palsied by the will of their constituents, I shudder for the consequence."

Jackson got it. Adams did not.

It was not just voters who hated the direction Adams and Henry Clay wanted to take America. Southern politicians had their own, specific misgivings about the policies. They despised the goals of Clay and Adams's so-called American System. Most of the proposed infrastructure projects were roads or canals that would tie the North and East to the West. The South saw their tax dollars going to projects that would not help them at all. They believed that the Constitution did not allow the federal government to spend taxpayer money in such a way. They also saw it as a threat to the institution of slavery. As historian Lindsay M. Chervinsky points out, "If you have more and better forms of travel and communication it is easier for enslaved individuals to self-emancipate and to run away. It is easier for the federal government to encroach on what they call the Southern ways of life, so they really saw any measure of federal intervention as a threat to slavery."

Jackson allies had already united in opposition. In October of 1825, the Tennessee legislature nominated Jackson as a candidate for 1828. While Andrew Jackson stood for the antithesis of everything Adams believed, he was mostly the figurehead behind a loyal network of supporters and followers who did his bidding in Congress. And the man leading Jackson's rabid sympathizers was New York Senator Martin Van Buren.

Van Buren was a Northerner, who, like many, did not necessarily like Jackson. But where others saw widening political division, he saw opportunity. He saw a chance to do what Jefferson had managed decades earlier—unite the Southern planter class with the plain republicans of the North who could live with slavery.

Van Buren wanted to bring back a Jeffersonian way of overcoming sectionalism by dividing political allegiances by ideology. And for him, the winning strategy was Jacksonian populism. Martin Van Buren would be the Karl Rove to Andrew Jackson's George W. Bush. In just a few years, what they created would become known as the Democratic Party. And that system has evolved into the two-party system that largely exists today.

The new party was still just an idea in Van Buren's head when the midterm elections of 1826 rolled around. But the divisions were real. Jacksonian candidates won a vast majority in both chambers of Congress. In the words of George W. Bush in 2006, Adams's party took a thumping.

The voters and Congress soundly rejected the American System. John Quincy, like his father, believed to his core that it was the president's duty to doggedly pursue what was best for the nation and to rise above party politics. The midterm election of 1826 proved that this belief—while laudable—was not a strategy for political success. New York City Mayor Philip Hone later said of Adams, "His desire to avoid party influence lost him all the favor of all parties."

John Quincy had a tough 1826. His agenda had stalled in Congress, blocked by obstructionists. His opposition had swept the midterm elections. But perhaps the most tragic moment of that hard year came on July 4, 1826. At ten minutes past one in the afternoon, Thomas Jefferson died. Two days later, the news reached Washington and President Adams. The irony was not lost on anyone. It was the fiftieth anniversary of the Declaration of Independence. But the news got even worse. On July 8, John Quincy received several letters from Massachusetts with the news that his father was close to death. At five the next morning, he and his son John left the President's House in a carriage. Later that morning, Adams stopped at Merrill's tavern in Waterloo, Maryland. The tavern keeper, John A. Merrill, informed Adams that he had that very morning come from Baltimore where he heard the news that Adams's father had died on July 4, at five o'clock in the afternoon. John Adams, the second president of the United States, had survived Thomas Jefferson, the third, by four hours. The news crushed John Quincy. His mentor. His hero. His father was dead.

Upon learning about his father's death, John Quincy wrote, "My father had nearly closed the ninety-first year of his life: A life illustrious in the Annals of his Country, and of the World—He had served to great and useful purpose his Nation, his Age, and his God—He is gone, and may the blessing of Almighty Grace have attended him to his Account." For the nation, the deaths of John Adams and Thomas Jefferson, two of the nation's founding fathers, passing on the very same day within hours of each other, was divine coincidence. For John Quincy, it may have been an omen.

The death of his father. A thumping in the midterms. John Quincy was in deep despair. Putting his father's affairs in order, he pitied himself, "From an active and much agitated life, to pass suddenly and forever to a condition of total retirement and almost of solitude, is a trial to which I cannot look without some concern."

Adams knew any hope of passing his agenda depended on the votes of Southerners already suspicious of internal improvements. A rare Southern ally, Senator John Gaillard of South Carolina, told Secretary of War James Barbour that the administration should say something "conciliatory" to calm the South about their enslaved property. The "friends of the Administration" from the region were under a lot of pressure as of late from the followers of John C. Calhoun. Calhoun's transformation from nationalist to fire-eating nullificationist was now complete.

South Carolinians, both in Congress and the state legislature, believed that President John Quincy Adams wanted nothing more than to confiscate their slaves. Adams had no intention of going that far, but he was still at odds with the state's governor over the Negro Seaman Act of 1823, enacted in the wake of the Denmark Vesey insurrection conspiracy. South Carolina was still imprisoning free Black sailors while their ships docked at the port of Charleston. The law was as much of a headache for President Adams as it was to Secretary of State Adams. Adams refused any reconciliation with South Carolina as long as the unconstitutional law remained on the books. The South Carolina governor did not even respond to a formal complaint made by the British government. At some point, Adams confessed, if the state did not comply, the federal government would have no other choice than to challenge South Carolina's doctrine of nullification. As much as he tried, President Adams could not entirely avoid the issue of slavery, including one instance in which Lundy's and Adams's personal interests intersected. In December 1826, Adams received a visit from men who sought a pardon for William Hill, a.k.a. William Bowser, the man whose hanging inspired Benjamin Lundy's attack on Austin Woolfolk. Itinerant preacher John Edwards and Gulian Crommelin Verplanck, a New York lawyer and politician, had each carried letters from clergy and citizens of New York pleading to have Hill's sentence commuted. Adams weighed the situation carefully. "I could grant a pardon upon no other principle, than that of formally determining that I would in no case whatever permit a capital execution during my Administration. This I did not feel myself justified in doing." Adams declined, and Hill went to the gallows.

However, John Quincy was able to secure the freedom of an enslaved African prince, Abdul Rahman Ibrahima. In 1788, Ibrahima had been taken prisoner during an attack against a rival tribe in Timbuktu when he was twenty-six years old. His captors auctioned him on the American domestic slave market, where he became the property of Colonel Thomas Foster, the owner of a large Mississippi cotton plantation. Word of Ibrahima's enslavement spread and eventually reached the sultan of Morocco. The sultan reviewed Ibrahima's case and requested his release from the United States government. The Adams administration obtained Ibrahima's emancipation from Colonel Foster on the condition the federal government send him back to Africa. After his release, the prince visited Adams at the President's House and petitioned for the release of his five sons and eight grandchildren. Ibrahima was unable to gain their freedom and died in 1829 after contracting a fever in Liberia, the colony established through the efforts of the American Colonization Society. The ACS eventually secured the release of some of Ibrahima's children.

Adams wrote in his diary that he "abhorred Slavery," and he did not suffer it in his family. But the truth is complicated. If you lived in Washington, DC, in the 1820s and moved in the social circles in which the Adamses did, it would be impossible to avoid encountering enslaved persons. The nation's capital was powered by enslaved labor, and the city of Washington had become a hub for slave traders and slave pens. John Quincy did not own enslaved people, but there is evidence that he lived with them and benefited from their services. In 1817, John Quincy and Louisa took in her sister's eleven-year-old daughter, Mary Catherine Hellen. Mary's deceased father, Walter Hellen, was the owner of several enslaved persons. When Walter Hellen died, it is likely they became the possession of Mary and her older brother,

Johnson Hellen. Johnson, a lawyer who practiced in Rockville, Maryland, lived in the President's House with the Adamses starting in 1826.

The strongest evidence of an enslaved person living under John Quincy's roof comes from three consecutive days in February 1828. On February 23, Adams wrote, "Holzey, the black boy belonging to Johnson Hellen, and who has been several years with us, died about five O'clock this afternoon. He has been sinking several months in consumption." The following day Adams wrote, "Johnson Hellen's black boy was buried" and included a verse from a poem written by the Roman poet Horace:

> Pale death, impartial, walks his round: he knocks at
> cottage-gate
> And palace-portal. Sestius, child of bliss!
> How should a mortal's hope be long, when short his
> being's date?

John Quincy was genuinely moved by Holzey's death.

Mary Hellen inherited an enslaved girl named Rachel Clark, possibly bought as a playmate by Walter Hellen. Mary's presence caused turmoil in the Adams household, with all three of Adams's sons falling for her. Initially engaged to George, she later chose his brother John II, marrying him on February 25, a day after Holzey's burial. George and Charles Francis did not attend the wedding. Notably, Mary signed Rachel Clark's manumission papers that same day, likely due to John Quincy Adams's opposition to slavery. It should also be noted that neither John Quincy nor Louisa were happy with John II marrying Mary Hellen. The stress of the situation added to George's quickening emotional crisis.

As Adams wrestled with issues involving slavery from around the nation and within his own household, his political enemies' plan to oust him from power was well underway. In December of 1827, the *Richmond Enquirer*, a paper not known to extend kindness to the Adams administration, published this account of a recent meeting of citizens "friendly to the election of General ANDREW JACKSON" from Goochland County and Elizabeth City County, Virginia. Jackson's supporters believed that having "danced attendance at foreign courts" was no measure of a president. Particularly, "at *this period*, when *regal customs and court etiquette* have become the order of the day," Jackson's supporters preferred "one disposed to administer the Republic agreeably to that simplicity of olden times." According to the citizens of Elizabeth City County, Virginia, Andrew Jackson was going to Make America Great Again! The endorsement continued. Emphasizing that while President Adams "qualified to discharge the duties of a *Professorship*," he lacked the "*talent* best calculated to conduct the affairs of a *frank* Republic." What America needed now was "that man who is prepared with the *remedy* to eradicate the disease and restore the body to its pristine health and vigor: this man we believe to be General Jackson."

The election of 1828 was a rematch. Voters love rematches. (Not really.) But this time Jackson was prepared to win. And it was going to get ugly. When people say that politics today are nastier than ever, they are not wrong, but I would argue that 1828 needs to be in the conversation for the nastiest election in American history. Talk all you want about the twenty-four-hour news cycle, in the 1820s, newspapers were political instruments of personal destruction. The party or friends of the politician financed newspapers. Good luck finding fair and balanced. In President Trump's 2024 hush money trial, many were shocked to learn that during the 2016 campaign, the *National Enquirer* printed false stories about Donald Trump's primary and general election opponents. The owner of the *National Enquirer*, David Pecker, had an agreement to support the Trump campaign. In

1828, that is the way all newspapers operated. Newspapers on both sides were brutal and unforgiving in their attacks. From the Jackson press, it was the 24/7 corrupt bargain that amounted to a stolen election. But the Adams press engaged in more personal attacks. You might even call them cruel.

An Adams-supporting newspaper in Cincinnati ran a headline saying that Jackson's mother was a prostitute. Jackson fumed at the attacks on his mother, Elizabeth. His father died before he was born, so he felt fiercely protective of the only parent he knew, a woman who had given literally everything to her children and her country. When the British captured Jackson and his guerrilla-fighting brothers during the Revolutionary War, they sent them to a prison camp. While working as a nurse on a ship, his mother came down with cholera and died, leaving Jackson an orphan when he was just fourteen years old.

When John Quincy Adams supporters dragged Jackson's mother through the mud, it cut Jackson to the quick. But that was just the beginning. What really set him off were the attacks on his wife, Rachel. When Andrew Jackson met Rachel Donelson, she had separated from her jealous husband, Lewis Robards. Hearing that her ex-husband had filed for divorce, Rachel married Jackson in 1791. But Robards had not filed for a divorce and instead brought a suit against her for adultery. When they realized Rachel was still legally married to Robards, she and Jackson separated and then remarried once the whole affair was over. Jackson and his wife claimed the whole thing had been an honest mistake. But from then on, accusations of adultery and bigamy followed the couple. Nothing ignited Jackson's short fuse like an attack against his wife or mother.

The newspapers that were sympathetic to Jackson gave no quarter to Adams or his family. One of the attacks against Adams was that while he was serving as the minister to Russia, he had pimped out one of his female servants to Czar Alexander I. This, of course, is false. The truth was that the czar developed an infatuation for Louisa's younger sister Kitty.

The Jackson press did not let Louisa off the hook. They accused her of being British. Because she was British. Besides Melania Trump, the only other foreign-born First Lady in American history is Louisa Catherine Adams, born in London in 1775. When the Revolutionary War began, Louisa's father, a patriot from Maryland living there, fled with his family to France. When the war was over, they returned to London. It was there in 1795 that Louisa met John Quincy Adams, a young diplomat from the fledgling United States dressed in a boxy dress coat, at a party at their home. Louisa came from a large family and had six sisters and a brother. The Johnson sisters were educated, fashionable, social, and very pretty. And they played music. One Louisa Adams biographer, Louisa Thomas, said of John Quincy, "I think he somewhat fell in love with the scene at first. He wrote in his diary about the beautiful music and the good food and the good conversation, and the daughters." John Quincy found himself falling in love with one of Louisa's sisters. Eventually, though, he listened to his heart and chose Louisa. In 1797, John and Louisa got married. Fast-forward thirty years, and now her name was smeared across the front pages of newspapers across America, feeding into existing conspiracy theories about Northern and antislavery sympathy to Great Britain. According to these attacks, Louisa's sympathies lied with the monarchs, not with the common men and women of America.

For the most part, at this point in American history, only white men could vote. In the election of 1828, more white men than ever cast ballots, many for the first time. For these new voters, intellectuals and establishment politicians like John Quincy Adams were what was wrong with the nation. However, Jackson, an adventurer from the West who rose from humble beginnings to become a war hero? That was someone with whom the people could relate.

Adams knew that he was going to need a miracle to defeat Jackson this time. While contemplating his prospects before the election, he compared himself to the Roman general who, after conquering Britain, laid down his arms and retired to the peace and quiet of his farm. "Prospects whether of public or of private life, without an interposition of Providence, which it were absurd in me to expect, I am reduced to wish myself the end of Agricola; to be spared the agony of witnessing the futurity before me."

In the suffocating heat and humidity of Washington in July, Adams experienced what may have been two of the brightest moments of his administration. Treasury Secretary Richard Rush came by to report that, during the Adams administration, the public debt had been slashed from over $16 million down to under $5 million. It was a worthy accomplishment any president would tout, but alas, it came too late to help John Quincy in the election.

The other moment of reprieve came on the Fourth of July, when Adams presided over the groundbreaking ceremony for the Chesapeake and Ohio Canal. The goal of the project was to connect the Potomac with the Ohio River Valley. It was an infrastructure project close to the president's heart. After a brief address to a crowd of around two thousand people, Adams picked up a spade to turn over the ceremonial first shovel of dirt. He lifted the shovel high off the ground and when he dropped it . . . hit a stump. Stunned, Adams stumbled back a few feet. The crowd hushed. Adams again lifted the shovel, and this time brought it down with even more force onto the unforgiving stump. Adams tried a third and a fourth time, "without making any impression." Finally, in dead silence, the president took off his coat, raised the spade above his head in a show of defiance, and brought the shovel down, this time into an even clump of soft earth. The crowd roared with approval as Adams lifted the shovel full of dirt with a big smile on his face. Later, Adams reflected in his diary that it was not his rhetoric that moved people; it was the theatrics of removing his coat and making a show of it at his own expense. It was much too little too late to make a dent in the public's opinions of him, but John Quincy Adams was beginning to "get it."

In late fall, Jackson was the clear winner of the popular vote, again. But he had also won a *decisive* 178 electoral votes. It was a landslide that completely wiped out John Quincy. Unlike the 1824 vote, there could be no doubt: The people had rejected Adams and his plans for national improvement. Jackson's limited government and states' rights agenda prevailed.

But Jackson's victory came at a great cost. Just weeks later, his wife, Rachel, died. She had suffered from debilitating health issues for years. President-Elect Andrew Jackson blamed her death on the brutal attacks that Adams and his allies broadcast during the campaign.

Jackson was devastated. Already in less than perfect health and with Rachel gone, Old Hickory was a shell of his former self. In some ways, he would never recover. "May God Almighty forgive her murderers," Jackson was heard to mutter at her funeral, "as I know she forgave them. I never can." For the rest of his days, his thirst for vengeance against Henry Clay and John Quincy Adams is what kept him going.

The election came at a great cost for John Quincy as well. The enormous pressure of being the son of the great John Adams weighed heavily on him all his life. Both of his parents placed the burden of the nation upon the shoulders of their son. He had spent his whole life trying to live up to their aspirations for him. After losing the presidency, he was consumed by despair. He had let the country down. He had let his late father and mother down.

Maybe it was the pressure his parents placed on him. John Quincy had struggled with depression on and off his whole life. Months prior to losing the election, Adams reflected on an inner pain that sounds a lot like clinical depression. Adams complained,

"My health has been languishing," confessing to getting only "four to five hours of Sleep," as well as suffering "indigestion, failure of appetite, uncontroulable dejection of Spirits, insensibility to the almost unparalleled blessings with which I have been favoured; a sluggish carelessness of life, and imaginary wish that it were terminated."

Upon learning that he lost the election, Adams confessed, "I have only to submit to it with resignation. . . . The Sun of my political life sets in the deepest gloom." It looked as though Adams's long career as public servant was over.

Like his father before him, John Quincy Adams did not attend the inauguration of his successor.

On March 4, 1829, Andrew Jackson became the seventh president of the United States. Jackson's inauguration was a raucous affair. There are reports of office-seekers climbing through windows and farmers walking through the President's House in their muddy boots. Washington socialite Margaret Bayard Smith recalled, "*The Majesty of the People* had disappeared, and a rabble, a mob, of boys, negros, women, children, scrambling, fighting, romping. What a pity. What a pity." She added, "The carpets and the furniture are ruined." Not just the carpets and the furniture, but the throng of the crowd also shattered the cut glass, which had been handpicked by Louisa.

After Jackson's inauguration, John Quincy and Louisa lingered in Washington waiting for their eldest son, George, to arrive to help them make the trip back to Quincy. Louisa was devastated. The stress of the campaign exacerbated her many physical afflictions.

But George had also taken a bad turn. Shortly after the election, Louisa received a letter from her youngest son, Charles Francis, telling her that George was not doing well. "I write this without any intention of unnecessarily alarming you. He is well enough in all bodily respects, but he pines for want of some excitement to action which now does not exist."

George was never adept at handling the pressure of being born into one of the most influential families in New England. He was an alcoholic and a womanizer. His behavior was getting worse. Louisa and John Quincy had watched their son slowly unraveling. Feeling helpless, they hoped a trip to Washington would do him good.

As an almost sixty-two-year-old newly retired ex-president, Adams tried to stay busy. He wrote in his diary, "After fourteen years of incessant and unremitted employment, I have passed to a life of total leisure—and from living in a constant crowd to a life of almost total Solitude." But do not fool yourself into believing that Adams gracefully accepted his forced retirement from American political life.

Adams filled his days with miscellaneous activities and trifles. He sat for the sculptor Luigi Persico as he cast a mold of him for a bust. He worked on a long essay, a rebuttal to a recently surfaced letter written by Thomas Jefferson in 1825, critical of Adams's first message to Congress. He also began work on a political history of the United States. Neither project was published until after his death.

Adams mostly read novels and entertained visitors who would drop by his house to share gossip about the new administration. One of Jackson's campaign pledges was to fire all the "corrupt" appointees from the Adams administration and replace them with loyal Jackson men. These "removals and new appointments to office" were the talk of Washington. Adams wrote that the firings were coming, "a few at a time, and in such manner as to keep up a constant agitation and alarm among the Office-holders." Who was getting the appointments? According to Adams, "The vilest purveyors of Slander during the late electioneering campaign."

Among the visitors Adams entertained during this period was a Quaker who wanted to discuss the successes of the American Colonization Society. As previously noted, Adams was no fan of the ACS. The Quaker gentleman also spoke of the horrors slaveholders perpetrated against their slaves. Adams also disagreed with this, remarking that "There are no doubt cases of extreme oppression and cruelty . . . but I believe them to be very rare and that the general treatment of Slaves is mild and moderate." This admission shows that, although Adams deplored slavery, he could still be insensitive to its ugly reality. It is hard to believe he was aloof to the extreme cruelty most enslaved people experienced.

On May 2, John Quincy and Louisa were still waiting for George to arrive when his brother-in-law showed up instead. He told them he read a brief report in the *Baltimore American* newspaper that morning that George had gone overboard the steamship *Benjamin Franklin,* somewhere between Providence and New York before dawn the previous Thursday. Within an hour, three letters arrived by mail carrying the same soul-crushing news: John Quincy and Louisa's firstborn son, George Washington Adams, was dead. He was only twenty-eight.

Louisa was inconsolable. In his diary, John Quincy wrote that, upon learning the news about George's death, Louisa's condition "is not to be described." Dr. Hunt, the family physician, came as soon as he heard the news. John Quincy lamented, "There was no medicine for this wound."

It took a few days to piece together exactly what happened to George aboard the ship. But by all accounts, George was sociable and talkative during the day. At night he became restless and appeared to be hallucinating. He entered a few passengers' cabins thinking others on board were conspiring against him. He begged the captain to take him to shore and let him off the boat, but the captain refused. Last seen making his way to the stern of the ship, George disappeared into the fog, never to be seen again.

Six weeks later, George's body washed up on the shore in Long Island Sound. In his "pockets: a watch, chain, and seal; an account book; a penknife; a comb; a silver pencil case; and eight $5 bills." Later, while going through a box of George's papers, Charles Francis found a note from George addressed to him. Should he die in the year 1828, George asked his brother to pay off his debts "and the balance given to a little girl he had seduced." Charles, circumspect, blamed George's death on the family darkness, remarking that, had George not died, he would have only caused more misery for his family and friends and that he was "unfit for the duties and common occurrences of life."

Louisa blamed herself and resented her husband. George's death opened old wounds. In 1809, when John Quincy received his appointment as minister to Russia, he decided that Louisa Catherine and Charles Francis, not yet two years old, would join him in St. Petersburg. But George, eight, and middle son John, five, would stay with Abigail Adams's older sister, Mary Cranch, and her husband, Richard.

There is no evidence Louisa had any say in the matter at the time. The arrangements were made by John Quincy and his mother. John Quincy did not even break the news to her. That task was left to John Quincy's younger brother, Thomas.

"Oh this agony of agonies!" She had written, "Can ambition repay such sacrifices? never!!—And from that hour to the end of time life to me will be a susession of miseries only to cease with existence." George and John would not see their mother and father for six years.

John Quincy leaned on his faith. He tried to accept George's death as God's will, a heartbreakingly mysterious part of God's plan. Utterly crushed by his defeat in the election and the death of his eldest son, John Quincy retreated to the solitude of his father's home, appropriately named Peacefield. There he spent his days tending to his garden and focusing on his next project:

organizing and publishing a collection of his father's papers. But God's plan for John Quincy was even more mysterious.

On the crisp late summer morning of September 17, 1830, the ex-president was an honored guest at the second centennial celebration for the settlement of Boston. Escorted by two marshals, the former president joined the procession as it passed through the Common by the great elm tree where, in 1659, the Quaker martyr Mary Dyer was hanged for believing God speaks directly to individuals, not through a preacher. After moving through the city, the procession made its way along Tremont Court and State Street to the wharf, winding its way back up State Street to Cornhill before arriving at the Old South Meeting House where John Quincy's distant cousin Samuel Adams rallied the Sons of Liberty a little over a half century before. There a choir sang Psalm 100, "his truth endureth from generation to generation."

By 1829, a lot of history had taken place in Boston: good, bad, and ugly. The Adams family certainly played their part. During the ceremony, John Quincy bumped into the retiring congressman for Plymouth, the Reverend Joseph Richardson, and John B. Davis, the editor of the *Boston Patriot.* They asked if they could come by Adams's house sometime to talk. Recently, the *Boston Courier* had printed an op-ed with the suggestion that Adams should run for the retiring Richardson's congressional seat.

Run for Congress? Adams had reached the pinnacle of political success in America. What would it say about him sitting in a legislative body in which his voice was but one of many? But then again, public service was the air he breathed, not to mention tinkering around the house was starting to get boring.

Adams downplayed the article in the *Boston Courier,* suggesting it was sarcastic in nature. The gentlemen argued the presence of a former president in Congress would only elevate the body. Adams agreed, "No person could be degraded by serving the People as a Representative in Congress—Nor in my opinion would an

Ex-President of the United States be degraded by serving as a Selectman of his town if elected thereto by the People."

John Quincy made clear that he would not actively campaign for office. When he was asked if he would accept the office if elected, Adams replied, "To say that I would accept, would be so near to asking for a vote." He wished for the people to act "spontaneously." And they did.

On November 6, 1830, John Quincy Adams won election to Congress as the representative of Plymouth, Massachusetts. Adams once again allowed himself to smash against the "Breakers of the Political Ocean." Unlike each of his predecessors in high office, Adams refused the solitude of retirement to ponder his service to the country. A seat in Congress would give Adams the opportunity to shape the nation's future and provide him with a shot at redemption.

There are probably many reasons Adams ran for Congress. But Louisa's wishes were *not* one of them. In fact, his wife did not know he was even considering it until she read about it in the newspaper! She. Was. Furious. Louisa essentially told John Quincy: Enough is enough! How much of your family are you willing to sacrifice to satisfy your ambition? But back then, that's how it was, and Louisa knew it. "In the marriage compact there are as in every other two parties, each of which have rights strictly defined by law and by the usages of society. In that compact the parties agree before the face of heaven to promote as far as in their power the welfare and happiness of each other. . . . The woman being the weaker of the two is expected and does nine times out of ten make great sacrifices for her husband." The sacrifices were gut-wrenching. "The grave of my lost child? The grasping ambition which is an insatiable passion swallowing and consuming all in its ever devouring maw."

John Quincy Adams entered Congress during the second half of Andrew Jackson's first term. By that time, Jackson had notched a few foreign policy wins. His administration negotiated a favorable trade deal with Great Britain and took on the French over their failure to pay damages to American shipping incurred during the Napoleonic Wars. On the domestic front, Jackson vetoed the Maysville Road Bill, a federal infrastructure project in Kentucky that would have applied federal funds to expand the nation's primitive system of roads, a project favored by Adams. The day after Jackson vetoed the measure, in late May 1830, he signed into law the Indian Removal Act, which once and for all dispossessed America's Indigenous populations west of the Mississippi.

The greatest struggle of the first two years of Jackson's presidency came from within his own cabinet and involved the relationship between his cabinet members' wives. The affair was a gossip columnist's dream. Floride Calhoun, the wife of the vice president, ostracized Peggy Eaton, the young wife of the war secretary, Major John Eaton, over Peggy's alleged promiscuousness and the mysterious circumstances surrounding her first husband's death. The scandal set off a war between the president and vice president and led to the resignation of the entire cabinet with the exception of the postmaster, William T. Barry, before the end of the first term. In a letter to Charles, Louisa wrote of the controversy, "War is declared between some of the ladies in the city, and . . . ladies' wars are always fierce and hot." After leaving the vice presidency, Calhoun would take up a seat in the Senate from which he would torment Adams and Jackson for the rest of his days.

Enter Congressman John Quincy Adams. Himself no stranger to personal and political backstabbing and infighting, from his desk in Congress Adams was to face down his own mortal enemy, the slavocracy. A faction so greedy it would stop at nothing to spread its seed of human bondage across the four corners of the United States and its territories.

But there were winds of change blowing across the country. In Baltimore Harbor, a wind of freedom blew a schooner carrying the itinerant Quaker abolitionist Benjamin Lundy, who was escorting a group of free Blacks to Haiti, leaving *The Genius of Universal Emancipation* in the hands of its new co-editor and the young antislavery acolyte, William Lloyd Garrison.

The winds of populism blew past the President's House in the District of Columbia as President Andrew Jackson and his cabinet plotted the destruction of the Bank of the United States. Winds of revolution blew southward where immigration posed a significant problem for the Mexican government, headquartered in far-off Mexico City. In the Tejas region, a swelling community of American expats from the United States were growing restless. The Guerrero administration had recently abolished slavery, and although they exempted immigrant slaveholders from the antislavery law, they passed another outlawing future immigrants from north of the border. The Texans made it clear to their kinfolk serving in the US Congress that they, too, viewed abolition as an infringement on their personal liberty. Soon, intrigue and chaos across the border would bring together the itinerant Quaker abolitionist and America's founding son.

END OF ACT ONE

· ACT TWO ·

· 9 ·

THE LION'S DEN OF SLAVITES, SLAVE TRADERS, AND ALL THE DEVILS IN HUMAN SHAPE

In Sean Wilentz's epic tome *The Rise of American Democracy: Jefferson to Lincoln*, Wilentz notes the populist fervor that brought Andrew Jackson to power was not limited to the inner working of American politics. As the 1820s gave way to the '30s, "popular movements redirected public loyalties and unleashed fresh ideas and programs."

Perhaps in no other realm was the breadth and scope of change in American society felt more powerfully than in the outbreak of religious revival known as the Second Great Awakening. Across the North, thousands of souls were captured in the name of Jesus Christ. For those abolitionists filled with the Holy Spirit, it was simple: Slavery was a sin. Man stealers had better repent if they had any hope for salvation.

The struggle for Black freedom was one piece in the holy cause for reform. From the Burned-Over District of New York to the Western Reserve in Ohio, the faithful engaged in the great moral struggles of their time by establishing temperance societies, Sabbath schools, and missionary societies, all in the name of bringing about the kingdom of God on earth.

At the center of the movement was Charles Grandison Finney, an ex-lawyer turned evangelist, whose sermons sent many a young man down on his knees to repent. Finney challenged the traditional Calvinist doctrine of predestination and limited atonement, which left anxious Christians wondering whether they were bound for salvation or eternal damnation. Unlike the Presbyterian preachers of the day, who talked down to their flocks in self-righteous, high-and-mighty tones, Finney spoke straight to people's hearts in the same commonsense, plainspoken way a lawyer addressed a jury. He was sick and tired of the same old "you can and you can't, you shall and you shan't, you will and you won't; you'll be damned if you do, and damned if you don't" rhetoric. Finney thumped on his Bible, prodding his listeners until they reached a state of excitement. "Mankind will not act until they are excited," Finney said. "How many there are who know they ought to be religious, but they . . . are procrastinating repentance until they . . . have secured some favorite worldly interest. Such persons never will . . . relinquish their ambitious schemes till they are so excited that they cannot contain themselves any longer." Finney believed excitement was the key to changing a heart with a "preference for self-interest" into one with a "preference for disinterested benevolence."

Finney's preferred venue for mass conversion was the revival. Religious revivals had occurred in western New York for decades. A revival typically consisted of a somewhat spontaneous gathering of souls at an outdoor venue that lasted anywhere from several hours to multiple days. At a revival, a preacher would whip up the crowd into an emotional frenzy of religious devotion. A Finney-led revival was known to attract thousands.

Of the many young men Finney lifted out of spiritual poverty, Theodore Dwight Weld showed the most potential to fill his mentor's shoes. Weld had been a student at Hamilton College in New York when he experienced a profound conversion at a revival in Utica and joined Charles Finney's holy band of itinerant preachers. Weld exhibited a natural eloquence and passion on behalf of temperance and manual labor education that earned him a reputation as a charismatic speaker. But Weld did not only exude confidence behind the pulpit or from the stage of the revival tent. A sister of the abolitionist poet John Greenleaf Whittier, Elizabeth Hussey Whittier, recorded in her diary that when Theodore Weld showed up at her door, it was as if "an archangel had entered our home!" The young woman found Weld in possession of "Godlike attributes of his very presence."

Weld's fervor for the gospel was matched only by his willingness to defy convention, such as encouraging women to speak openly at meetings. He continued his training for the ministry at the Oneida Institute, a manual labor school in New York. The quintessential example of the age of reform, the belief behind manual labor schools was that hard physical work, combined with intensive academic rigor, developed a person's "ability and responsibility" to serve God in their occupations. At manual labor school, young men learned farming, printmaking, and mechanical skills, all of which helped pay for their tuition and kept their schools financially solvent.

And so, it was in his capacity as a representative for the Executive Committee of the Association for the Promotion of Physical Education in Literary Institutions in which a young Theodore Weld wrote to John Quincy Adams seeking his opinion on "the influence of physical exercise upon health, intellect, moral feeling, habits and character." Weld posed five questions to the scholarly politician, including, "Has your experience and observation convinced you of the importance of regular exercise for the preservation of health?" Adams, perhaps one of our fittest nineteenth-century presidents, was known to time how long it took him to walk a lap around the Capitol and took regular swims in the Potomac buck naked. He replied to Weld that his experience had convinced him of the importance of regular exercise but that he did not believe it had to always be the same kind of exercise. Exercise should be "*varied* as much and as often, as the circumstances of individual condition will admit." He added, "I believe Exercise to be indispensable to bodily *health*—And that all the intellectual operations of the mind are invigorated by *health.*"

This new generation of abolitionists, of which Weld was a member, were more radical than Benjamin Lundy's generation. All were inspired by a democratizing wave of evangelical zeal, but some found inspiration in a string of slave uprisings that had occurred in recent decades. The Haitian revolution, the Gabriel Prosser rebellion, and the Denmark Vesey conspiracy helped radicalize the antislavery movement and scare the hell out of slaveholders. These events taken together amounted to a palpable shift in attitudes toward slavery in the North and the South. Nothing crystallized this combination of religious fervor and violent radicalism better than the writings of a free Black man named David Walker.

The facts surrounding David Walker's early life are vague. Walker is believed to have been born on September 28, 1785, in Wilmington, North Carolina, to an enslaved father and free mother. According to the law, the offspring of a freed woman was born free. Walker claimed he attended the AME church in Charleston while staying there in 1822 and may have taken part in the Denmark Vesey conspiracy. What we do know about David Walker is that he cemented his legacy as the most crucial Black abolitionist of the era while in Boston, working as a used clothing salesman. In the cradle of liberty, David Walker wrote *Appeal to the Coloured Citizens of the World.* The most influential pamphlet since Thomas Paine's *Common Sense*, Walker's *Appeal* was a jolt of energy to white and Black abolitionists. Historian Richard Newman describes Walker this way: "He represents all those African American musicians in the 1940s and fifties and sixties who influenced all of those white rock and rollers . . . including Elvis Presley. You can't look at the rise of rock and roll without

David Walker

looking at black musicians. You can't look at the rise of all these white abolitionist politicians and activists in the 1830s and 40s without looking at the influence of David Walker."

It is no surprise that Walker's writing offended Andrew Jackson, but it also offended Benjamin Lundy. Walker exhorted free and enslaved Blacks, "God will not suffer us, always to be oppressed. Our sufferings will come to an *end*. . . . Then we will want all the learning and talents among ourselves, and perhaps more, to govern ourselves.—'Every dog must have its day,' the American's is coming to an end." While Walker respected Lundy, placing him in the company of Wilberforce and Granville Sharp, who "have gone, and will go, all lengths for our good," Lundy, always pragmatic, was troubled by Walker's writings. Walker "indulges himself in the wildest strain of reckless fanaticism . . . [*Appeal*] is a labored attempt to rouse the worst passions of human nature, and in flame the minds to whom it is addressed." Garrison had the opposite opinion, publishing multiple articles in support of Walker and his *Appeal*.

The ground beneath the antislavery movement had shifted. For Garrison, Walker's *Appeal* confirmed what he had long suspected. The gradualist philosophy, which had undergirded Quaker abolitionists like Benjamin Lundy for so long, moved too slowly. Half measures like colonization, which most Black abolitionists had found racist, were a waste of time. The time had come for a new battle cry: immediate emancipation!

Garrison's heated rhetoric left Lundy shaking his head. He knew that fiery sermons and speeches would not free even one enslaved human being. It confirmed the belief held by many Americans that abolitionists were hotheaded radicals looking to rip apart the social fabric of the nation. He and Garrison went their separate ways. Forty-one years old, broke, his newspaper on the verge of collapse, Benjamin Lundy relocated to Washington to begin again. He was on a search for new subscribers and new allies. He thought he may have found one after reviewing the recent congressional election returns.

By capturing two hundred years of pent-up anger, David Walker's *Appeal* became but another paranoid bundle of kindling on the fire of the Southern psyche. If David Walker and his *Appeal* were a log, Nat Turner's uprising was a freaking bonfire.

An atmospheric aberration turned the sky an odd bluish green that day in late August 1831. People up and down the Atlantic coast stared at the heavens, wondering what it all meant. One Virginia preacher had been expecting this sign from God. He confessed to seeing apocalyptic visions. "While laboring in the field, I discovered drops of blood on the corn . . . representing the figures I had seen before in the heavens."

The time had come. When the last strands of the fantastical colors faded from the night sky, he got to work. He gathered six other men and crept through the swamps of Southampton County, Virginia, stealing horses, knives, hatchets, and axes. Within two days, a group of more than seventy had joined the preacher's movement. They went house to house, slaughtering every white enslaver they came across, freeing the enslaved people as they went.

Nat Turner's rebellion had begun.

When it was over, Nat Turner and his band of enslaved African Americans had killed some sixty white people, including women and children. The backlash was immediate and severe. A mob of three thousand tracked down the rebels just outside of Jerusalem (now Courtland), Virginia. When they caught up with Turner, they tore his body limb from limb. Turner would kill no more. But an idea cannot die. The ideas articulated by Walker, Garrison, and even Rufus King's writings would not die. In response, white Southerners murdered dozens of Black men and women across the region, most with no connection to the rebellion. Nat Turner's rebellion was an earthquake. State legislatures wrote oppressive laws restricting slave literacy, the possession of Northern abolitionist propaganda, and the movement of free and enslaved Blacks. From port to plantation, marshland to main street, the landscape of servile labor would never be the same again.

On December 5, 1831, at eleven thirty in the morning, John Quincy Adams walked through the columned entrance of the House of Representatives. The sixty-four-year-old once again took an oath to protect and defend the Constitution. He could not have realized the threat it faced.

The floor of the House was cold and dark in December. Adams noted in his diary that the temperature hovered in the teens all month. Fireplaces ringed the hall, the echoes of nonstop crackling bouncing off the marble walls.

The Speaker of the House selected Adams as the chair of the Committee of Manufactures—a position for which he considered himself ill-equipped. The chair of the foreign affairs committee was more in line with his vast experience. He served in multiple diplomatic posts around the world, negotiated the Treaty of Ghent, negotiated with Great Britain access to Oregon Country in the Northwest, and a deal with Spain that gave the nation Florida. But politics is politics, and he and his party were in the minority. Did he expect to receive a warm welcome from Jackson's allies? He did not. Adams even found another congressman willing to swap committees with him, but the Speaker refused. Adams would quickly see all his goals upended by the intense response to the recent slave rebellions and hot rhetoric on the topic. And in time, he'd be forced to either come out fully against slavery or accept its evils.

An invigorated abolitionist movement started to quicken the volume and pace of antislavery petitions to the House. I can imagine Southern lawmakers using them to fuel the fireplace or light a cigar. Enter John Quincy Adams. His desk was covered with petitions just a week into his term. Recall what he wrote in his diary during the Missouri debates in 1820. He hated slavery, but he did not consider himself an abolitionist, and did not believe Congress had the power to abolish slavery. It did not matter to Adams what was *in* the petitions. He saw it as his duty to give voice to them on the House floor, whether he agreed with them or not.

So, during his first session, in his first actual speech, John Quincy stood up from his desk, cleared his throat, and read one abolitionist petition after another. "I presented fifteen Petitions signed numerously by Citizens of Pennsylvania, praying for the abolition of Slavery and the Slave-trade in the District of Columbia . . . I moved that one of the Petitions presented by me should be read; they being all of the same tenor, and very short. It was accordingly read—I made a very few remarks chiefly to declare that I should not support that part of the Petition which prayed for the abolition of Slavery in the District of Columbia." With that speech, John Quincy Adams, unbeknownst to himself, became an unwilling antislavery crusader.

Adams did not see a relationship between offering a few petitions on behalf of constituents resembling anything remotely like the radical behavior of abolitionists such as William Lloyd Garrison. It was his job. He worked in the "People's House" doing the "People's business," and petitions were the "People's business." But there was, let us call it, the synergy between Adams's personal beliefs and those who were zealous in the cause of emancipation. You see evidence of this in Adams's diary. Commenting on the news of the day, he tries to reason what is moral against what is practical and possible. Take, for example, his comments on the news that the British were moving toward the abolition of slavery in the West Indies. "It may aggravate the condition of the Slaves in our Southern States; but the result of the Missouri Question, and the attitude of Parties, has silenced all the declaimers for the abolition of Slavery in the Union—This State of things however is not to continue forever—It is possible that the danger of the abolition doctrine, when brought home to the Southern States, may teach them the value of the Union; the only thing that can maintain their system of Slavery."

On February 13, 1831, Adams was just leaving services at the Unitarian church, where the preacher had spoken on 1 Corinthians 15:53, "For this corruptible must put on incorruption, and this mortal must put on immortality." When he bumped into William Seaton, publisher of the *Register of Debates* as well as the *National Intelligencer*, Mr. Seaton said he had written a letter of introduction on behalf of a "young Quaker from North-Carolina" who wished to visit him. When Adams arrived at his home later that afternoon, he found two men waiting for him, a man named Lindley, to this day a mystery to historians, and another man who we know very well, Benjamin Lundy. Adams did not go into any detail about what the men discussed. He noted sparingly in his diary that Lundy was "Editor of a weekly paper, called the Genius of Universal emancipation . . . first published in Tennessee, afterwards in Baltimore and now comes out in this City—Its object is to promote the abolition of Slavery; of which Lundy freely expressed his confidence and hopes." The way Adams records the meeting is as if it was just another in the longer tally of mundane comings and goings of politicians, thought leaders, and lobbyists he entertained daily. But from our perspective, it was fate. Lundy would not appear in Adams's diary again until 1836. In between, Lundy traversed thousands of miles north, south, east, and west. Adams made clear to Lundy he was no abolitionist. But in Adams, Lundy saw a powerful ally to the antislavery cause long before Adams realized it himself.

* * *

Through the fall of 1831 and winter of 1832, legislatures throughout the South passed ever more restrictive laws against free and enslaved Blacks. Free Black communities across the country were on the receiving end of unrelenting threats and violence from their white neighbors. Many chose to flee rather than risk suffering at the hands of white brutality. Some fled to Liberia, and others went to New York and New England. Lundy published a report of four hundred free Blacks from Cincinnati passing through New York to Canada. The band of pilgrims braved the cold and wet of the Great North as they made their way to the safety of a fledgling colony near present-day Ontario called Wilberforce.

In the early nineteenth century, Cincinnati had the potential to be the land of opportunity for free Blacks migrating from the East or those escaping bondage in the South. Its location on the Ohio River supported its most significant economic drivers, manufacturing, pork packing, and steamboat building, providing abundant free labor jobs for Blacks and whites. The Northwest Ordinance restricted slavery in Ohio, but that did not deter white city leaders from passing "Black Laws" aimed at stemming the flow of migration. The code stripped Blacks of their civil rights and demanded they pay a $500 bond within twenty days of arriving in the city to guarantee "good behavior." White leaders did not strictly enforce Black codes until the late 1820s. Between 1820 and 1829, Black population growth outpaced the white population by four to one. In the summer of 1829, city leaders decided it was time to enforce the laws already on the books. The crackdown led leaders in the Black community to plan a mass exodus from the city. But where in North America could this thriving Black community flee? Upper Canada.

The community elected two land agents, Thomas Crissup and Israel Lewis. The men traveled to Upper Canada and met with

Lieutenant Governor John Colborne. Colbourne promised the men that any Blacks who migrated to the region would share the "privileges of the rest of His Majesty's subjects," including suffrage. Any realtor will tell you it's all about location, location, location. Biddulph Township had four thousand acres of fertile soil less than twenty miles from Lake Huron and the Thames River and was just eight miles from Lake Erie. And the best part? No neighbors! Crissup and Lewis jumped on the deal. And not a moment too soon. In August, a mob of three hundred white men attacked the predominantly Black Fourth Ward neighborhood, destroyed businesses, assaulted people, and burnt homes to the ground. For over a week, the rampage continued, terrorizing the more than two thousand Blacks who had made the Queen City their home.

In the aftermath, an estimated 1,500 Blacks left Cincinnati. Many risked the 377-mile journey deep into the Canadian frontier. Lundy reported their progress in the pages of his newspaper. He published maps detailing the safest routes through the wilds of Canada. Lundy admitted he had reservations about how the emigrants would fare in such an unforgiving climate. In January 1832, he decided to conduct a fact-finding mission.

Benjamin Lundy crossed into Canada and headed west. By now, a seasoned adventurer and budding travel writer, he had noted the beautiful and "exceedingly fertile country, partly clothed with a thick forest and partly checquered with fine farms." When he arrived at Wilberforce, he found a productive community of more than thirty Black families: Baptist and Methodist churches and three schools. Lundy reported that the schools were of such quality that some of the nearby white frontier families sent their children. The community was also home to three sawmills, a gristmill, general stores, and taverns, not to mention a temperance society. The members of Wilberforce had a semblance of citizenship they would have never enjoyed in the United States.

They even elected their own representatives in the form of township commissioners.

All was not rosy at Wilberforce. The community faced many challenges. Lundy looked on grimly as a meeting "degenerated into a display of the factionalism that had nearly rent the settlement." Lundy sat there like an awkward guest at a dinner party where the host couple publicly aired their dirty laundry. From what Lundy could gather from the incident, some settlement members thought the land agent, Israel Lewis, was a "scoundrel." The visit confirmed Lundy's prior reservations about Canadian emigration. And while he continued to publicly endorse Wilberforce as an option for free Blacks, privately he thought there might be a more suitable and appealing location south of the border.

After leaving Wilberforce, Lundy dipped back into the United States through Detroit. There, he visited his old friend Elizabeth Margaret Chandler in the recently settled Quaker community of Hazlebank in Lenawee County in the territory of Michigan. A Quaker abolitionist and poet originally from Philadelphia, Elizabeth Chandler was the editor of the Ladies Repository section of the *Genius*, encouraging women to form antislavery societies and convert "friends" to the cause. The fate of abolitionism and feminism would become intertwined for the rest of the nineteenth century. Lundy and Chandler discussed the situation of Wilberforce in Canada. As usual, Lundy sought new subscribers during his stay in Michigan.

After leaving Michigan, the path grew treacherous as Lundy continued his journey through Ohio. "The worst travelling ever experienced . . . but one house in 20 miles. Had to wade from half leg to knee deep more than 20 times while snow falling fast & it was *freezing* rapidly!! . . . cloak, coat, pantaloons, stockings, all a glare of ice. feet benumbed!!"

As Lundy spent the next few weeks recuperating near Cincinnati, he could not help pondering the fate of the

Wilberforce colony. The unforgiving climate added to the tension within the community. He thought Mexico might be a better option. So, Lundy once again packed his bags in preparation for a trip South.

Since the publication of David Walker's *Appeal* and Nat Turner's uprising, Lundy and Garrison had become wanted men in the South. Lundy reasoned it would be safest if he traveled in disguise. He dressed "rough," threw on a knapsack, and took the alias J. Dynul. Mr. J. Dynul embarked on a five-hundred-mile convoluted journey deep into "The lion's den of slavites, slave traders, and all the devils in human shape that infest those 'nether regions' the slave golgothas of the South!" He met kind souls in Louisville and Nashville who "wished him well" and "God speed," but his ruffian disguise was looked upon with contempt by the "more elegant passengers" afraid to speak to him on the deck of a steamship from Nashville to New Orleans. When he arrived at the French trading post of Natchitoches, he put on his knapsack and hiked 120 miles through the Louisiana low country. To quote Bob Marley, "cold ground" was his bed, and "rock" was his pillow, but above were heaven's sparkling skies, a magisterial blanket that held the hope of freedom for all. In a letter to Elizabeth Margaret Chandler, he told of what happened one night when he slept at a "creole tramster encampment." Awakened by a violent thunderstorm in the middle of the night, he "crept under one of the wagons for shelter. I had not been there long before a great surly Dog disputed my right to that place! However, he was a reasonable Dog and somewhat . . . contented himself with barely room for his own accommodation."

Revolution was in the air when Lundy arrived in Nacogdoches, then a part of the Mexican state of Coahuila. The town was on high alert as the military garrison expected an attack from a band of what Lundy called "insurrectionists." A law passed on April 6, 1830, by the central government in Mexico City outlawed slavery,

Benjamin Lundy, seeking shelter from the storm,
shares a little dry space with a surly, yet reasonable dog.

restricted American immigration, and encouraged Mexican settlers in the Mexican state of Texas. It also called for constructing military garrisons like the one at Nacogdoches. American immigrants were using the fertile soil, producing crops, and raising livestock on hundreds of acres of Texas land. The April 6 law was Mexico City's attempt to promote Mexican settlement while trying to tamp down the flow of Southerners crossing the border with their enslaved. Some of the American migrants, like William B. Travis and Jim Bowie, were fleeing debt collectors and bad marriages on the other side of the border.

The military commander of the garrison at Nacogdoches was a man by the name of José de las Piedras, who had recently tried disarming American settlers in the area. In response to Piedras's actions, the settlers revolted. Lundy did not seem to properly understand what the conflict was really all about. He was more focused on obtaining a promise for a land grant to settle a colony of free Blacks. Lundy stayed in Nacogdoches only six days, but it might have been the most profitable week he had that year. He made the acquaintance of a former secretary of finance, Lorenzo de Zavala, who offered to help. Zavala wrote an introduction to the governor, "introducing me in the most flattering terms, urging my proposition upon his attention." Lundy petitioned the government of Mexico for a land grant and permission to settle four hundred families.

In the first nine months of 1832, Benjamin Lundy's winding journey took him from the unforgiving forests in the upper reaches of Ontario in the cold of winter down to Nacogdoches in the heat of summer. Many of the miles he covered were on foot, and each step was in pursuit of the cause of his enslaved brothers and sisters in America.

10

I HAVE BEEN DEEPLY DISAPPOINTED IN HIM, AND NOW EXPECT NOTHING FROM HIM BUT EVIL

As John Quincy settled into the role of congressman, he soon found slavery permeating every nook and cranny of the Capitol and Southern lawmakers seeking every opportunity to solidify the institution into the bedrock of the republic. However, he remained wary of acting against it. One day, Adams received a visit from a Quaker abolitionist who asked him his sentiments on slavery. "I told him I thought they did not materially differ from his own—I abhorred Slavery; did not suffer it in my family, and felt proud of belonging to the only State in the Union, which at the first census of population in 1790 had returned in the column of Slaves—none." But Adams added he believed any discussion of slavery in the House "would lead to ill-will—to heart-burnings, to mutual hatred" between North and South. Adams then showed off his debate skills and turned the tables on his guest. "I asked him what he should think of the Inhabitants of the District of Columbia, if they should petition the Legislature of Pennsylvania to enact a Law, to compel all the Citizens of that State to bear arms in defence of their Country? He said he should think they were meddling with what did not concern them—I said the People of the District of Columbia, might say the same of Citizens of Pennsylvania, petitioning for the abolition of Slavery, not in that State itself but in the District of Columbia."

As chair of the Committee on Manufactures, Adams recognized slavery as the root of all the business of the House: the tariff, banking, and the lack of investment in infrastructure. But of the three, the tariff posed the most immediate threat of dissolving the Union.

President Jackson was in favor of tariffs. He understood they brought money into the treasury and could be used to reduce the federal debt—one of his campaign promises. John Quincy also supported tariffs. It was the one issue that cut through the bitterness Adams felt for Jackson and vice versa. But it created new enemies.

In 1816, Congress enacted the first protective tariff to support the nation's emerging manufacturers. This tariff raised rates to approximately 20 percent. Although most manufacturers were located in the Northeastern and mid-Atlantic states, the tariff of 1816 was generally supported across the country, including by some Southern legislators.

In 1824, Congress passed another tariff, which expanded protection to include products like glass, lead, iron, and wool. This measure was well received in the North and West but faced mounting opposition in the South where manufacturing never took hold. The economy of South Carolina, which was dependent on agricultural exports like cotton, faced retaliatory measures from Britain and Europe.

Southern hostility toward tariffs grew increasingly intertwined with grievances over the Missouri Compromise, adding fears of economic oppression by the North to the paranoia of slave uprisings. The combination of financial and racial anxieties created a highly combustible situation.

When John Quincy Adams signed the 1828 tariff—infamously dubbed the "Tariff of Abominations"—into law, authorities in South Carolina perceived the tariff as an attack on their sovereignty, leading many to advocate for nullification.

You might recall John C. Calhoun was not only Andrew Jackson's vice president. He was also John Quincy's vice president. You might also recall that when Calhoun and Adams served together in Monroe's cabinet, they did not agree on every issue, but they were both what you might call nationalists and elevated the good of the Union over sectional issues.

As the 1820s dragged on, Calhoun began to rethink his support for federal authority. Tariffs were wildly unpopular to the folks back home in South Carolina. There, tariffs were not just a tax on imports, but the usurpation of power by the federal government and the consolidation of one section of the country against another. John C. Calhoun and Southern lawmakers championed states' rights. This battle over where power should lie was as old as the Constitution: With the states? Or with the federal government? Tariffs became the centerpiece of that power struggle.

I want to pause here because this is important. Southern politicians have this aha moment. They say, "We don't have to honor the tariff. States have the power of nullification." The idea behind nullification is that the Union is a compact between the states. The federal government had certain "delegated powers," but if the states believed the feds overstepped their bounds with a particular law, they had the right to supersede it. In theory, nullification allowed states to say, "No, we don't like that federal law. We're not going to follow it. It's null and void." The debate over nullification carried on into the Civil War. The burning question was then and still is: Is the Constitution a compact between the states or a compact between the people?

You have heard the phrase *constitutional crisis.* That's pretty much what this was. What power do the Constitution and the federal government have if states don't listen? President Jackson was not a fan of nullification. Sure, he was a Southerner and a big supporter of states' rights. But he was the president of the United States, the head of the federal government, charged with preserving the Union and protecting the Constitution. So, all this nullification nonsense? He did not want to hear it. And that exposed a rift between Jackson and his vice president, Calhoun. A bitterness simmered silently between the two. And like any couple with unresolved issues, this bitterness tends to boil over at the worst possible and most public moment.

Scene: The Jefferson Day Dinner, April 12, 1830
Location: The Indian Queen Hotel, Washington, DC

It was to become one of the most critical political gatherings of the century. A regular Who's Who of Washington's elite political players gathered in tribute to the late scion of democracy, Thomas Jefferson. In some ways, it was the Democratic Party's coming out. The guests of honor were President Andrew Jackson and his vice president, John C. Calhoun. Most of the men in attendance were backers of states' rights and allies of Calhoun. It was his home crowd. During these dinners, every man in the room would stand up and make a toast to this or to that. And then they'd give more toasts! By some accounts, more than a hundred toasts occurred at one of these dinners. Sean Wilentz describes it this way: "They'd get very drunk slowly 'cause they'd make all these toasts and every time they did a toast, they knocked something back. Usually something very stiff."

President Jackson could feel the tension in the room. His vigorous opposition to nullification put him at odds with almost everyone there. Hateful eyes weighed heavily on him like sharp daggers all around. But he was the president, and he knew he needed to bring it. According to Jon Meacham, Jackson arose early that morning and wrote three different toasts. He showed them to two of his aides. When they both favored the same one, Jackson knew he nailed it. When it was time, Jackson stood up and raised his glass. Straightening his spine as much as the bullet lodged in his shoulder allowed, he sneered over at his vice president and let it rip, "Our federal Union: It must be preserved!"

The words hit Calhoun like a slap in the face. Not to be outdone, Calhoun immediately pushed back his chair and rose to his feet, raising his glass high in the air. Locking eyes with Jackson, he bellowed for the crowd, "The Union, next to our liberty the most dear; may we all remember that it can only be preserved by respecting the rights of the States and distributing equally the benefit and burden of the Union." If they had microphones in 1830, Calhoun would have dropped his. The crowd of Calhoun cronies burst into applause. If they had twenty-four-hour cable news channels, the toasts would have scrolled across the bottom of the screen for weeks.

Just two years later, in 1832, Calhoun put nullification to the test. He joined with the leaders of South Carolina in a push to ignore the federal tariff. The governor called up the South Carolina state militia to defend the port of Charleston. In response, Jackson threatened to send the army to secure the port and collect the tariff themselves. As the commander and chief of the United States, Jackson was not afraid to use military force against a state that was in revolt. Now Calhoun was engaged in a duel of sorts with Jackson. But this time, Jackson was armed with the US military, not a pistol. This was precisely the kind of aggressive behavior Adams and Clay feared Jackson was capable of during the election of 1824. They could not imagine he would turn against the South. Jackson issued a proclamation to the state of South Carolina in late 1832. "You are free members of a flourishing and happy union. There is not settled design to oppress you. . . . The power to annul a law of the United States, assumed by one State, is incompatible with the existence of the Union, contradicted expressly by the letter of the Constitution, unauthorized by its spirit, inconsistent with every principle on which it was founded, and destructive of the great object for which it

Calhoun's rebuttal:
"The Union. Next to our liberties most dear"

was formed." Jackson made the repercussions of their actions crystal clear to the South Carolinians: "Disunion, by armed force, is TREASON."

Calhoun could feel the pressure mounting. He had no idea how far Jackson would go in this stalemate and had none of the seasoned veteran duelist's steely resolve. Was it the Nixon playbook? *Make the other guy think you are unhinged.* Or the Trump playbook? *Be unhinged.*

In the end, Calhoun and South Carolina backed down. The Congress negotiated a lower tariff, allowing both parties to win, but nullification was yet to have its day. Once again, Sean Wilentz put it in the most straightforward terms: "[The] Civil War's not going to be fought over nullification. It's going to be fought over secession. But secession was kind of the ultimate step beyond nullification." Jackson had won the duel over nullification. Calhoun resigned the vice presidency and took a seat as senator from South Carolina, which he held for the rest of his life. Like Adams, Jackson saw the future. In May 1833, he said, "The tariff was only the pretext and disunion & a Southern confederacy the real object. The next pretext will be the . . . slavery question." Jackson—an enslaver—had held the slave powers in check. But it was just a matter of time before things got out of control.

Adams followed the nullification crisis with great concern. He had his own issues with nullification. While he was president, the governor of Georgia refused to honor federal treaties with the Native American populations. The Adams administration backed down, allowing the Georgia governor to run roughshod over the Native American tribes in his state. John Quincy supported Jackson against South Carolina and lamented the role his old friend Calhoun played in the affair. Reflecting on their time in the Monroe cabinet the year before, Adams wrote, "Mr Calhoun was a member of Mr Monroe's Administration, and during its early part pursued a course from which I anticipated that he would prove an ornament and a blessing to his Country—I have been deeply disappointed in him, and now expect nothing from him but evil."

As a result of President Jackson's standoff with Calhoun and the nullifiers, debate was underway in the House over a revised tariff bill. Adams listened patiently for days as supporters and detractors hashed out the details of the legislation. Now it was his turn.

Rising at his desk, Adams held in one hand a copy of the Constitution, in the other a declaration from a convention recently held in South Carolina addressed to the people of the other twenty-three states of the Union. Adams then put forward an eloquent discourse on the doctrine of "We the people" versus the doctrine of nullification. "With respect to the doctrine of protection, South Carolina expressly declared that there should no longer be a protecting tariff." In that regard, they had called on their citizens to support nullification. Adams agreed protection is the "right of the citizen, and the duty of the government."

South Carolina argued that the tariff enacted by the federal government protected Northern interests at the expense of Southern interests. "Wherever any great interest existed in the community, there the protection of Government must, of right, be extended." Adams admitted that "the interests of one portion of the community could often be protected only at the expense of some other portion of it." But South Carolina, too, had a protected interest. "An especial protection peculiar to itself."

Adams was referring, of course, to slavery and the Three-Fifths Compromise. In a nod to a comment recently made by a Georgia representative who referred to enslaved persons as "the machinery of the South," Adams replied, "That machinery had twenty odd representatives . . . elected, not by the machinery, but by those who owned it."

Adams sneered, "Did the manufacturers ask for any representation on their machinery? . . . their looms and factories had no vote in Congress." Adams made clear that he was not complaining about it; he was just pointing out the "South possessed a great protected interest—an interest protected by that instrument," the Constitution of the United States, a copy of which he now waved above his head.

The Three-Fifths Compromise was a bargain, and Adams was "adhering to the bargain because it was a bargain. Not that he would agree to it if the bargain were now to be made over again."

A Southern congressman shouted that Adams "had thrown a firebrand into a hall."

Adams took his shot at the nullifiers; next he turned his attention to his old nemesis, Jackson. Nowhere was the specter of Jacksonian populism clearer than in December of 1832, in Andrew Jackson's fourth annual message to Congress, in which he declared, "The wealth and strength of a country are its population, and the best part of that population are cultivators of the soil. Independent farmers are every where the basis of society and true friends of liberty." Jackson suggested that Southerners were the true Americans. The president's message disturbed Adams so much that he wrote a rebuttal.

These days, some rising star for the party out of power goes live on television from their kitchen and reads a prewritten rebuttal to a speech that the president gave ten minutes before. Adams took two months to craft a fiery yet insightful response to the president's message, which he couched in a Minority Report for the Committee of Manufactures.

"That the President of the United States should in a public document, addressed to the Representatives of the whole people of this union, peremptorily declare one part of the population . . . better than the rest, appears to the subscribers little compatible with that equality of rights upon which our whole social system is . . . believed to be founded." Adams was growing older and bolder. In no uncertain terms, Adams charged "a vast proportion of the cultivators of the soil, are in a state of servitude—possessing no rights, civil or political—and existing only as the property of another part of the same population." Adams reasoned what Jackson was really saying was that "the best part of the population . . . and the friends pre-eminently of freedom, are the *wealthy landholders*." Adams warned that using this philosophy as a "foundation of a system of national policy" threatened not only the nation's prosperity, but "the dissolution of the Union by a complicated, civil, and servile war."

Adams charged that there were four discernible features to Jackson's message that attacked the Constitution and put the wishes of the Southern states over the Northern states.

1. The abandonment of all appropriations of public money for purposes of internal improvement.
2. A reduction in the protective tariff for all domestic industry, whether agricultural, manufacturing, or mechanical.
3. Ending federal revenue from the sale of public lands but donating them to "privileged" voluntary settlers.
4. Denunciation of the Bank of the United States, depreciating the value of stock held in it by the nation.

Adams believed these actions represented an unprecedented takeover of the whole government by the executive branch.

Adams had found his groove as the congressman from Massachusetts. He had written a comprehensive Minority Report outlining the anti–state rights and antislavery position. And now he had a name for the opposition: the slavocracy.

The last night of the congressional session in March 1833 was a raucous voting marathon. The body struggled to form a quorum at varying points throughout the evening. After the president reported to Congress that he had no further "communications," the Speaker slammed the gavel to end the session. Adams looked up as he passed under Clio's chariot on the way out of the hall. It was 5:00 a.m. The old man walked down the stairs into the frozen, snow-covered Washington morning. He noted, "Thermometer at 6. the extremest cold of the winter." As he lay down in his bed, body aching, ears ringing, the sixty-five-year-old prayed his gratitude "to the Supreme disposer of Events, for the merciful dispensations of his Providence, in bringing the affairs of the Country to a condition more favourable to Peace and Union than it has been of late, and though still surrounded with dangers . . . My Career is yet to be closed. It is in its last and lingering Stage—May its remaining afflictions be mitigated—May its last moments be serene—May its transition be to a happier state of existence."

Louisa Catherine Adams also felt the ravages of age. All through 1833 and 1834, Louisa suffered from one illness after another, erysipelas, never-ending coughing fits, ulcerated throat, and repeated bleeding, afflictions brought on at times by physical maladies and on other occasions by fits of sorrow and shame. Somehow Louisa always managed to recover. Her son John was another story. Young John was John Quincy and Louisa's middle son. As with his older brother, George, the pressure of being an Adams was often too much to bear. To cope with the pressure, he self-medicated with alcohol. Charles Francis suspected alcoholism ran in his family. More than one hundred years before the American Medical Association declared alcoholism a disease, Charles speculated, "I do not know whether vices are hereditary in families, but it would almost seem so from the number of examples which one meets with. The Smith blood [Abigail Adams's side of the family] seems to have had the scourge of intemperance dreadfully applied to it."

Louisa believed that if only John and his family had come to stay with her, she could save them. She pleaded, "I shall be perfectly miserable until I hear that you have left the city as the health of yourself your wife and Fanny's make it essential, and the season leaves no time for deliberation." Louisa recommended John sell her silver breadbasket to cover travel expenses. "Do not hesitate to take this step as they are my own and if they can prove serviceable, they will yield me more pleasure and more solid wealth than they ever have since I have owned them."

Back in Massachusetts, John Quincy spent the better part of Saturday, October 18, 1834, on his Mount Wollaston farm inspecting his apple trees and making plans to plow the east side of his property. He returned home that afternoon and sat down to dinner. A few hours later, Charles arrived from Boston with a letter from his cousin in Washington letting him know that his brother John was "extremely ill" and that his mother, father, or Charles himself should come immediately. It was the letter John Quincy and Louisa had always feared. Within hours of hearing the news about John, Louisa fell into shock. John Quincy said she was "seized with excessive sickness, faintings and cramps." She was too sick to travel to see her boy. John Quincy would go.

The next morning at church, Adams found comfort in Reverend Lunt's sermon on Mathew 11:28: "come unto me, all ye who labour and are heavy laden, and I will give you rest." As he left Boston, Adams scribbled a prayer in his diary. "I feel the duty and the difficulty of resignation to the Will of God—I invoke his mercy, profoundly conscious as I am of my own unworthiness to obtain it—And still cherish hope, where hope is without rational support." John Quincy took the steamship *Benjamin Franklin* from Boston to Providence. He must have been aware of the sad irony as he stepped onto the same ship from which his eldest son had jumped to his death five years before. The enormous burden Adams carried, for a few hours at least, was redirected toward the "multitude of passengers," some with whom he was previously acquainted. Under clear, starry skies, Adams discussed religion and politics with his fellow travelers until after midnight. The topics of conversation included the "controverted character and divinity of Christ" and "the prospects of universal emancipation, and the intellectual capacity of the African race." The evening must have been a rare diversion from his sorrows.

Upon arriving in Washington, John Quincy Adams rushed to his son's home and found him on the brink of death. As the life drained from his son's body, Adams stood helplessly, watching in silent agony. He bent down and tenderly kissed his son's sweaty brow. "I went to his bed-side twice, and saw and heard him; he had no consciousness of any thing on Earth," he lamented. John's wife, Mary, also ill in the upstairs bedroom, burst into tears at the sight of her father-in-law. With a heavy heart, Adams promised her that he would be a father to her and to her two children.

Exhausted from his journey and feeling unwell, Adams finally lay down at 2:00 a.m., hoping to snatch some sleep, only to wake at half past four. He stepped into his son's room just in time to see his brother-in-law, Nathaniel Frye, gently close his departed boy's eyes. John Quincy had lost another son. "May God, in his infinite mercy have received him to the joys of Heaven!" he prayed, his heart heavy with sorrow.

John Adams II was born on the Fourth of July, just like the nation his father and grandfather had given up everything in service of. His was another lost soul crushed by the impossible expectations of the family name. John's death once again filled John Quincy and Louisa's lives with sorrow and grief. And for all their love and caring, they couldn't help but feel like they had failed their children. When Louisa Adams learned of her son's death, she became incapacitated. She crumbled into a deep depression. Her son Charles Francis wrote, "She lay in a state of almost stupor for some time, followed by violent and indefinite emotion." I can imagine her at Peacefield, staring out her window at a yellowwood tree still there today, the one Louisa had planted when her other son George had died five years earlier. Its yellowing leaves float to the ground in the cool autumn air.

Charles Francis processed his grief with great reserve. He always knew he was different than his brothers. Perhaps it was due to almost a decade-long estrangement at such a young age when he went to Russia with his parents and his brothers stayed behind. In a diary entry from July 1827, after an argument with his brother John, Charles pondered his brothers' struggle to find their way to a productive life. "If I do not draw instruction from the characters of my elder brothers it is my own fault. They have points of contrast verging to the extreme. In one there is an openness, a confidingness if there is such a word. . . . In the other there is an affected mystery which repels all the good feelings of the heart, the more unfortunate as it is not known by himself to produce the effects which it does." At least for the time being, Charles cast his emotions aside and assumed the burden of being the remaining heir to the Adams name.

Down in Washington, John Quincy grieved as he always had. He threw himself into his work in the House of Representatives.

· 11 ·

IT CRUSHES THE BODY . . . BREAKS THE HEART AND KILLS THE SOUL

Theodore Weld had come a long way from promoting the value of manual labor education at the Oneida Institute. Weld had earned a reputation as a charismatic lecturer after renouncing a career in ministry that would confine him to a pulpit. Arthur Tappan sent Weld on a westward journey to seek out a location for a national manual labor college. As word of Weld's quest spread, he received requests to visit sites east and west of the Alleghenies.

Weld received a letter from a J. L. Tracy encouraging him to check out Cincinnati. "You are well aware of the fact that this western country is soon to be a mighty giant that shall wield not only the destinies of our own country but of the world," the correspondent wrote. "Tis yet a babe. Why not then come and take it in the feebleness of its infancy and give a right direction to its powers that when it grows up to its full stature we may bless God that it has such an influence?"

Mr. Tracy had a point. As the populations of the Northeast and New England spread westward, so did the fervor for self-improvement. Cincinnati's growth had been fueled by its burgeoning industries and strategic location. The race riots of the 1820s had driven much of the Black population to Canada, but the city remained a thriving hub of commerce. Sugar mills, cotton gins, and a branch of the Bank of the United States remained as a testament to its prosperity. Goods flowed in and out of the city; iron, wood, lumber, cotton, hemp oil, furs, and whiskey were shipped to New Orleans, while liquor, molasses, salt, and coffee returned from the Big Easy. Cincinnati had blossomed into a booming Northwestern city infused with Southern charm and sentiment.

In 1828, a wealthy merchant from New Orleans named Ebenezer Lane, along with his brothers, envisioned the establishment of a seminary in Cincinnati. Lane donated a tract of land and had gained the approval of the Ohio legislature for a Lane Seminary. But there was no money to finish the project. In fact, the agent for the project had sought funding from Arthur Tappan. Now it appeared as though Tappan was in search of a location for a manual labor college and Cincinnati had a seminary in need of a benefactor.

When Weld arrived, the only thing that existed of Lane Seminary was the foundation of a building on a hilltop. Walnut Hill, as it was known, enthralled Weld. He deemed it ideal for a "National Manual Labor College." Tappan offered Weld a professorship at the future school. Weld, however, preferred to join the mission to transform the West not as a professor, but as a student.

The inaugural class of Lane Seminary in 1833 comprised a mature group of freshmen. Many had already distinguished themselves as doctors, politicians, and theologians, having studied at renowned seminaries in the East such as Oneida and Andover. They were attracted to Lane Seminary to study under the esteemed Boston preacher and university president Lyman Beecher, known as "The Unvanquished Puritan." Among the students, one individual stood out: Theodore Weld, the thirty-year-old protégé of Charles Finney.

College campuses have long been centers of free thought and open discussion. But every so often, those conversations take on a life of their own. In the twentieth century, students on college campuses across the country came together and made their voices heard on a variety of issues from the Vietnam War in the 1960s to South African apartheid in the 1980s, and recently over the war in Gaza. In February 1834, Lane Seminary was the epicenter of the most extraordinary campus protest of the nineteenth century and one of the decade's defining antislavery moments.

Weld and his fellow students proposed a series of public discussions on the issue of slavery centered on two controversial questions: "Ought the people of the Slave holding States to abolish Slavery immediately?" and "Are the doctrines, tendencies, and measures of the American Colonization Society, and the influence of its principal supporters, such as render it worthy of the patronage of the Christian public?" Faculty ears perked up when they learned about the proposed conversation. Here was the student body of a brand-new seminary, still in search of adequate funding, planning a talk on slavery in a Northern city steeped in Southern culture. Lyman Beecher issued a statement enumerating his reservations that a free and open conversation on these questions would cause "unpleasant and permanent divisions" within the student body. When Weld and the others refused to yield, Beecher threw up his hands and said the faculty would not stand in the way of the students. "They have given their advice, with the reasons for it: and do not feel called upon to do any thing more."

The discussion commenced on the night of February 5, 1834, and continued for the following seventeen days, two and a half hours a night—nine evenings for the first question and nine evenings for the second question. The highlight of the debate on the first question was the testimony of a Black seminary student, James Bradley. As a young child, Bradley had been kidnapped from Africa and brought to the United States. He grew up to become the manager of his owner's plantation and eventually purchased his freedom. Fifty years later, a former student reflecting on Bradley's speech wrote, "I doubt if there was a dry eye in the chapel." The following week, when the case against colonization was discussed, it was so convincing that Augustus Wattles, the former president of the Colonization Society at the Oneida Institute, wrote, "I believe its doctrines, tendencies and measures are calculated to subvert the best interests of the colored people, to strengthen prejudice, to quiet the conscience of the slave-holder, and put far off the day of emancipation." At the end of the discussion, the student body held a vote. Only one student still supported colonization. After two and a half weeks of debate, the students formed an antislavery association with the goal of immediate emancipation.

Immediate emancipation was a vague platitude that meant different things to different people. For many, a more palatable slogan read, "immediate emancipation, gradually accomplished." For Theodore Weld, it was immediate emancipation—full stop. Which meant an end to bondage and an end to what we today consider racism: "God has committed to every moral agent the privilege, the right and the responsibility of personal ownership. This is God's plan. Slavery annihilates it, and surrenders to avarice, passion and lust, all that makes life a blessing. It crushes the body . . . breaks the heart and kills the soul."

In Cincinnati, all this talk about immediately freeing enslaved people made white folks uncomfortable. James Hall, a reporter for the *Western Monthly Magazine*, denounced Lane students for starting an antislavery society. "There certainly ought to be some spot hallowed from the contests of party, sacredly protected from the contamination of the malignant passions, where the mind might be imbued with the lessons of truth, and peace, and honor, unalloyed with prejudice." Hall criticized the "young gentlemen" of the school for making "sophomoric declamations" on a subject as disruptive and divisive as slavery. Weld shot back at Hall in an essay. The student body at Lane, he noted, consisted of mature men, many with families of their own, who had already distinguished themselves in ministry, medicine, and education. Why "should not students examine into the subject of slavery? Is it not the business of theological seminaries to educate the *heart*, as well as the head? To mellow the sympathies, and deepen the emotions, as well as to provide the means of knowledge? If *not*, then give Lucifer a professorship."

Fired up by the mantra "faith without works is dead," the students of Lane spread out into the local Black community. Weld visited thirty families in one week. Lane students set up Bible and Sabbath schools and another school that taught "grammar, geography, arithmetic, natural philosophy, etc." They taught many older Blacks to read and created a library. They visited Black homes, sat at their tables, and broke bread with them. Occasionally, after spending hours teaching and studying, they stayed the night. There were even two Black members of the Lane student body, including James Bradley. These interracial interactions repulsed the city's white residents. The word *integration* was not a part of the vocabulary. Beecher leaned on Weld to tamp down the rhetoric. Weld refused.

Lyman Beecher went back east for the summer to raise funds for the seminary. Weld and some of the other students involved in the debates remained on campus to tend the manual labor farm and tutor their Black neighbors. But as reaction to the student antislavery society spread across the academic world of the North, pressure mounted for the trustees of Lane Seminary to do something about its radical student body.

Lyman Beecher gave Arthur Tappan his word he would not interfere with the students' right to free speech. However, other university administrators were not as supportive. At the time, only a few colleges condoned student antislavery societies. The ones that did were in locations where there had long been a strong antislavery impulse, like Western Reserve, in Ohio, and Andover and Amherst in Massachusetts. But on campuses like Harvard, Princeton, and Wesleyan, students held anti-abolitionist protests and demanded that all antislavery agitation should be suppressed. In response, university administrators shut down antislavery societies throughout the North. The trustees at Lane followed. They abolished the antislavery society and convened a censorship board to investigate the students' activities. They said students were to cease all discussion of the topic, even "communications with students at their meals, or when assembled on other ordinary occasions." So much for free speech. The trustees gagged the students.

Beecher heard the news while he was back east. A panicked faculty member told him there was a crisis on campus and he needed to return to Cincinnati immediately. The unvanquished Puritan urged patience: "In the meantime pray much, say little, be humble and wait." In other words, "Let God and let go." When classes resumed in the fall, harsh restrictions were still in place. Weld led a massive walkout in protest. A local religious leader coined the term *Weldite.* "This is the name of a most deluded sect, the leader of which was a fanatic by the name of Theodore D. Weld . . . he excited a great tumult on the subject of abolishing slavery at once, amalgamating blacks and whites, overturning the order and peace of the country, for the sake of giving liberty and equality to a set of men who were incapable of self-government." Lyman Beecher lost a large percentage of his student body to the cause of immediatism, a cause that, with time, his own children would come to support. In 1851, his daughter, Harriet Beecher Stowe, so deeply moved by Theodore Weld and his later writings, published a fictional series about the horrendous conditions of the enslaved called *Uncle Tom's Cabin.*

Upon leaving Lane Seminary, the "Weldites" scattered. Some went home, while others enrolled at a new seminary on the edge of the Western Reserve called Oberlin. Lane Seminary did not pan out as an abolitionist training ground the way Arthur Tappan hoped it would, so he invested heavily in Oberlin. Weld refused the offer to serve as president, so Tappan recruited Charles Finney. With an integrated student body, Oberlin would become what Lane could not.

Theodore Weld became a traveling lecturer for the newly formed American Anti-Slavery Society. The organization held its first gathering in Philadelphia in December 1833, just a few months before the Lane debates. The AASS was the brainchild of a group of abolitionists—William Lloyd Garrison, Elizur Wright, and a young publisher named Joshua Leavitt. Of course, the Tappan brothers funded the organization; Arthur was chairman. The addition of Theodore Weld was a boon for the AASS. Weld had the personal charisma and magnetism that Lundy lacked, with none of Garrison's ego. Weld believed if the American people knew the ugly truth about slavery, they would join in its overthrow. Over the next few years, Theodore Weld would make a lot of converts as he organized antislavery societies across Ohio and New York. But to do so, he would have to face down the most violent mob in American history.

· 12 ·

I FEAR I MUST

The slavery issue was a vexing one for Adams. On August 11, 1835, he wrote, "There is a great fermentation upon this subject of Slavery, at this time in all parts of the Union." Adams shook his head as he read newspaper reports of mob violence in response to the growing momentum of the antislavery movement. "The theory of the rights of man has taken deep root in the soil of civil Society. It has allied itself with the feelings of humanity and the precepts of Christian benevolence. It has armed itself with the strength of organized association. It has linked itself with religious doctrines and religious fervour." The spread of abolitionism bred fear and resentment in many Northern towns and villages, where citizens desired the status quo to preserve the Union. Tradesmen and artisans in Massachusetts, New York, and Pennsylvania feared that immediate emancipation would lead to millions of freed Blacks taking their jobs.

In the South, the belief was not *if* another Nat Turner–style uprising would occur, but *when.* In early July 1835, in Madison County, Mississippi, one such plot was uncovered. "Various circumstances excited some suspicion in the minds of a few respectable citizens in Madison County . . . of an insurrection of the slaves of that settlement being about to occur." The alleged leaders, two white men named Cotton and Sanders, were hanged in public on the Fourth of July. The chilling details paralyzed the community. Cotton had signed a written confession detailing his role in a plot he hoped would spread across "the whole slave region from Maryland to Louisiana . . . and contemplated the total destruction of the white population of all the slave states." Authorities executed ten to fifteen Black co-conspirators.

In Philadelphia, a mob terrorized a community of free Blacks after the attempted murder of an older man named Mr. Stewart by his servant. Fifteen hundred white men assembled and ransacked the homes of four or five free Black families. According to one newspaper account, "The cry of the mob when a colored man was caught was 'Kill him—beat him—place him under the pump. . . .' In many cases, the treatment of the poor defenseless blacks was barbarous in the extreme." Black men hiding in a chimney were smoked out.

Today, there is a belief that the South was for slavery and the North was against it, but in the 1830s, most Northerners could not imagine a society where Blacks and whites lived together as equals.

John Quincy understood the gravity of the situation but remained resolute. He maintained that Congress was powerless to do anything about the institution of slavery. Adams also knew there was no moral argument abolitionists could make to convince slave owners to give up their human property. In 1820, Adams confessed in his diary that the only way he could conceive of emancipation was if the Union was somehow dissolved and then reconstituted. The most likely means by which this would occur would be through a violent and bloody civil war. Silence would be his course of action, for now.

Silencing abolitionist propaganda was the tactic authorities chose in Charleston, South Carolina. Local politicians, including a former governor, raided the mail to "purify it of the abolition pamphlets." The seized mailbags full of antislavery propaganda kindled a bonfire that burned William Lloyd Garrison and Arthur Tappan in effigy. President Jackson proposed a federal law to ban abolitionist propaganda in the mail, but the Senate refused to back him up.

Another powerful rejection of abolitionism occurred right in Adams's own backyard. In the city of Boston, a meeting was held in opposition to the antislavery movement at Faneuil Hall. Among the organizers was the city's former mayor Harrison Gray Otis. In what became known as the Boston Resolutions, some of the most esteemed citizens of Boston "Resolved" abolitionists must sacrifice their "opinions, passions and sympathies upon the altar of the laws . . . [and] the supremacy of those laws is the rule of our conduct . . . to deprecate all tumultuous assemblies, all riotous or violent proceedings, all outrages on person and property." Boston had declared it was going to go along to get along with their Southern brethren. The relationship between New England manufacturers and Southern slave interests ran deep. Northern hands sewed the sacks that slung across enslaved shoulders and wove the baskets their callused hands clutched day after blisteringly hot day in the fields. The machines of the North empowered slave labor in the South.

In 1835, the slavery issue was tearing the fabric of the nation apart. Its threads tossed into a smoldering furnace of bigotry and hate. And there was Adams. A witness to all of it. Sitting on the fence. Waiting for his moment.

Meanwhile, as mobs terrorized towns and cities around the country, Theodore Weld was battling it out in the trenches for the cause of abolitionism. He had spent months in northeastern Ohio giving speeches and making converts. In a letter to his good friend and fellow abolitionist Elizur Wright, Weld wrote of how he had recently signed up fifty new members to the Chester Anti-Slavery Society in Geauga County.

The next day, protestors attended Weld's speech in the county seat of Chardon. While he was speaking from a pulpit, a man stood up and interrupted. The president of the Chester Anti-Slavery Society tried to maintain order—"There is a gentleman on the floor"—but the man insisted on being heard. When the president again demanded order, the protestor announced in a loud voice, "The abolitionists are always clamoring about free discussion. I wish to discuss, and you refuse to hear." Weld told the man that if he could just wait until after he concluded his remarks, he would happily discuss "the question as long as he pleased." At which point the man began reading from the Boston Resolutions, his voice getting louder as he went until he was screaming. When other men in the crowd egged the protestor on, it became plain it was a coordinated disturbance.

The situation became untenable. Weld and the antislavery society moved the gathering to a schoolhouse across the street. There, Weld tried to pick up where he left off, but as he began speaking, a mob soon returned, this time bringing "sleigh bells, drums etc., and ding dong'd like bedlam broke loose." The assault escalated. Angry protestors pelted women with rotten eggs. At the conclusion of the evening, Weld still boasted converting thirty to forty souls to the cause.

Theodore Weld had a reputation for keeping his cool in the face of mob violence. At one meeting, he was hit in the face with an egg. As it dripped from his forehead down to his chin and shirt, he responded soberly, "I beg the audience will be composed," and continued without missing a beat. On another occasion, Weld was hit in the head with a rock while speaking from the pulpit at a church. The projectile came through the window and, "for a moment stunned me." He paused briefly to let the dizziness

Theodore Dwight Weld

subside and just as quickly picked up the lecture as if nothing had happened. The injury was not serious. Weld did admit, "though for a few days I had frequent turns of dizziness."

When Weld spoke, it was not just a meeting, it was a revival, reminiscent of the ones given by his mentor, Charles Finney. Weld wrote, "In most places I have lectured from six to twelve times—sometimes sixteen, twenty and twenty-five, and once thirty times." In speeches that lasted as long as five hours, he was never guilty of "exhausting his subject nor his hearers." One convert wrote, "I have seen crowds of bearded men held spell-bound by his power for hours together and for twenty evenings in succession." At the end of a speech, Weld held an altar call and asked the converted to rise. Edwin Stanton watched Weld from the front pew of a church and heard him say, "Friends, will all of you who believe . . . please rise to your feet?" Stanton stood up and turned around with arms lifted high above his head and noticed the rest of the congregation standing too.

For all the danger, welts, and bruises, Theodore Weld succeeded at making converts and establishing new antislavery societies across central and northern Ohio. But one task remained: the formation of a statewide society. Weld called delegates to the town of Zanesville sixty miles east of Columbus. When he and his fellow activists arrived, they found Zanesville to be "locked up." The convention managed to find just one public room that would allow them to meet across the river in the town of Putnam. A mob from Zanesville followed the convention delegates across the river. They smashed the gate and broke all the windows of the meeting place. Weld was stoned and clubbed as he exited the venue. Undaunted, the convention continued in a private room. A few nights later, the mob returned. This time they listened to Weld as he testified to the horrors of slavery, families separated, the mothers willing to murder their own children rather than have them endure a lifetime of bondage. A few nights later, officials from Zanesville called him back across the river. Finally, on the sixteenth night, like John the Baptist baptizing converts in the Jordan, Theodore Weld won hundreds over to the cause and cleared the way for the convention to begin in earnest.

The state convention drew over a hundred attendees, including some of the most important abolitionists of the time like James G. Birney, a former slaveholder who Weld had converted years ago during a trip through the South. Weld was joined by members of the Lane Rebels, and students from Oberlin College and Negro schools in Cincinnati. Many older abolitionists and Quakers showed up as well. The seeds of the Lane rebellion had bloomed. Convention attendees took a pledge to uphold what was known as the New York doctrine: "By immediate emancipation we do not mean that the slaves shall be . . . turned loose"; they must be subjected instead to "the salutary restraint of laws appropriate to their condition." The Ohio State Anti-Slavery Society was established.

As the cause of abolition moved forward in the state of Ohio, it slid backward in the House of Representatives. Since the 1790s, the House dedicated the first thirty days of business to presenting, hearing, receiving, and referring petitions. Thereafter, petitions were typically presented every other Monday. But by 1835, the American Anti-Slavery Society quickened the pace and volume of antislavery petitions making their way into the hands of any congressman willing to present them. That was just the beginning; between 1837 and 1838, 130,000 petitions with one million signatures would show up at the Capitol.

Southern congressmen felt threatened by the number of petitions. When the Twenty-Fourth Congress opened in December 1835, they decided it was time to do something about them. The

Register of Debates reported on petitions, including those that were immediately tabled. The debates in Congress were reprinted in local newspapers across the country. Citizens carried those newspapers from dock to plantation, tavern to slave quarter, and from there, by word of mouth. As we would say today, antislavery debates in Congress went viral. Slaveholders in South Carolina, Alabama, Georgia, and other states were acutely aware of the danger posed by the enslaved population sharing stories about noble Northern allies who paralyzed the House of Representatives with a flood of antislavery petitions. It might inspire another Denmark Vesey or Nat Turner. Southern congressmen decided to test a new tactic: Petitions would not simply be tabled—they would be rejected. Abolitionists would be denied their First Amendment right to petition the government.

A couple of weeks into the session, Nathaniel Briggs Borden, Adams's fellow Massachusetts representative from Wrentham, read a petition for the abolition of slavery in the District of Columbia. James Henry Hammond of South Carolina, a roommate of John C. Calhoun, made a motion that the petition should be rejected, meaning not accepted in any way. The proposal seemed to come completely out of left field. It even caught Speaker of the House and future president James Knox Polk by surprise.

Adams wrote that Hammond's motion "disconcerted [Polk] and he blundered in the tangles of the Rules—a debate of four hours arose." Borden, flustered, caved to the Southerner's demands and sat down without reading the petition. Dismissing petitions out of hand denied American citizens their right to petition their government for a redress of grievances. The time to remain silent had passed. A few days later, two Northern congressmen, Abbott Lawrence and Francis Granger, visited Adams at The National Hotel and encouraged him to address the House about the petition issue. Adams confessed to his diary, "I fear I must."

For three long days, Southern politicians bloviated about why Congress must reject all these antislavery petitions. Like listening to your drunken uncle drone on and on about his insane politics at the Thanksgiving dinner table, Adams's irritation built . . . and built . . . and built . . . until he had had enough. He sprung from his desk and spoke directly to the Southern delegation. "Will you introduce a resolution that members of this House shall not speak a word in derogation of the sublime merits of slavery? . . . Well, sir, you begin with suppressing the right of petition; you must next suppress the right of speech in this House. . . . You suppress the right of petition; You suppress freedom of speech; the freedom of the press, and the freedom of religion; for in the minds of many worthy, honest and honorable men, fanatics if you please so to call them, this is a religious question, in which they act under what they believe to be a sense of duty to their God."

In Philadelphia, Benjamin Lundy, back from his journey to Mexico, cheered Adams's bold stand as he reflected on the progress the antislavery movement had made throughout the violent year of 1835. Across the North, many new antislavery societies had been established, and there had been a boom in journals to support them. "The good work has progressed with a rapidity unparalleled, within the space of a few years." Lundy also warned his fellow freedom fighters, "In advocating the cause of emancipation, a high degree of circumspection, and the entire command of our own tempers, are requisite. Though it is difficult for human nature calmly to endure the obloquy which is heaped upon us, and the malice and violence with which we are assailed, yet it becomes us to restrain our indignant feelings, and appeal to the reason and judgment, instead of the passions of others." Lundy encouraged abolitionists to take the high road: "The language of cutting retort or severe rebuke is seldom convincing, and it is wholly out of place in persuasive argument."

Sadly, Lundy also wrote an obituary notice for his dear friend and assistant editor Elizabeth Margaret Chandler, who died from a fever in Lenawee County, Michigan, at just twenty-four years old. No one did more to inspire women to join the cause of abolition. In just a few short years, women would carry the work of abolition on their shoulders, work from which the suffrage movement would be born in earnest.

On his way to New York to spread the gospel of emancipation, Theodore Weld read John Quincy's speech on the House floor. Weld had the same thought Benjamin Lundy had years before: What if Adams could be a voice for the antislavery movement *in* Congress? John Quincy's support for freedom of speech had put him on an ideological collision course with enslavers but made him a hero in the eyes of abolitionists. Adams wanted to stay neutral. But the ground was shifting all around him. And then . . . war came to the southern border. And it changed everything.

13

AM I GAGGED?

The Mexican Army surrounded the mission. When one of the leaders of the Texans, Jim Bowie, looked over the walls, he saw a sea of Mexican soldiers: nearly two thousand against fewer than two hundred Texans.

When the Texans refused to surrender, Mexican General Antonio López de Santa Anna ordered a red flag flown from a nearby church. It was a sign to those holed up in the mission: No quarter would be given.

The Battle of the Alamo had begun.

By the fall of 1835, Texas was in a state of all-out war. Outnumbered, undisciplined, and scattered, Texans fortified an old mission called the Alamo at a crucial crossroads and waited to ambush the Mexican Army. Unbeknownst to the 150 or so Texans in the mission, including the soldiers' families, the Mexican Army had orders to destroy the rebellion once and for all.

Days into the siege of the Alamo, reinforcements still had not arrived. Bowie's co-commander, William B. Travis, penned a letter to his countrymen and all the world from within the Alamo walls. "Fellow Citizens & compatriots, I am besieged, by a thousand or more of the Mexicans under Santa Anna. I have sustained a continual Bombardment & cannonade for 24 hours & have not lost a man. The enemy has demanded a surrender at discretion, otherwise, the garrison are to be put to the sword, if the fort is taken. I have answered the demand with a cannon shot, & our flag still waves proudly from the walls. I shall never surrender or retreat . . . I am determined to sustain myself as long as possible & die like a soldier who never forgets what is due to his own honor & that of his country. Victory or Death." Just before the break of dawn on the thirteenth day of fighting, the Mexican Army stormed the mission, sparing only women, children, and enslaved people in the slaughter. Every fighting man met his end with either a bullet . . . or a bayonet. The message was clear. The Mexican Army was happy to abide by William Travis's terms: victory or death.

They were not the only ones to receive a message. Among the dead at the Alamo, former Tennessee Congressman David Crockett (he hated when people called him Davy). Outrage and calls for vengeance rippled across hundreds and hundreds of miles, through the plantations of the South, northward to Washington, DC, and the floor of Congress. US citizens had been killed at the hands of the Mexican Army. The bloodbath in Texas was a tragedy quickly becoming a national disaster. Lawmakers were bombarded with calls to send US troops to Texas. At the heart of this decision was a Texas-size elephant in the room. What would happen if the Northern Mexican territory seized its independence? Would it join the United States? And what would happen if a slave state the size of Texas joined the Union? The outcome of the rebellion had the potential to upset the balance of power in the United States for generations.

When news of the massacre in Texas reached the US Capitol, John Quincy Adams took to the House floor. He spoke out against the United States getting involved in a war with Mexico. But before he or any other lawmaker could even decide whether to send troops to Texas, the direction of the war had shifted dramatically. Following the Alamo, the Texas Army—a ragtag group of rebels—was on the run, retreating eastward from San Antonio to the Gulf of Mexico, the Mexican Army close behind, committed to ending the rebellion. The former governor of Tennessee, and close friend of Andrew Jackson, Sam Houston led the Texans. With their backs to the gulf and the Mexican Army bearing down on them, Houston ordered his men to make a final stand. Turn and attack, rather than flee. On April 21, 1836, just weeks after the Battle of the Alamo, Texans launched an assault against the Mexican Army near modern-day Houston. Screaming "Remember the Alamo," Houston's troops attacked mercilessly, catching their enemy off guard. The Mexican Army—surprised—scattered. The battle lasted just eighteen minutes. At the end, Mexican general Santa Anna stood in shackles. In exchange for his freedom, he agreed to take his army and leave Texas for good. The Alamo had been avenged. The Republic of Texas was now an independent nation.

Events were moving fast, but news of Santa Anna's surrender would not reach Congress for a few weeks. Newspapers filled with copies of Adams's recent speeches against American intervention in Texas caught the eye of Benjamin Lundy in Philadelphia.

During Benjamin Lundy's second and third trips to Mexico, he sought to finally obtain a land grant for a proposed free-labor farm on which Blacks from the United States would produce sugar, cotton, and rice. The trips took a toll on Lundy. On his way South, he suffered a bout of cholera in Tennessee. Both trips combined, Lundy spent over a year walking across the state, sleeping on the ground, and recording the amount of dew that fell on him overnight. He endured threats of violence from American expat enslavers. At one point he ran out of money so he set up a pop-up saddle shop in Monclova just so he could eat. Eventually, he made it all the way to Coahuila, and after meeting with government officials, and a lot of waiting on Mexican bureaucratic red tape, Lundy secured a grant of 138,000 acres from the State of

Tamaulipas. The deal was conditioned on whether he could guarantee he could settle 250 families. Excited, Lundy returned to the United States and was gathering investors when war broke out. After Houston's victory at San Jacinto, the deal went up in smoke.

Upon returning to Philadelphia, Benjamin Lundy was buoyed by reports of former President John Quincy Adams diving into the deep end of the antislavery pool in Congress. However, Lundy faced other problems. The recent success of the antislavery movement meant that *Genius of Universal Emancipation* now had competition, with abolitionist newspapers sprouting up all over the North.

A Philadelphia district court issued a $300 judgment against him for failure to pay one of his creditors, resulting in a week in debtor's prison. Ever faithful to God and the cause of antislavery, Benjamin Lundy wrote from his prison cell, "We meet with many obstacles in the pursuit of happiness; and they are most likely to attain it, who submit in quiet resignation to the will of an unerring Providence."

A victim of historic forces beyond his control, Lundy never accepted defeat. Like Thomas Edison, Lundy found ten thousand ways that did not work. And if you like mixing your metaphors, he made lemonade out of the situation. Benjamin Lundy took all the information he had gathered over the previous few years on his trips through Texas, took up his pen, and published a series of nine letters under the pseudonym Columbus in the Philadelphia daily newspaper the *National Gazette.*

Lundy sent a copy of the letters to Adams. "There can be *no doubt* of the fact, that the grand object of the insurgents is, the re-establishment of Slavery in Texas . . . I rejoice that the subject has presented itself to thy mind in its true light. . . . My acquaintance with *various* proceedings connected with it, for a period of eight or ten years past, enables me to state, that the remarks of the writer of these essays are strictly correct . . . if I can be of any service to thee hereafter . . . I shall be happy to render any aid that may be in my power."

Lundy and Adams wrote frequently during 1836 and 1837. The two men shared more than a partnership; they developed a bond. Their letters are filled with sentiments like "My esteemed friend" and peppered with the Quaker marks of "thee" and "thou." Abolitionists wanted nothing more than to claim Adams as one of their own. Lundy repeatedly tried coaxing him. "Our friends are highly pleased with thy public course, especially of late, and will be glad to evince their satisfaction by some mark of personal respect. . . . They are desirous to have from thee a *public address*." Lundy candidly expressed his own wish that Adams would come out publicly for abolition, but he knew it was unlikely.

With Mexico no longer controlling the vast stretch of borderlands along the American Southwest, a power vacuum had been created. According to Richard S. Newman, it made the ground fertile for anxious speculation that international meddling was afoot: "Great Britain is going to step in or some other European power, and you'll have this big anti-slavery border land in the Southwest. Slaveholders and their allies really want to get Texas into the American Union, and then maybe they want to create several states to boost their political power on top of that."

Adams was way ahead of them. He believed that the annexation of Texas was the South's golden ticket to upsetting the fragile balance in Congress. But now he had a man on the inside. There was no doubt that Texas would be a slave state. But Southern politicians had grand machinations. Lundy had long speculated that the plan was to annex Texas and carve it up into several slave states. You might as well tear up the Missouri Compromise and use it to fire up your barbecue smoker. However, Adams had no time to focus on his Texas-sized problem. At just about the same moment the news arrived at the Capitol confirming Houston captured Santa Anna, John Quincy Adams was on the floor of the House of Representatives firing the opening salvo of his own war.

By 1836, the petition controversy had become a crisis. In the Senate, Adams's old ally John C. Calhoun took charge. After a measure that would make it illegal to send abolitionist pamphlets through the United States Postal System failed, he pivoted to the massive number of petitions that as of late were arriving at the Capitol. "The peculiar institution of the South—that on the maintenance of which the very existence of the slaveholding States depends, is pronounced to be sinful and odious, in the eyes of God and man; and this with a systematic design of rendering us hateful in the eyes of the world. . . . The subject is beyond the jurisdiction of Congress; they have no right to touch it in any shape or form, or to make it the subject of deliberation or discussion."

Presidential politics has a way of raising the stakes of any and every issue, creating problems that otherwise would not exist and making everything out to be a conspiracy. Case in point, the election of 1836. Jackson's heir apparent, Martin Van Buren, was desperately trying to hold together a coalition of Southern slaveholders and Northern republicans able to stomach their neighbors' peculiar habits. The smartest political operator of his day, Van Buren knew coalitions are tenuous and can easily unravel over petty policy disagreements and personal insults. As a Northerner, he had to keep Southern politicians happy if he was going to win the presidency. One thing that would make them very happy, besides annexing Texas, would be putting an end to the discussion of slavery in Congress for good.

The Democratic Party, like all political parties, consisted of factions inside of factions. Van Buren's allies in the lower chamber, including Henry Laurens Pinckney of South Carolina, knew the House needed to figure out a way to dispose of antislavery petitions in the most expedient and palatable way without infringing upon the petitioners' First Amendment rights. However, more extreme members, like fellow South Carolinian James Henry Hammond, did not believe the petitioners had any First Amendment rights. The dynamics in the House were not unlike what we once saw between establishment Republicans and the Freedom Caucus, or MAGA Republicans.

To understand what happened next, we need to go over some of the parliamentary rules of the House governing petitions. To save time, the rules prohibited discussion of petitions on the day they were presented. After congressmen presented a petition, they could move that it be received and referred to the appropriate committee. In some cases, a congressman could move for a petition to be received and printed. This allowed it to go into the record and, politically importantly, printed in newspapers for the benefit of their constituents back home. Or a petition could be received, read, and tabled. Meaning the petitioner was heard but the petition itself would go on to, in Adams's words, "Sleep the sleep of death."

Adams was of two minds about what to do with all these antislavery petitions. He agreed with his Southern counterparts who believed discussion of slavery would inflame Congress and divide the nation. But he took offense to the idea that there was a "sublime benefit of slavery," which made them willing to deny citizens the right of petition.

Adams's nemesis in waiting, Virginia Whig Congressman Henry Wise, said, "Slavery is interwoven in our political existence, is guaranteed by our Constitutions, and its consequences must be borne by our Northern brethren as resulting from our system of Government. They cannot attack the institution of slavery without attacking the institutions of our country, our safety, and welfare."

When Adams presented his first petitions in 1831, he explained why he disagreed with the petitioners before referring them to the Committee on the District of Columbia, where they went to die. But the petitions were received, and the petitioners heard. Hammond and the other members of the slavocracy had worked themselves into such a lather over the issue, they did not want them to get that far. Which brings us back to Henry Laurens Pinckney from South Carolina. He wanted these petitions disposed of as much as Hammond did. But Pinckney, being an ally of Martin Van Buren, also had to consider the Northern Democrats who did not love the institution but were willing to go along with it to achieve, eh, um . . . more important policy goals. Put simply, Pinckney was a member of the establishment wing of the Democratic Party, and Hammond was from the . . . (clears throat again) Freedom Caucus. Hammond and his fellow hard-liners wanted to dismiss the petitions outright. They did not want them to make it on to the wagons that carried them through the mail into the Capitol where they lined the hallways and piled up on the desks of John Quincy Adams and the small group of Northern congressmen brave enough to present them. To defuse the issue, Pinckney chaired a committee at the start of 1836 to figure out what to do with the thousands of antislavery petitions flooding into Congress. The committee finished its work in May, right around the time news of Houston's victory at San Jacinto arrived. The report put forward three resolutions for how to handle the troublesome petitions.

As William Lee Miller puts it in his incredible, must-read *Arguing About Slavery: John Quincy Adams and the Great Battle in the United States Congress,* "If Pinckney's committee had followed the instructions the House had given them . . . the petitions would have been respectfully received and respectfully referred, as before, and then respectfully forgotten, as before." The three resolutions were read out over consecutive days.

The first resolution read, "*Resolved, That Congress possesses no constitutional authority to interfere in any way with the institution of slavery in any of the States of this Confederacy.*" This was a bow to Southern democratic hard-liners like James Henry Hammond and Waddy Thompson. Adams tried to seize the floor while the motion was under debate. A Georgia congressman, an ally of Pinckney, moved to end debate and proceed to the vote. Adams demanded the motion be withdrawn. He had something to say on the matter. Pinckney and his allies refused. Adams turned and appealed to House Speaker James K. Polk. He too refused. Adams shot back, "I am aware there is a slaveholder in the chair!" The House devolved into chaos. Polk refused to let Adams speak. Adams froze. Turned to the Speaker. And asked, "Am I gagged, or am I not?"

The next day, the second resolution was read: "*Resolved, that Congress ought not to interfere, in any way, with slavery in the District of Columbia.*" This enraged the extremists. They wanted to add a resolution declaring Congress did not have the power to abolish slavery in the District of Columbia. They considered "*ought not*" a slippery slope.

It was the final resolution that hit the House floor like a lit stick of dynamite, and it came accompanied with a brief prologue that stated it was included so that the "*agitation of this subject should finally be arrested, for the purpose of restoring tranquility to the public mind.*" Pinckney proposed that all petitions or other correspondence to the House about slavery should "*be laid upon the table and that no further action whatever shall be had thereon.*"

He's basically saying (my words not his): *We are not just going to ignore all these antislavery petitions in Congress . . . we are going to ban even mentioning them. They. Do not. Exist.*

Adams was in shock as the vote to silence petitions proceeded. His voice now also silent. When his name was called, he got in one last jab. Voting nay, he added, "I hold the resolution to be a direct violation of the Constitution of the United States." His objections fell on deaf ears. The resolution to ignore antislavery petitions on the House floor passed. It would become known as the gag rule. The discussion—even mention—of slavery was now banned in the House of Representatives. However, his enemies would soon realize that John Quincy Adams was an indomitable force. Nobody could shut him up when he had something to say.

Adams was just getting started. The next issue before the Congress was a relief measure for the citizens of Alabama and Georgia at risk of starvation in the aftermath of violent attacks by the Creek Indians. Adams rose to speak and made it known that he was going to vote for what he called the "scalping-knife and tomahawk laws." He would not "withhold from those appeals a responsive and yielding voice." Adams reminded the assembly that Congress had voted for a similar measure for the inhabitants of Florida. Twenty years earlier, Congress also sent millions from the public treasury to aid the people of Caracas after they suffered a devastating earthquake, famine, and civil war. The goodwill of the American people and Congress was unquestioned. But Adams was quick to point out, "Mere commiseration, though one of the most amiable impulses of our nature, gives us no power to drain the Treasury of the people for the relief of the suffering object."

Where did Congress derive its constitutional ability to fund such humanitarian efforts? Adams suggested it was the war powers given to Congress to provide for the common defense and general welfare—the true intent of the Constitution. But it was a power given to Congress that must remain narrow in scope. "Step one hair's breadth out of the circle bounding the true intent and meaning of these words," Adams warned, "and you have no more authority to pass this resolution, than you have . . . to saddle the people of the United States with the insupportable burden of the whole system of the poor laws of England."

Adams took his fellow members to task for the way Congress mishandled its war powers privileges. "In your relations with the Indian tribes, you never declare war, though you do make and break treaties with them, whenever either to make or to break treaties with them happens to suit the purposes of the President and a majority of both Houses of Congress. For, in this matter, you have set aside the judiciary department of the Government as effectually as if there were none such in the constitution."

Hours earlier, he had been gagged from speaking on the slavery issue; fine. Adams now held the floor speaking on behalf of the motion to provide rations to the inhabitants of Alabama, and he was about to put on a demonstration of the verbal jujitsu that would define the rest of his career.

On the previous question of the abolition petitions, "the freedom of debate has been stifled in this House to a degree far beyond any thing that ever happened since the existence of the constitution of the United States." If he had been given the opportunity, he would have explained that Congress had as much a right to interfere with slavery as it did to provide millions of dollars in relief to the citizens of Alabama and Georgia. Both actions are examples of congressional war powers. "The existing law [of 1808] prohibiting the importation of slaves into the United States from foreign countries, is itself an interference with the institution of slavery in the States."

Then Adams mused, "Suppose Congress were called to raise armies, to supply money from the whole Union, to suppress a servile insurrection: would they have no authority to interfere with the institution of slavery?" Adams imagined, what if to bring the war to an end, the president made a treaty of peace that granted emancipation? In that situation, surely Congress has the power to do something about slavery. James Traub points out that John Quincy Adams was once again gifted with the uncanny power of foresight as he gave an interpretation of war powers that "formed the constitutional foundation of Lincoln's Emancipation Proclamation."

Adams was like an expert prosecutor, methodically building his case against the slavocracy. Without missing a beat, he next turned the focus of his speech to Mexico, his correspondence with Lundy fresh on the brain: "The war now raging in Texas is a Mexican civil war and a war for the re-establishment of slavery where it was once abolished. It is not a servile war, but a war between slavery and emancipation, and every possible effort has been made to drive us into the war, on the side of slavery." Headfirst down the rabbit hole, Adams painted the Southerners in the audience with the brush of warmongering racists. "Do not you, an Anglo-Saxon, slaveholding exterminator of Indians, from the bottom of your soul, hate the Mexican-Spaniard-Indian, emancipator of slaves and abolisher of slavery?" Adams then spun the very meaning that the American Revolution was a war fought against oppression in the name of freedom by pointing out "Great Britain has recently, at a cost of one hundred millions of dollars, which her people joyfully paid, abolished slavery throughout all her colonies in the West Indies. After setting such an example, she will not . . . stand by and witness a war for the re-establishment of slavery where it had been for years abolished." If the defense of Texas is our mission, America might be the oppressors in a war in which Great Britain is the champion of freedom.

Adams's prestige kept growing among abolitionists. His correspondence with Lundy is warm and personable. The Quaker zealot sat in awe of the old man's eloquent, outspoken stand against slavery. Lundy tried to nudge Adams to accept a leadership role in the movement. Adams responded, saying he was not an abolitionist. Lundy agreed. Adams was more than an abolitionist. "The eyes of *millions*, my dear and honoured friend, are now *turned to thee.* No mortal ever held a part of greater usefulness, more enviable distinction, or higher moral responsibility, than is thine at the present moment."

The two men sealed their bonds of friendship in Philadelphia the week of Adams's sixty-ninth birthday. Lundy introduced Adams to newspaper editor Lewis C. Gunn. Lundy and Gunn begged Adams to address the antislavery societies. Flattered, but not swayed, Adams also entertained a visit from a committee of four members of the Pennsylvania Anti-Slavery Society and the Philadelphia Anti-Slavery Society. They brought with them resolutions of thanks for his recent speeches in Congress and pressed Adams to become a spokesperson for the antislavery issue. "I gave them a full and candid exposition of my own principles and views with regard to the Institution of Domestic Slavery differing from theirs under a sense of the compact and compromise in the Constitution of the United States . . . I believed the cause itself would be more benefited by such Service as I could render to it, in the discharge of my duty in Congress than by giving notoriety to any action on my part in support of the Societies, or in connection with them."

The morning of Adams's birthday, Lundy again visited and asked him to become a supporter of a new newspaper. Adams was noncommittal. That evening, the two men went to a party at the home of noted abolitionists James and Lucretia Mott. Reading his journal, you get the sense that, hanging out with Quaker abolitionists, Adams had found "*his people.*" "I had free conversation with them till between ten and 11 O'Clock, upon Slavery—the abolition of Slavery and other topics—of all which the only exceptionable part was the undue proportion of the talking assumed by me, and the indiscretion and vanity in which I indulged myself."

After they left the Motts' home, Lundy and Adams had their own after-party and stayed up talking past midnight.

As Adams cozied up to his new abolitionist friends, Louisa worried her husband's antislavery stance put him in physical danger. A Southerner by birthright, Louisa's father was a Marylander, her sisters slaveholders. Louisa and John Quincy were hemorrhaging friends over his stance against slavery. She wrote in her diary that supporting her husband meant "losing the love, the friendship and the society of my own nearest and dearest connections." She had grown accustomed to the name-calling and sideways glances, but things kept getting uglier. Adams received death threats, some specific and graphic: "On the first day of May next I promise to cut your throat from dart to ear." Louisa wrote again and again to try to convince her husband to chill his rhetoric. She must have known her words were in vain from the moment she scribbled them on the page.

· 14 ·

WHAT IS A MOB?

Theodore Weld received so many death threats he could have used them to wallpaper his home. If he had a home. By 1836, Weld proved himself to be the American Anti-Slavery Society's greatest orator. History has long remembered the name William Lloyd Garrison as the most recognizable pre–Civil War abolitionist, but that title could have gone to Weld if only he had not refused to own it. Weld was determined to keep the focus off himself and on the enslaved as he tore up the Ohio countryside, making converts and setting up antislavery societies. He refused to allow the American Anti-Slavery Society to print pamphlets of his speeches. He did not want newspapers to cover his revival-like meetings whereby the sheer strength of his voice converted hundreds of people at a time.

His friend and AASS board member Henry B. Stanton said of him, "Do you think it possible for an individual to go thro' the United States in this age of free enquiry . . . and produce in the public mind 'an intelligent, rational, abiding Excitement' . . . and at the same time entirely screen himself from public observation through the medium of the press?" Weld refused invitations to address the national antislavery anniversary in New York City and the Rhode Island, Connecticut, and Pennsylvania state legislatures. The very definition of a grassroots activist, Theodore Weld knew that if he could convert the folks in the countryside to the cause of antislavery, the politicians would have no other choice but to follow.

In the summer of 1836, there was no place in the North more dangerous for an abolitionist than western New York. In Utica, the place where Weld fell to his knees before Charles Finney in 1826, a violent mob drove the first state antislavery convention out of town. Weld went to the church the mob attacked and began giving nightly lectures to packed-out crowds for sixteen nights and won the city over. A local man reported, "Mr. Weld is one of the most astonishing men of the age."

Weld barnstormed New York State. Buffalo fell next, then Rochester, but it was in the city of Troy that Weld finally met resistance. A ring of the town crier's bell called out to the mob, "All you who are opposed to amalgamation, meet in front of the courthouse!" The mob charged Weld as he spoke from the church pulpit. The scene turned bloody as Weld's bodyguards repelled the attackers three times. Weld retreated to his hotel under a hail of rocks. Determined to win over the city, Weld refused to back down, but each time he tried to even walk around the city, attackers pelted him with rocks.

Courting sainthood, Weld penned a farewell call to arms. "Let every abolitionist debate the matter once and for all, and settle with himself . . . whether he can lie upon the rack—and grasp the fagot—and tread with steady step the scaffold—whether he can stand at the post of duty, and having done all and suffered all . . . fall and die a martyr . . . God gird us all to do valiantly for the helpless and innocent. Blessed are they who die in the harness." Eventually, city leaders gave Weld an ultimatum: Leave or face the wrath of the mob. His frail frame was covered in welts from the rocks hurled his way. After months of being constantly under attack and in continuous motion, Weld retreated. He did not know it at the time, but his days as an itinerant orator were over.

Despite the violent resistance Weld met in western New York, the American Anti-Slavery Society pivoted from sending thousands of antislavery pamphlets through the Southern mail and instead focused on the type of grassroots revivalism Weld had so instinctually employed. The organization asked Weld to raise an army of seventy new recruits to spread the good news of freedom across the North. They were known as the Seventy, based on the biblical notion of the seventy elders assembled by Moses in the Old Testament book of Numbers and the seventy apostles Jesus sent out to preach in the gospel of Luke in the New Testament. The remnants of the Lane Rebels formed the core of the group. From there, Weld scoured the universities of the North and dragged the best ministers away from their pulpits.

The recruits gathered in New York City in November of 1836. It was a boot camp like no other. From sunup to sundown, for two weeks, Weld filled their heads with "facts and fervor." Still physically weak and hoarse from the attacks in Troy, Weld soldiered on and gave the men every argument against slavery imaginable and a rebuttal to every rebuttal conceivable. The doctrine of immediatism confused a lot of people and terrified others. "*What do you plan to do*?" asked doubters. "*Ask a state legislature to pass a law freeing enslaved men and women immediately and set a massive uneducated, untrained population loose throughout the country?*" "*What is your plan?*" For Theodore Weld, it was simple: If slavery be a sin, it must be ended immediately, and the rest will work itself out, or as William Lloyd Garrison put it, "Duty is ours and events are God's."

During those weeks of training the Seventy, something else happened to Theodore Weld. Something new. He fell in love with a woman named Angelina Grimké, a Southern-born Quaker abolitionist, who along with her sister Sarah were the only two women trained at the convention. Angelina and Sarah Grimké were born and raised in Charleston, South Carolina. Their father was a judge, and their family owned slaves. Angelina refused to be confirmed into the Episcopal faith that her family practiced and could not tolerate the local Presbyterian churches' embrace of slavery, so she and her sister Sarah became Quakers and moved to Philadelphia.

The Grimké sisters became followers of William Lloyd Garrison. They were present at the birth of the American Anti-Slavery Society. They were two examples of a new radical group of women abolitionists in the mold of Elizabeth Margaret Chandler and Lucretia Mott, who while working to end slavery lit the spark for the women's suffrage movement.

In an 1835 letter to Garrison, Angelina wrote, "It is my deep, solemn, deliberate conviction that this is a cause worth dying for." Angelina was chagrined when Garrison published the letter in the *Liberator*. A quote like that coming from a woman got a lot of attention. It caught the eye of Theodore Weld. Weld caught Grimké's eye, or maybe more accurately, her imagination as well. Angelina made note of him when the *Emancipator* published details of his exploits in Circleville, Ohio. William Lee Miller points out that it's one of the "more unusual instances of a couple finding each other through the columns of the newspaper."

Angelina's fame—or should I say, infamy—grew. Her detractors called her "Devilina." In 1836, she penned *Appeal to Christian Women of the South* for the American Anti-Slavery Society. Grimké argued to the women of her native South Carolina that the Bible does not just outright reject the practice of slavery, citing the jubilee proclaimed in Leviticus 25:10, and Deuteronomy 23:15–16: "Thou shalt not deliver unto his master the servant which is escaped from his master unto thee: He shall dwell with thee, even among you, in that place which he shall choose in one of thy gates, where it liketh him best: thou shalt not oppress him." She also referred to the Declaration of Independence: "We must come back to the good old doctrine of our fore fathers who declared to the world, 'this self-evident truth that all men are created equal, and that they have certain *inalienable* rights among which are, life, *liberty*, and the pursuit of happiness.'"

Grimké's *Appeal* is an antislavery argument wrapped in a feminist call to action. "But perhaps you will be ready to query," she writes, "why appeal to *women* on this subject? We do not make the laws which perpetuate slavery. No legislative power is vested in us; we *can* do nothing to overthrow the system, even if we wished to do so." With a tone reminiscent of Abigail Adams's "Remember the Ladies" letter to John Adams during the Revolution, Grimké makes the case to her fellow Southern women: "You are the wives and mothers, the sisters and daughters of those who do; and if you really suppose you can do nothing to overthrow slavery, you are greatly mistaken." She tells her audience they can read on the subject, pray over the subject, speak on the subject, and act on the subject.

Theodore fell in love with Angelina's mind and passion for abolition. In her, he found his equal. Divisions in the abolitionist movement had formed over women taking up prominent positions. The Garrisonians fully supported women playing an equal role in the fight, but conservative abolitionists thought it would only turn off those already suspicious of immediate emancipation. As much as Weld expressed his own reservations, he could not, and would not, try to hold Angelina back.

They were the nineteenth century's greatest power couple. As the courtship of Theodore Weld and Angelina Grimké blossomed, it was Angelina who became the bigger celebrity. While Weld felt compelled to slow down and take on a behind-the-scenes role in the movement, Angelina became the first woman to address the Massachusetts legislature, or any state legislature for that matter. Weld's mighty voice was still his greatest weapon against slavery, but now it came through in the words he wrote rather than those shouted from a pulpit. In 1837, Weld wrote *The Bible Against*

Slavery, which was a point-by-point takedown of slaveholders who believed that the Bible sanctioned the vile practice.

Until 1837, the petitions inundating Congress mostly originated from state and local antislavery societies. The managers of these efforts hired freelancers to gather signatures, reminiscent of the college students today who pace the city block and approach with a clipboard asking you how you feel about this or that issue. Because signature collectors were not necessarily members of the movement, detractors accused antislavery societies of fraud. And even if a petition did make it to Washington, the language was sometimes so offensive that members of Congress would not read it.

The American Anti-Slavery Society looked to streamline the petition process to hone their message, increase their numbers, and be acceptable to the congressmen who read them. Theodore Weld worked on the petition committee, along with AASS financial manager Henry B. Stanton and the abolitionist poet John Greenleaf Whittier. Weld labored all day long in the AASS office. At night he would return to a small apartment in the Black section of New York City. He refused a paycheck and took only a small allowance to help maintain a vegetarian diet and keep the simple clothes on his back. No longer a charismatic leader, Theodore Weld saw himself as a foot soldier.

The first thing the committee did was survey the number and location of antislavery societies in the North and West. Best estimates showed there were more than one thousand societies with over one hundred thousand members spread across New York, Ohio, and Massachusetts. Other cities and states also had impressive numbers. Philadelphia boasted many active Quaker women like the Grimké sisters. Vermont was notable for being the only state where the antislavery society controlled the legislature.

Rhode Island, Connecticut, Maine, and New Hampshire all had a substantial number of members as well. Weld and his colleagues also reported seeing green shoots of abolitionism in Indiana and Michigan, as well as in Illinois, where Elijah Lovejoy edited the antislavery newspaper the *Alton Observer* and seemed to be attracting as many enemies as converts.

Once the committee knew the location of societies and members, they constructed a system to circulate, receive, and send petitions to the Capitol. Thanks to the county-level success of the Seventy, the committee appointed two agents from every county to receive blank petitions from the national society in New York. The county agents handed off the petitions to township-level agents along with detailed instructions on how to fill them out and where to send them. Local agents circulated petitions and got them signed. Signed petitions were then handed over to county agents who checked and verified the information before sending them to state offices, or the New York headquarters. If the home congressman was favorable to abolitionists, petitions would be sent to him, and he would present them on the floor of the House of Representatives. If not, the state or New York office would send them to a friendly congressman. An army of antislavery activists peppered towns and villages with antislavery petitions, door to door, church to tavern, in general stores and county fairs. Antislavery petitions were everywhere.

Everywhere indeed. Petitions burst out the sides of the thick binder Adams carried as he shuffled up hundreds of steps to the doors of the Capitol. It was the lame-duck session of the Twenty-Fourth Congress and there was a new gag rule in place; the previous expired with the end of the last session. Undeterred, Adams got creative. On February 6, 1837, Adams presented what must have been the two strangest petitions sitting in his folder. The point of presenting these two petitions was for Adams to stir the pot a little and get a rise out of his Southern colleagues. It worked.

The first was "the petition of nine ladies of Fredericksburg, in the State of Virginia." Adams "would not name them, because, from the disposition which at present prevailed in the country, he did not know what might happen to them if he did name them." It was a petition praying for Congress to put a stop to the slave trade in the District of Columbia. Adams made it known to the House that, "This was one of those petitions which had seemed so strange to him when he received it, that he did not feel a perfect security that it was genuine." Congress voted to table the petition per the rule of the House. So much for the nine ladies from Fredericksburg. Maybe? Maybe not.

The trap had been set. Curiosity got the best of James Patton, a Democratic representative of Richmond but a Fredericksburg native. Patton walked over to look at the petition as it sat on the clerk's desk. Adams was already on to the next. "He held in his hand a paper on which, before it was presented, he desired to have the decision of the Speaker. It was a petition from twenty-two persons, declaring themselves to be slaves. He wished to know whether the Speaker considered such a petition as coming within the order of the House." Polk replied that he could not say until he examined the petition in question. *Former* President Adams told *future* President James Knox Polk he wished to do "nothing except in submission to the rules of the House." The petition Adams held in his hand "purported to come from slaves, and it was one of those petitions which had occurred to his mind as not being what it was purported to be." Adding to the suspicion, the signature on the document consisted of "marks" that you might expect to come "partly by persons whose handwriting would manifest that they received the education of slaves."

Southern congressmen shouted objections as the blindsided Speaker processed what Adams had said. Polk admitted, "It was the first time, in the recollection of the chair, that persons not free had presented a petition to this House." Some Southerners, like Henry Laurens Pinckney, did not want the House to devolve into "a protracted discussion on the subject, which could only lead to useless excitement and confusion." Others, like Dixon Lewis from Alabama, took the bait: "If the House would inflict no punishment for such a flagrant violation of its dignity as this," the rotund Lewis suggested, "it would be better for the Representatives from the slaveholding States to go home at once." Another congressman suggested they burn the petition.

Amid all the drama, James Patton, still fixated on the earlier petition from the nine ladies from Fredericksburg, stood up to make a motion. Patton grew up in Fredericksburg, and after a close examination of the signatures on the petition, determined "the name of no lady was attached to that paper. He did not believe there was a single one of them of decent respectability." The only name he recognized was that of a "free mulatto woman of the worst fame and reputation . . . the others were names of free negroes, all of whom he believed to be bad." Patton requested the tabled petition returned to Adams.

By this point, the entire House of Representatives was in a rage. While Patton was making his speech, Waddy Thompson from South Carolina made an amendment to Patton's motion, which gave him the floor. Thompson "resolved, that the honorable John Quincy Adams, by the attempt just made by him to introduce a petition purporting on its face to be from slaves, has been guilty of a gross disrespect to this House, and that he be instantly brought to the bar to receive the severe censure of the Speaker."

John Quincy Adams had unleashed a terror. Southern congressmen took turns launching venomous attacks on the "honorable gentleman" and offered their own modifications to the censure resolution. Adams stood up to correct the record: "I did not present the petition, and I appeal to the Speaker to say that

I did not. I said I had a paper, purporting to be a petition from slaves; I did not say what the prayer of the petition was; I said it was a paper purporting to be a petition from slaves . . . I stated distinctly to the Speaker that I should not send the paper to the table until the question was decided, whether a paper from persons declaring themselves slaves was included within the order of the House."

Adams had the fat mouth of the slavocracy dancing on the end of the line. It was time to reel them in. Looking Dixon Lewis in the eyes, Adams said, "If the House should choose to read the petition, I can state to them they would find it something very much the reverse of that which the resolution states it to be; and if the gentleman from Alabama shall still choose to bring me to the bar of the House, he must amend his resolution in a very important particular; for he probably may have to put into it, that my crime has been for attempting to introduce the petition of slaves that slavery should not be abolished." The petition, which many including Adams believed may have been a hoax, prayed not for the abolition of slavery but for the end of the antislavery actions of Adams and his abolitionist friends.

Adams now turned toward a Northern critic, Francis Granger from New York, who asked why an "Honorable man" like Adams would spend his time offering the petitions of slaves and alleged free mulatto prostitutes. Adams responded, "Where, in the land of freemen, was the right of petition ever placed on the exclusive basis of morality and virtue? Petition is supplication—it is entreaty—it is prayer! And where is the degree of vice or immorality which shall deprive the citizen of the right to supplicate for a boon, or to pray for mercy . . . the right of petition belongs to all."

Then Adams turned his attention back to Patton.

"The gentleman from Virginia says he knows these women, and that they are infamous. How does the gentleman know it?" Patton shot back, "I did not say that I knew the woman personally.

I knew from others that the character of one of them was notoriously bad." Adams replied, "I am glad the gentleman now says he does not know these women, for if he had not disclaimed that knowledge, I might have asked who it was that made these women infamous—whether it was those of their own colour or their masters. I have understood that there are those among the coloured population of slave-holding States, who bear the image of their masters."

Chaos erupted in the House. Shouting, screaming, and cries of "order!" drowned out the Speaker's gavel. For four long days Southerners howled at Adams. Waddy Thompson accused Adams of attempting to incite a slave insurrection and suggested he be brought before a grand jury in the District of Columbia. Talk about lawfare. Adams responded to the South Carolinian, "If a member of that Legislature is made amenable for words spoken in debate, not only to the Legislature, but also to the grand and petit juries—if that, sir, is the law of South Carolina, I thank God I am not a citizen of South Carolina!"

Attacks like Thompson's spewed forth with a venom Congress had rarely witnessed, yet they were a harbinger of things to come. Between assaults against the nearly seventy-year-old former president, the Southern congressmen honed and crafted the censure resolutions. Adams did not mind censure, not at all. He knew these controversial petitions would get a rise out of them. He knew they would froth at the mouth and hurl charges at him. He also knew that if he was censured, he would have a right to a rebuttal of the charges against him. In doing so, he would have the ability to speak free of the gag. Which is exactly what he did.

In his defense, Adams reiterated that he meant no offense to the rules of the House. That is why he asked the Speaker before he offered the petition. He also admitted that the petition allegedly from slaves was probably a forgery sent to tempt him into presenting it. Adams warned about what happens when the

First Amendment right to freedom of speech is denied to the citizen who sent the petition and the congressman who offered the petition. "If you once admit the principle that the right of petition is limited, and will not apply to slaves, the next thing will be to limit it still further, by extending the limitation to free colored people . . . the next limitation will be to the question of the character of the petitioners; then the next limitation will be to inquire on what side of political parties are the petitioners; and then, sir, from one side all petitions will be perfectly good and receivable, but on the other side all the petitions will be from people of bad character. . . . To this state will things come if the right of petition shall be limited by peculiar distinctions, and shall be made to rest on such grounds as these which have been relied upon in this debate."

Adams's speech was one for the ages. The *Boston Daily Advertiser* wrote, "The effect of this speech on the House has been rarely if ever exceeded by the influence of any speech on any assembly." If they wanted to censure him, Adams's enemies had the votes to do it. Many congressmen realized it would set a bad precedent to censure a congressman for speaking his mind on the floor of Congress. Only twenty-one members voted in favor of the censure resolutions. The vote to censure John Quincy Adams failed, but in the following days, the House passed a few face-saving resolutions to make sure nothing of the kind would ever happen again. One stated, "That this House cannot receive the said petition without disregarding its own dignity, the rights of a large class of citizens of the South and West, and the constitution of the United States." And another that denied slaves "the right of petition secured to the people of the United States by the Constitution."

The issue of slavery was an ironic drag on Martin Van Buren's quest for the presidency. The Little Magician (a nickname he despised) stood atop Old Hickory's strong, broad shoulders. But political gravity is real, and by 1836, even Jackson felt its weight. Jackson's battles with the South over the tariff and nullification had weakened the administration's standing with an important part of the Democratic coalition. For Van Buren, the petition battles in Congress reminded slaveowners in the South and West that Van Buren might be a plain Northern republican who could live with slavery, but he was still a Northerner and, therefore, could not be trusted.

Opposition to Andrew Jackson had hardened into a coalition of strange bedfellows who called themselves the Whigs. One part of the Whig Party coalition was the Anti-Masons, a movement begun in western New York State after the mysterious kidnapping and murder of a former Freemason named William Morgan. A conspiracy theory spread throughout the region that the secretive fraternal organization had murdered Morgan to keep him quiet. The Anti-Masons joined National Republicans like Henry Clay, disaffected nullifiers like John C. Calhoun, and former Jacksonians who broke with Old Hickory for what they perceived as the brazen way he wielded executive power.

The only thing that gave Van Buren a chance was that the Whigs were as divided as the Democrats. So divided that the Whigs put forward two candidates, Hugh Lawson White from Tennessee and William Henry Harrison from Ohio. Three, if you count Daniel Webster, who refused to step aside, and ran in Massachusetts.

Adams had no regard for any candidate. "White and Harrison are men of moderate capacity, but of varied public service, and of long experience in the affairs of the Nation—They are as competent for the Presidency at least as Jackson, and like him, if elected to his Station, would rule by the proxy of subalterns—By party management and political love potions, White and Harrison are now the golden calves of the People, and their dull saying are repeated for wit, and their grave inanity is passed off for wisdom." Equally unimpressed with Van Buren, Adams found a campaign biography about the vice president to be "much of that fraudulent democracy by the profession of which Thomas Jefferson rose to power in this Country, and of which he set the first successful example." Adams added, "Van Buren's personal character bears however a stronger resemblance to that of Mr. Madison than to Jefferson—They are both remarkable for their extreme caution in avoiding and averting personal collisions."

A scan of the occasions in which Van Buren appears in John Quincy Adams's diary reveals that the men shared a good rapport. Van Buren called on Adams at his home regarding a settlement with France over disputed claims going back to 1800. The two men had dinner with each other on a few occasions, and on others it appears Van Buren visited with Adams for mere conversation.

At the end of the day, however, Adams never felt inhibited to tell the world or his diary how he really felt about Martin Van Buren. That truth-telling continued through the Van Buren administration, as Van Buren carried fifteen states and won 170 electoral votes. Martin Van Buren did not ride into the President's House on a populist wave, but thanks to his predecessor—the man who put him in office—his presidency was doomed from the moment he raised his right hand to take the oath.

Andrew Jackson's greatest nemesis was neither Henry Clay nor John C. Calhoun; it was the Bank of the United States. Years before he became president, Jackson speculated in lands in the West and, as a result, faced severe financial struggles due to a bank collapse. This episode stung Jackson, leading him to view banks as corrupt institutions controlled by elites that were dangerous to democracy.

In 1834, when the rechartering of the Second Bank of the United States (BUS) came before Congress, Jackson came out in full force against it. By executive order, Jackson stopped depositing federal funds in the BUS. Instead, he spread them out among so-called pet banks in the states. Jackson's enemies denounced him as a contemptible despot whose actions were unprecedented executive overreach. Adams called Jackson and his supporters "grifters" and predicted that the Bank of the United States was the glue holding the financial system together. In the Senate, Henry Clay and his allies voted 26 to 20 to censure President Jackson.

Jackson was determined to destroy the Bank of the United States. He believed paper money was at the root of the problem. To encourage the use of hard money—gold and silver, also known as specie—he supported the Coinage Act of 1834, which altered the ratio between gold and silver to make gold more attractive and promote gold imports. The Distribution Act of 1836 deposited $28 million in federal surplus funds into pet banks. Finally, the Specie Circular declared that only hard money could be used in the purchase of federal lands.

Jackson's policies shifted specie reserves from brokerage houses in the East to Western banks where land speculation was occurring. With no BUS, there was nothing in place to stabilize the money supply in case of a crisis, which is exactly what was unfolding as Van Buren was moving his things into the President's House.

The major brokerage houses in Great Britain, heavily invested in American cotton, had become insolvent, so they called in loans to their American counterparts. Brokerage firms in cities stretching from New Orleans to New York did not have enough specie in reserve. A panic ensued, the worst since 1819. There was a run on banks. Many were forced to close their doors. Three months into Van Buren's term, the nation faced a liquidity crisis. Before long, one in thirty-four Americans lost their jobs. Food costs skyrocketed. Angry mobs rioted in the streets of the nation's major cities. The populist wave that Andrew Jackson rode to the presidency looked like it might carry Martin Van Buren out with the tide.

The financial crisis consumed Congress. Members had to decide whether to approve a fourth installment of deposits from the federal treasury to state banks. At the same time, Adams presented a steady stream of petitions against the annexation of Texas and the slave trade in the District of Columbia. Adams was so busy that he had to get out of bed between three and five in the morning to keep his journal and correspondence up to date. Some nights he did not return home from the Capitol until midnight or later.

One day in late October 1837, while reading the *National Intelligencer,* Adams came upon an advertisement that caught his eye. The ad, posted by local slave trader James Birch and auctioneer Edward Dyer, announced the sale of enslaved persons Birch had recently bought from a man named Rezin Orme. There was nothing unusual about advertisements for enslaved persons in Washington newspapers. The nation's capital boasted a thriving slave industry, but this ad became more curious and disturbing with every new detail. The ad claimed the enslaved were "warranted sound in bodies and in mind, to wit, Dorcas Allen and her two surviving children, aged about seven and nine years." It made sense to ensure the mental and physical fitness of the enslaved persons for offer. But what Adams read next shocked him: "The other two [children] having been killed by said Dorcas in a fit of insanity, as found by the jury who lately acquitted her." The ad then requests the presence of Rezin Orme, "who refuses to retake the same and repay the purchase money."

Adams asked his brother-in-law, Nathaniel Frye, the relative who cared for John in the days and weeks leading up to his death, what he knew about Dorcas Allen. Frye, a slave owner, seemed reluctant to discuss the matter. After a pause, he told Adams that James Birch purchased Dorcas and her children and placed them in the Alexandria slave pen for holding. It was there that Allen slit the throats of her two youngest children, aged four and two. She also tried to murder her two older children, according to the *Alexandria Gazette*, "by beating them on the face and the head with a brick bat." Allen then tried to slit her own throat before someone intervened. Dorcas Allen was charged with murder, but the jury found her not guilty by reason of insanity. Now Birch was looking to recoup his money.

The sad tale of Dorcas Allen tortured Adams. He had been prosecuting the case against the gag rule in the House of Representatives and narrowly escaped a censure for it. Not only was Adams hailed as a hero in the abolitionist press, but the Massachusetts legislature and many of his constituents commended him for his principled stand on behalf of the First Amendment and freedom of speech. In the pages of his diary, it is easy to see that Adams weighed the pros and cons of getting involved. He understood there was a fine line between defender of free speech and antislavery activist. If he overstepped, it would not only jeopardize his own political future, but it would also be a grave setback to the movement. "It is a case of Conscience with me, whether my duty requires or forbids me to pursue the enquiry in this case—to ascertain all the facts, and to expose them in all their turpitude to the world."

John Quincy Adams mentally transported back to 1820 and once again turned over in the soil of his mind what authority the federal government had over slavery. "The prohibition of the internal Slave-trade is within the Constitutional power of Congress, and in my opinion is among their incumbent duties . . ." Adams rationalized. "I have gone as far upon this article, the abolition of Slavery, as the public opinion of the free portion of the Union will bear—and so far that scarcely a slave holding member of the House dares to vote with me, upon any question." Sure, his constituents rallied around him after his censure battle. But how much further would *they* be willing to go? "I have as yet been thoroughly sustained in my own State; but one step further, and I hazard my own standing and influence there; my own final overthrow, and the cause of Liberty itself for indefinite time." As it was in 1820, Adams mused about the arrival of an avenging angel to lead the fight against slavery—anyone but him. "Were there in the House one member capable of taking the lead in this cause of universal emancipation . . . I would withdraw from the contest, which will rage with increasing fury, as it draws to its crisis, but for the management of which my age, infirmities and approaching end totally disqualify *me*—There is no such man in the House."

A few days later, Adams saw another advertisement for the auction of Dorcas Allen and her children. This time, he could not help himself. At 11:00 a.m. on October 28, 1837, a former president and sitting member of Congress stepped foot in the dank, dark confines of Edward Dyer's slave auction room. Someone enslaved in the cell could see the Capitol from their window. There, he found Dorcas Allen, "weeping and wailing most piteously." Adams enquired of Dyer whether Allen and her children had been purchased. Dyer told him they were, last Monday by Allen's husband, Nathan, a free man who worked as a waiter at Gadsby's, a well-known Washington hotel and tavern. Allen had promised to pay $475 for his family's freedom but was unable to come up with the money, so they were for sale again.

Adams learned that Dorcas Allen had been the property of the wife of a War Department clerk by the name of Gideon Davis. On her deathbed, Mrs. Davis made her husband promise to free Dorcas when she died, which he did. But Davis never gave Allen the required papers to make it official. Allen lived the next twelve to fifteen years in total freedom. She married Nathan, and the couple had four children. During that time, Mr. Davis got remarried and died. His second wife married Rezin Orme, and it was in August that Orme sold Dorcas Allen and her children to James Birch. As Dyer filled in the details of Dorcas Allen's backstory for Adams, Francis Scott Key walked into the room. The "Star-Spangled Banner" lyricist was the district attorney for Washington, DC, and was investigating whether Rezin Orme had a legal right to sell Dorcas. Orme had skipped town. His wife was holed up in her bedchamber and refused to talk. Key asked Adams to step outside where they could speak in private. Key, proslavery and a supporter of the colonization society, told Adams he thought a "subscription" could be raised to help Nathan purchase his family. Adams pledged fifty dollars.

Adams's thirst for more knowledge about the case inspired him to pay a visit to his cousin Judge William Cranch, who adjudicated the Dorcas Allen trial. Cranch went over his trial notes with Adams. The only evidence of insanity was the murder of her children; otherwise Dorcas was subject to epileptic fits and was known to be "passionate and violent" and "sometimes wild in her talk." When asked why she killed her children, "she said they were in Heaven—that if they had lived she did not know what would have become of them."

A few days later, Nathan Allen showed up at Adams's home hoping to receive the promised fifty-dollar subscription to gain his wife and children's release. Adams assured him he would give him the money if Nathan raised the remainder of the balance first. Adams asked Nathan for more information about his wife. Nathan said that Dorcas suffered seizures that often left her ill for the next ten to twelve days. Her owner would leave her in the care of Nathan because they refused to pay her medical expenses.

By now completely obsessed with the case, Adams returned to Dyer's auction house on November 2, and the two men argued over Orme's ownership of Dorcas Allen. Dyer told Adams that Orme was "one of the best and most respectable men in the world." Dyer contended that it did not matter whether Orme had a rightful claim to sell Dorcas. Mr. Davis died insolvent, so ultimately his creditors could claim ownership of the woman and her children. Adams went home feeling depressed by the whole situation.

On November 13, Nathan Allen once again appeared at Adams's door, this time with his wife, who was on temporary release. Nathan came with a promise from the commander of the DC militia, General Walter Smith, that if Adams would remit his fifty-dollar subscription, Smith would pay the rest. Adams wrote a check for fifty dollars, and it was the last time he ever saw the couple, but it would not be the last time he spoke the name Dorcas Allen.

In the fall of 1837, while Adams was in the throes of investigating the Dorcas Allen case, he received a visit from a Mr. Thomas Munroe, an old acquaintance of thirty years. According to Adams, Mr. Munroe suffered from hypochondria, due at least in part to grief over the death of two of his adult children and his wife's ill health. Munroe told Adams he suffered from a case of the "blue devils." He asked Adams whether he had "experienced the like" and if he might "prescribe a remedy for his disease." Adams replied, "I had occasionally been afflicted with it; always when I had nothing to do—never at any other time." Adams said the remedy was simple: "intense occupation." It was a "principle and habit" for Adams "to keep myself always busy—with serious affairs as much as possible—With trifles, for exercise, variety and relaxation." Adams asked Munroe whether he had tried riding on horseback. Munroe replied he had, "sometimes, and with good effect." Adams asked, "Had he sought cheerful company?" To which Munroe replied, "he could not endure company, and was often annoyed even by visitors in his family." Having lost two adult children of his own, John Quincy assuredly could relate. "I told him my materia medica was exhausted—exercise, active exercise—open air, temperance, cheerful company and above all constant employment of body or mind were all the remedies I knew for the blue devils."

It does not take much historical or psychological analysis to come to understand Adams absorbed himself in the slavery issue to in some way remedy his own "blue devils." But now it had him caught in a cycle of internal conflict. He knew joining the abolitionist ranks would "ruin me and weaken and not strengthen their cause." At home, Louisa, Charles Francis, and other family members pressured Adams to cease this senseless crusade. "My own family . . . exercise all the influence they possess to restrain and divert me from all connection with the abolitionists, and with their cause . . . my mind is agitated almost to distraction." Becoming the most recognizable voice against slavery put more than his career and personal relationships in danger. Attacks by proslavery mobs were occurring with more frequency.

To Adams's mind, "The most atrocious case of mob rioting whichever disgraced [the] country" took place on November 7, 1837, in Alton, Illinois. There, a proslavery mob broke into a warehouse and murdered the antislavery *Alton Observer* editor Elijah Lovejoy. Lovejoy had attempted three times to import a printing press. Each time, a mob broke in and destroyed not only the press but also the office that housed it. On November 7, a fourth press was delivered to a merchant's warehouse in the dead of night, hoping to elude the notice of the mob. Unfortunately, the angry crowd of anti-abolitionists had spies keeping lookout. In no time at all, the warehouse was surrounded and set ablaze. A battle ensued between the forces of slavery and the forces of freedom. Lovejoy was shot five times and died shortly afterward. His body lay where it fell until the next morning. The rioters threw his press into the river. Lovejoy had written to Adams the previous January. Adams warned him that he was in danger, but the harder the mobs pushed, the more ferocious Lovejoy pushed back. After his murder, Adams wrote that Lovejoy was "fated to be a martyr to the cause of human freedom." Shaken, Adams agreed to write a preface to a memoir written by Lovejoy's brothers.

Adams believed the country teetered on the edge of a knife. Lundy could see it too. In March of 1838, he wrote Adams while visiting his aging father in New Jersey. Lundy believed Northern opposition to Texas annexation was stiffening, but "The bane of political partyism *may* yet baffle all the cherished hopes of the philanthropist and the patriot." He encouraged Adams to take heart that by warning the nation about the true intent of Texas annexation, they had done their duty to their country and God. Still, "If our fellow citizens *will,* notwithstanding all the expositions that have been given, take to their arms that *Babylonish Harlot,* whose gates, politically and morally speaking, are the ways to hell, and whose embrace will be eventual death, why be the sin and its consequences upon them!" Almost fifty years old, Lundy had been making plans to move west to Illinois. Years of hard traveling had taken a toll on his already frail constitution. He told Adams that he "can perhaps, do little or nothing more than I have already done" and implored his brother-in-arms, "It may fall to thy lot, hereafter, to do much more than heretofore, in resisting the encroachment of slaveholding influence, and corruption." Before concluding, Lundy warned Adams that he looked "with sleepless anxiety to the termination of the present session of Congress" as it may decide the "prosperity, or *ruin,* of this Republic."

There was another who saw clearly the dangers facing the nation. It was a young lawyer and Whig state representative from the state of Illinois named Abraham Lincoln. Just twenty-eight years old, Lincoln delivered an address in Springfield before a local debating society, the Young Men's Lyceum, in which he warned of a rising danger to democracy. "At what point shall we expect the approach of danger?" Lincoln asked. "By what means shall we fortify against it?—Shall we expect some transatlantic military giant, to step the Ocean, and crush us at a blow? Never!—All the armies of Europe, Asia, and Africa combined, with all the treasure of the earth (our own excepted) in their military chest; with a Buonaparte for a commander, could not by force, take a drink from the Ohio, or make a track on the Blue Ridge, in a trial of a thousand years." Lincoln believed the real danger to American democracy would come from within: "If destruction be our lot, we must ourselves be its author and finisher. As a nation of freemen, we must live through all time, or die by suicide." The self-inflicted wound Lincoln referred to was mob violence, which "pervaded the country, from New England to Louisiana;—they are neither peculiar to the eternal snows of the former, nor the burning suns of the latter;—they are not the creature of climate. . . . Alike, they spring up among the pleasure hunting masters of Southern slaves, and the order loving citizens of the land of steady habits."

Lincoln sounded a lot like John Quincy Adams: "I know the American People are *much* attached to their Government;—I know they would suffer *much* for its sake;—I know they would endure evils long and patiently, before they would ever think of exchanging it for another. Yet, notwithstanding all this, if the laws be continually despised and disregarded, if their rights to be secure in their persons and property, are held by no better tenure than the caprice of a mob, the alienation of their affections from the Government is the natural consequence; and to that, sooner or later, it must come." To the dismay of Adams, Lundy, and Lincoln, things were about to get worse.

In the spring of 1838, antislavery activists in Center City, Philadelphia, completed construction on the crown jewel of the movement—Pennsylvania Hall. Hailed to be a center for free speech and discussion, not only for abolition, but science, philosophy, and religion, the hall sat on Sixth Street, just a short walk from where Adams's father signed the Declaration of Independence and where the Constitution was debated. Commissioned by the Pennsylvania Anti-Slavery Society at a cost of $40,000, Pennsylvania Hall was said to be the most elegant building of its kind in the city.

Adams received an invitation to come and speak at the dedication ceremony but declined so he could avoid any "indiscreet movements." He did, however, send a letter of congratulations to be read in which he congratulated the Pennsylvania Hall Association for erecting "a large building in your city, wherein liberty and equality of civil rights can be freely discussed, and the evils of slavery fearlessly portrayed . . . I rejoice that, in the city of Philadelphia, the friends of free discussion have erected a Hall for its unrestrained exercise."

Theodore Weld also declined an invitation to speak. The famed orator had reinvented himself as the author of the recently published *The Bible Against Slavery*. Angelina accepted an offer to be a part of the women's convention that also featured William Lloyd Garrison and Lucretia Mott. A crowd of three thousand people attended the mixed-race gathering. A newspaper later reported that "the hall had no negro pew, and of course the people all sat where they could find a place."

Not everyone welcomed the opening of Pennsylvania Hall. Outside, a mob completely encircled the building as Angelina Grimké ascended the rostrum to give her speech. Inside, patrons could hear the chants of the mob. They saw the flickering orange of the torches and the tips of brick bats reflected on the thick windowpanes.

Angelina was not intimidated. "Hear it—hear it. Those voices without tell us that the spirit of slavery is *here*, and has been roused to wrath by our abolition speeches and conventions: for surely liberty would not foam and tear herself with rage, because her friends are multiplied daily, and meetings are held in quick succession to set forth her virtues and extend her peaceful kingdom.

This opposition shows that slavery has done its deadliest work in the hearts of our citizens." Garrison would later write of Grimké that her "eloquence kindled, her eyes flashed and her cheeks glowed."

Angelina raised her voice to match the volume of the shouts coming from the outside. "When hope is extinguished, they say, 'let us eat and drink, for tomorrow we die.'" Just then, a rock hit the window, shattering the glass. Then another . . . and another. The audience let out a collective gasp. A large commotion overtook the hall.

Angelina stiffened her spine. "What is a mob?" she continued. "What would the breaking of every window be? What would the levelling of this Hall be? Any evidence that we are wrong, or that slavery is a good and wholesome institution? What if the mob should now burst in upon us, break up our meeting and commit violence upon our persons—would this be any thing compared with what the slaves endure?"

The mob harassed attendees as they left the hall at the end of the evening. Several of the Black patrons were snuck out the back door to safety. The mob was reacting to a fire hose of conspiracy theories about the hall and what was going on inside. Their shouts of "amalgamation" revealed their greatest fear had become reality; Blacks and whites mingling together as equals.

The women's convention was not the first mixed-race event to occur that week in the city of Philadelphia. Earlier that week, the wedding of Theodore Weld and Angelina Grimké took place at the Spruce Street home of Grimké's recently widowed sister, Anna Frost.

The guest list included Garrison and Weld's good friends and fellow abolition society associates Henry B. Stanton and James G. Birney, among others. Of course, Angelina's sister Sarah was there. Several Black guests were also in attendance including two former enslaved persons from Charleston, South Carolina,

Angelina Grimké

previously owned by the Grimké family. The ceremony was anything but traditional. "Obey" was dropped from Angelina's vows. A Black Presbyterian minister and a white Presbyterian minister read prayers. The wedding cake was made with free sugar. Sugar neither grown nor harvested by enslaved hands.

Proslavery forces plotted the destruction of Pennsylvania Hall before it opened its doors. Reports of a mingling of Blacks and whites of both sexes, "sat together on the platform of the pulpit," told the mob all they needed to know about what type of crowd Pennsylvania Hall was going to attract to "the city of brotherly love."

On the evening of May 17, a mob reported to be ten thousand strong assembled outside the empty hall. Within hours, the crowd swelled to thirty thousand. A report from Philadelphia published in the *Richmond Enquirer* a few days later characterized the men in the crowd as "generally respectable and well dressed, and determined, almost to a man to protect from interruption the immediate agents in the destruction of the building." At around eight o'clock, the mayor arrived with a small group of police officers. The mob made way for the mayor and law enforcement to reach the front doors of the hall. The mayor told the crowd to disperse. The mob refused, and after law enforcement tried to arrest some of the protestors, "the populace fell upon them."

Assailants surrounded the hall, throwing rocks and bricks through the windows. The mob broke down the door, and an army of well-dressed, angry men poured forth into the building and smashed the furniture as they went. They torched a stack of broken pews piled up in the center of the hall. Men ripped the gaslight pipes from the wall and used them to fuel the fire. According to one newspaper report, "Every window vomited forth its volume, and the roof cracked, smoke blazed before the progress of the devouring element."

Onlookers filled the streets for several blocks on all sides as the fire department arrived but did not spill one drop of water on the inferno of Pennsylvania Hall. Instead, they made sure none of the surrounding structures were set ablaze. The roof collapsed at 10:00 p.m., and within an hour only the charred walls of the building remained. The fire smoldered for a day. The charred remains sat untouched within sight of Independence Hall for decades to come, a message to all that the City of Brotherly Love would not tolerate the radicalism of the abolitionists.

Lundy used one of the storefronts on the first floor as an office. There, he kept his papers, letters, and diaries from his decade-plus of antislavery travels. Adams recorded in his diary, "Lundy says that all the valuable property that he had in the world was deposited there and is destroyed."

Benjamin Lundy was devastated, overcome by a weariness and exhaustion he had never felt before. He considered retirement. It was time for him to head west.

Pressure mounted on all sides to silence John Quincy Adams and the abolitionist movement. Violence in the streets. A gag order in the US Capitol. But John Quincy Adams was a lethal politician. He knew all the rules. And more importantly . . . he knew how to wield them against his enemies.

END OF ACT TWO

· ACT THREE ·

· 15 ·

YOUR FRIEND AND FELLOW CITIZEN, JOHN QUINCY ADAMS

Throughout 1837 and 1838, petitions for and against the annexation of Texas were making their way to the Capitol. These were added to the flood of petitions already being sent by antislavery activists. Adams would sift through them in his study at home. Organizing and reorganizing petitions had become his full-time job as it became evident to his fellow citizens that John Quincy Adams was their trusted voice in Congress regardless of whether they were his constituents or not.

Adams presented 350 petitions on February 14 alone. The bulk of them, 158, prayed for rescinding the gag resolution. One petitioner suggested the government fund building a wall that would separate the free states from the slaveholding states. A substantial number of petitions, 54, were against the annexation of Texas. All were tabled.

Adams's attempts to break the grip of the gag rule by repetition and volume of petitions had not gotten him anywhere. But when fellow Massachusetts Congressman George Nixon Briggs presented a resolution from the Massachusetts state legislature opposing the annexation of Texas, Adams saw an opening. He quickly moved that the resolution and all petitions pertaining to Texas should be referred for "study and report" to the Foreign

Affairs Committee. In a moment of weakness, the chair of the committee, Benjamin Chew Howard of Maryland, agreed.

Adams wanted to squelch any talk of Texas annexation. All the better if he could break the gag rule in the process. The potential for the United States to absorb Texas into the Union had been left dangling in the American conscience since the Republic of Texas declared independence in 1836. At present, President Van Buren had no appetite to annex the territory for fear of upsetting his Northern supporters. Still, there was no shortage of backroom machinations by pro-Texas men whispering in the ear of the president. The matter was never completely off the table.

John Quincy knew what was at stake. A few months earlier, Adams decried on the House floor that the annexation of Texas would mean the dissolution of the Union. Never "a nation 'damned to everlasting fame' by the reinstitution of that detested system of slavery, after it had once been abolished within its borders, should be admitted into union with a nation of freemen. For, Sir, that name, thank God, is still ours!"

The committee, with its 6–3 slaveholder majority, reported its findings in early June, just three weeks prior to the adjournment of Congress. Committee member from Virginia George C. Dromgoole stated that because there was no proposition for or against Texas annexation before the House, all state resolutions and the stacks of petitions signed by over one hundred thousand American citizens should be laid upon the table. Chairman Howard was ready to put the whole affair to bed: "I cannot anticipate a single good result from the prolongation of a general debate upon the subject of Texas."

But John Quincy Adams knew exactly what the committee was up to. They had not studied or reported on anything. They had not even read the resolutions and petitions in question.

When Adams asked whether these petitions received even five minutes of consideration, Howard swiped back at Adams, "How dare any member catechise the committee of its actions?!" These days, Howard would have just said: *Don't tell us how to do our job.*

The committee claimed they did not read the petitions because they had no intention of taking any action for or against Texas. But Adams knew the rules. The committee was required to at least read the petitions even if they did not address them. Committee member Hugh Legaré from South Carolina stood up and admitted he had been aware of the petitions and resolutions but didn't see the point in reading, as Legaré confirmed, "Not one."

Adams smiled. He proceeded to read the seventy-sixth standing rule of the House, which stated that it was the duty of the Foreign Affairs Committee to "take into consideration all matters which concern the relations of the United States with foreign nations, and which shall be referred to them by the House, and report their opinion on the same." Legaré argued he was familiar with the rule and did not break it.

Adams disagreed.

That was when Adams's Massachusetts colleague and Foreign Affairs Committee member Caleb Cushing stood up and said that he dissented from the committee's decision to table the petitions and resolutions, but he was not given the opportunity to issue a Minority Report on the subject. Cushing made a motion to reconsider the issue "more deliberately and argumentatively." Cushing's motion opened the door. Southern Congressman Waddy Thompson leapt through it.

Thompson offered an amendment to Cushing's motion, calling on President Van Buren to immediately annex Texas. Adams proposed an amendment to Thompson's amendment saying that neither the president nor Congress had the power to annex Texas.

There it was. According to House rules of order, an amendment to an amendment is the end of the line. Whoever makes an amendment to an amendment holds the floor. Adams's knowledge of parliamentary procedure gave him the high ground. The gentleman from South Carolina had unwittingly ripped the gag from Adams's mouth.

About to turn seventy-one, John Quincy Adams used a parliamentary maneuver and held the floor during the "morning hour," a time set aside for committee business, from June 16, 1838, until the session adjourned on July 9. Adams enjoyed defending the Constitution and democracy against its enemies, many of whom were his congressional colleagues.

For the next three weeks, Adams divulged details from Lundy's reports. He spoke against the annexation of Texas. He shared with his colleagues the sad tale of Dorcas Allen. He quoted the Constitution and Declaration of Independence. Recalling Chairman Howard's previous testimony calling most of the petitioners against Texas "meddling females," Adams launched into a full-throated defense of women's rights.

"Was this from a son? Was it from a father? Was it from a husband that I heard these words? . . . It is to the wives and to the daughters of my constituents that he applies this language. . . . Are women to have no opinions or action on subjects relating to the general welfare? Why does it follow that women are fitted for nothing but the cares of domestic life, for bearing children and cooking the food of a family? . . . I say women exhibit the most exalted virtue when they depart from the domestic circle and enter on the concerns of their country, of humanity, and of their God!"

While Adams's feminist outburst reflects his mother Abigail's famous letter to his father, in which she implored him to "remember the ladies," I must note here that John Quincy did not exactly extend the same deference to Louisa.

Eventually, a committee member asked Adams if he was ever going to shut up. Adams replied, if he so wished, he would be happy to "enter into a full and strict scrutiny of slavery. And so long as God will give me life and breath and faculty of speech, he shall have it, to his heart's content." Like Captain America, Adams was saying, *I can do this all day.*

Adams was like a hostage taker, and by the time he had released his hostages at the end of the congressional session, the administration of President Martin Van Buren backed off any designs for annexing Texas—at least for now. The press coverage of Adams's arguments against annexation rattled the administration and caused the Texas government to withdraw its request for admittance into the Union. Texas annexation had stalled, but the fight over slavery was more heated than ever. Within a year, it would boil over.

In early 1839, John Quincy shifted his plan of attack against the slavocracy. He was the unofficial leader of the antislavery faction in the federal government. He himself believed the movement had been "committed to [his] trust." But Adams found the idea of immediate emancipation something impractical for which there was no real plan to implement. Adams called out the foolishness of Northern abolitionists in speeches on the floor of the House before he proposed his own ill-fated plan for the limitation and gradual emancipation of slavery by constitutional amendment.

In early February, Adams received a letter from Benjamin Lundy. Neither man realized at the time that it would be their last correspondence. Now settled in Lowell, Illinois, the old Quaker had not lost the zeal that brought him to the fight two decades before. "I see, by the accounts from Washington, that thee is still engaged in battling for the *right of petition*. . . . It would, indeed, seem that the elements of anarchy and despotism have *combined* . . . and are about to overwhelm our cherished liberties and free institutions, with their resistless torment of corruption and wickedness. Yet, while God, in his mercy, spares *thy* valuable life, we shall not despair." I get a sense that Adams would not suffer a pep talk from just anyone. He and Lundy were connected on a deeper level. He wrote, "The prayers of thousands are constantly ascending to Heaven for thy protection amid the storm of demoniac malignity which threatens by night and by day. Suffer not spirits to flag, my dear friend, for great and glorious is the reward that awaits thee. Most enviable is thy situation—dangerous as it may seem to be, at the present moment. The highest meed of honor, that has ever been awarded to a statesman, is thine; and the soul-felt consolation, of which nothing, earthly, can deprive thee; will be eternal." Lundy signed off, "I remain, most truly, Thy Sincere Friend, B. Lundy."

Lundy's February 4, 1839, letter to Adams reads like a pep talk. But Adams turned around and penned a blistering attack—against the abolitionists.

In April and May, Adams published two public letters addressed to the "Citizens of the United States, whose Petitions, Memorials and Remonstrances have been intrusted to me." Published in the *National Intelligencer*, they were soon reprinted in newspapers across the country. The first letter was focused on the gag rule and the second the history of Southern slavery, its connection to the Declaration of Independence, and antislavery organizations.

Adams pointed out the inconsistencies between the doctrine of slavery and the founding documents. "There was obviously a gross inconsistency between the principles proclaimed in the Declaration of Independence and the practice of holding human beings in perpetual and hereditary bondage." Southerners had created a philosophical, religious, and scientific justification for the institution of slavery. He lamented that he "never imagined a day . . . when . . . public men, ambitious of a name and aspirants to popular favor, would be found to sophisticate slavery into a blessing, and to charge the Signers of the Declaration of

Independence with deliberate falsehood and perjury—with treason to their country and blasphemy to God."

Next, Adams took the American Colonization Society to task for trying "to establish colonies of free negroes on the coast of Africa, to disburden this continent from the load to its colored population, has, from its first inception, appeared to me a visionary and utterly impracticable though benevolent project."

Then, he turned his ire on the very organizations that had in recent years honored and courted him, practically elevating him to sainthood, the abolition societies of the North. Adams said that all throughout the fight over petitions and the gag rule, "the reason upon which I have declared myself not prepared to vote for the immediate abolition of slavery in the District of Columbia . . . is . . . its utter impracticability."

Only curmudgeonly John Quincy Adams could deliver such brutal honesty to a group of people who had so embraced him. Adams pulled no punches in explaining his position against immediate emancipation. "Public opinion," Adams wrote, "throughout the Union is against it. No member of Congress from any one of the States where slavery is established would dare to vote for it, nor could he return with safety to his person among his constituents if he should." Adams noted that, apart from Vermont, no Northern state would be favorable to it.

He acknowledged the political reality of the times. "All of the strength of Mr. Van Buren in the South rests exclusively upon the pledges that he has given against this particular measure."

Adams said although the cause they fight for is noble and just, the abolitionists are in their "martyr age," driven in large measure by "religious principle." He reiterated his opinion "that one human being cannot be made the property of another. That persons and things are, by the laws of Nature and of Nature's God, so distinct that no human laws can transform either into the other."

But if he were to offer a bill to end slavery in the district, it would fail tremendously. And for the federal government to impose emancipation on the citizens of the district, it would fly in the face of the Declaration of Independence.

He concluded that while he would continue to fight for the right of the petitioners to be heard and considered, "the time has not yet come when Justice herself would be satisfied with the immediate abolition of slavery in the District of Columbia." Abolitionist hearts snapped as the words of Old Man Eloquent unfolded on the page.

Adams admitted that slavery had embedded itself in the South and it would not be removed in his lifetime. "The spirit of slavery had acquired not only an overruling ascendency, but has become at once intolerant, proscriptive, and sophistical. It has crept into the philosophical chairs of schools. Its cloven foot has ascended the pulpits of the churches. Professors of colleges teach it as a lesson of morals. Ministers of the Gospel seek and profess to find sanctions for it in the Word of God!"

Adams was not telling the abolitionists to quit the field entirely. He pointed out that the battle he waged on behalf of petitions and resolutions for and against Texas annexation had, at least for now, prevented the consummation of a territory, "sufficient for the foundation of ten states with the new brand of irrevocable slavery."

Pointing to the very epicenter of the slavocracy, South Carolina, he charged that the South, with Calhoun and the nullifiers in charge, were engaged in a counterrevolution and had renounced the principles of the Declaration of Independence.

He closed with a similar prediction to the one he recorded twenty years earlier when the nation was in the deep darkness of the Missouri Crisis. The day of emancipation would be "preceded by convulsions and revolutions in the moral, political, and physical world" of the United States. There could be no longer any doubt about it, the slavocracy had corrupted American democracy.

Adams accused abolitionists with whom he had worked so closely of being in denial. He was right. The American Anti-Slavery Society was bankrupt, the abolitionist movement divided, and there was no real plan for immediate emancipation. America was not ready for emancipation. The end of slavery in the United States would be left up to future generations to figure out.

August 22, 1839, marked the end of an era in the fight for emancipation. Benjamin Lundy, just fifty years old, passed away in the small village of Lowell, Illinois. Years of relentless travel had taken their toll on his body, and he never fully recovered after his last trip to Mexico. While editing the weekly *National Enquirer* and trying to continue the *Genius* in Philadelphia, Lundy found himself overshadowed by the next generation of younger, more vigorous abolitionists. What was once a landscape dotted with a few antislavery journals had now become a field teeming with them. For Lundy, publishing an antislavery journal in the East had long ago ceased to be sustainable.

Lundy faced a significant blow when he lost his lifetime's work in the burning of Pennsylvania Hall. Recognizing it was time for a change, he decided to move west. His older daughters, Susan and Elizabeth, and his sons, Charles and Benjamin, had all relocated to Putnam County, Illinois. After years spent in constant motion, it was time to settle, though not retire. Just days after arriving in Hennepin, Illinois, Lundy attended an antislavery convention. There, he proposed resolutions supporting John Quincy Adams's efforts in Congress on behalf of the right to petition and against the annexation of Texas. Demonstrating his unwavering commitment, Lundy began publishing new editions of the *Genius*.

In early August, while farming his newly purchased land, Lundy caught a fever that had made its way around the community. Confined to his bed, he never recovered.

On September 16, Adams wrote, "I received this day, the Genius of universal emancipation N. 314. printed at Hennepin Illinois announcing the death of Benjamin Lundy, a pure and noble spirit as ever lived—He has left none better behind."

Benjamin Lundy may never have broken the chain of slavery, but he helped set it on a path to ultimate destruction. As previously noted, it was Lundy who converted William Lloyd Garrison to the cause, but he never managed to convert John Quincy Adams to abolition, but Adams, a keen observer of motives, saw in Lundy a pure and honest soul. Adams had relied on information that came directly from Lundy's journeys to Texas as the basis for his most effective arguments when he held the Congress hostage in the summer of 1838. In Adams's eyes, the former president of the United States and the fervent Quaker zealot were equals.

A few months before the death of Benjamin Lundy, on May 4, 1839, Theodore Weld completed his own transformation from orator to writer when he published *American Slavery as It Is*, a monumental indictment of slavery that would influence the next generation of antislavery activists. "Reader," Weld implores, "You are empannelled as a juror to try a plain case and bring in an honest verdict. The question at issue is not one of law, but of fact—'What is the actual condition of the slaves in the United States?' A plainer case never went to a jury. Look at it." Weld continues, "TWENTY-SEVEN HUNDRED THOUSAND PERSONS in this country, men, women, and children are in SLAVERY." With the help of Angelina and Sarah, Weld compiled the testimonials of current and former enslaved individuals, current and former enslavers, and others. The book was the most comprehensive analysis of slavery produced, influencing the daughter of Lyman Beecher, Harriet Beecher Stowe, when she wrote *Uncle Tom's*

Cabin, the book that would influence the next generation of abolitionists. It also moved John Quincy, who wrote, "The details of Theodore D. Weld's book—American Slavery as it is—The stomach heaves at the perusal of the numberless cases of human suffering inflicted by human hands." The man once considered the greatest antislavery spokesman was now its greatest writer.

· 16 ·

AMISTAD

It was a summer morning, 1839. The hatch leading below the deck of the ship lifted. A hard shaft of light shot through the dank, fetid ship's hold. Joseph Cinqué winced as he struggled to open his eyes. Dazed. Unsure of his surroundings. Pain shot through his legs. He tried to lift them. They wouldn't budge. He was chained to a long line of men, women, and children.

Months had passed since he was in his village in what is now Sierra Leone with no idea where he was, how he got there, or where he was going. When the sun shined, Cinqué and the other captives were brought to the deck for fresh air, while the cabin boy shoveled out the excrement from the slave quarters. Cinqué took the opportunity to familiarize himself with his surroundings, taking note of everything he saw aboard the ship—named *Amistad.*

There was a captain, a cook, and a handful of crew members. The details are murky, but somehow, perhaps with a nail he'd found in the ship's waterlogged boards, Cinqué unchained himself and the other captives. When night fell, they stormed the deck, found a cache of machetes, and seized the moment.

They slashed the captain, Ramón Ferrer, and bludgeoned the mulatto cook to death. And they forced the ship's owners, José Ruiz and Pedro Montes, to help them navigate back to Africa, back home to Sierra Leone. Montes was an experienced sailor. By day, the ship crawled eastward; at night, he navigated north and west at a steady clip in hopes of being spotted by a friendly vessel off the coast of the United States. Cinqué and the other Africans had no idea the men who were now *their* captives were enslavers—the very men responsible for their abduction.

Montes's gamble paid off. The *Amistad* was spotted off the coast of Long Island. A lieutenant named Thomas Gedney looked out from his ship to see a vessel in tatters: bedraggled sails and a colorfully dressed Black crew—quite a curious sight. Gedney and his crew boarded the suspicious vessel, and they could tell right away what had gone down. The human cargo of the *Amistad* had risen up and slaughtered their captors. Gedney took charge of the *Amistad* and brought the vessel to nearby Connecticut. Cinqué and dozens of other captives were arrested, charged with murder and piracy, and placed in a prison cell to await trial. Their story hit the newspapers the next day: "A bloody slave insurrection on the high seas." Overnight, it became a national sensation. Were these African captives heroes struggling for freedom? Or murderers?

The headlines shattered the peace and quiet John Quincy Adams was hoping to enjoy during a break at his home, Peacefield. He was preparing for the next session of Congress but couldn't get the *Amistad* case out of his head.

The case ignited America's debate over slavery like never before. The moment the *Amistad* was towed into the port of New London, Connecticut, word of the mutiny on a slave ship traveled quickly. It was as if the entire population of New London made their way to the docks to catch a glimpse of a barnacled ship sitting offshore with torn sails. Among the first individuals aboard the ship were sketch artists, who rendered Cinqué with his spine upright, his jaw squared, his almond-shaped eyes determined. He was wearing a buccaneer shirt and duck pantaloons and striking the pose of a Roman warrior. News reports quickly made their way from Boston down to Washington. At all points in between, people were talking about the *Amistad.*

Onshore, Lieutenant Gedney sent a message to Judge Andrew Judson of the district court in New Haven telling him of the murderous rampage and piracy committed by Cinqué and his fellow captives. Gedney also made a salvage rights claim worth an estimated $65,000 for the value of the ship and its human property. Of course, Montes and Ruiz also made the claim that they were the slaves' masters and that they should be returned to them. After a brief investigation, Judson ordered Cinqué and the others to stand trial for murder and piracy in a circuit court in Hartford. The roughly fifty *Amistad* captives, including four children, would be held in the jail in New Haven.

The abolitionist movement seized the moment. They rallied around the case. Raised money. Recruited new antislavery activists. Lewis Tappan visited the captives in their jail cell and joined with William Lloyd Garrison in fundraising for their legal defense. William Jay, son of founding father John Jay, published a letter he had written to William Lloyd Garrison in which he made a $20 donation to the legal fund and ticked through the many reasons the *Amistad* captives should not be held liable for murder and be returned to Africa at once. Jay wrote, "There was a treaty between Spain and Great Britain going back to 1835 declaring, 'the slave-trade on the part of Spain to be totally abolished in all parts of the world.'" Jay noted that the queen of Spain had issued a "Royal Order" to the "Captain General of their Cuban Colony," directing him "to apply the strongest zeal in dictating the necessary measures for preventing the deplorable contraband."

John Quincy Adams found it impossible to escape the *Amistad* case. He had been following it in the newspapers just like everyone else. Jay's righteous and well-researched assessment of the case got Adams's blood up. He could not help but write him a letter agreeing that the captives of the *Amistad* had "vindicated their own right of liberty . . . executing the justice of Heaven upon one pirate murderer, their tyrant and oppressor." Just like today, if you write it down, it is going to become public eventually. Abolitionists got the message. John Quincy Adams, the man who had spent the previous six months publicly humiliating them, was on their side once again.

Adams's first comments about the case in his diary appear on September 12, after a visit from New York Congressman Gouverneur Kemble and his brother-in-law, who happened to be the secretary of the navy. "He thinks . . . that the Slaves of the Spanish Slave ship who mutinied and captured here and have been brought into New-London, must be delivered up to the Government of the Island of Cuba.—I fear they will be."

Meanwhile, abolitionist lawyers representing the African captives tried to get *their* side of the story. But the captives didn't speak a lick of Spanish. This was surprising because the two enslavers aboard the ship *claimed* the captives came from Cuba, not Africa. And this is actually a *big* deal.

The American government prohibited the importation of enslaved individuals into the United States in 1808. According to the international slave trade ban, ships involved in this trade from other nations were not permitted to enter US ports. If an individual arrived in the country from Africa, they could not be legally enslaved in the United States. The slave traders Montes and Ruiz attempted to do something illegal yet common for the time. Essentially: slave laundering. The *Amistad* brought the captives from Africa to Cuba with forged documents that listed the captives as *ladinos*, which meant they were slaves "who had lived in Spanish territories since long before the slave trade had been outlawed." What slave launderers would do is land their human contraband on one part of the Cuban island, file false paperwork, board them on another ship, and land them on another part of the island.

If the lawyers for the captured rebels could prove this, they could shatter Montes and Ruiz's case. But these lawyers had never heard any of the languages spoken by Cinqué and the others. They were not Spanish-born, as Montes and Ruiz claimed. The defense had no way to speak with their clients . . . until Lewis Tappan came across an African sailor in New Haven who recognized that most of the captives were in fact known as Mende (MEN-dee) and spoke a shared second language of the Mende captives, a language called Vai. Finally, the captives were able to tell the story of violence and horror they had endured. Just weeks later, their case kicked off in a district court in Connecticut.

Their defense was led by Roger Sherman Baldwin, who came from an esteemed lineage. He was the grandson of Roger Sherman, a signer of the Declaration of Independence, who also served briefly as a United States senator from Connecticut. Baldwin would later serve as governor of Connecticut.

When the case kicked off, Montes and Ruiz, the Spanish government, and Lieutenant Gedney all claimed some form of ownership of the captives. Roger Baldwin argued that these African prisoners were not murderers or slaves. They were free men, women, and children who had been forcibly kidnapped from their homes. Unable to testify by speaking the English language, Cinqué sat on the floor of the court and dramatically held his hands together clenched in fists to show how they had been manacled on board the *Amistad*.

At the conclusion of the testimony, Judge Smith Thompson ruled that the captives were "natives of Africa and were born free and ever since have been and still of right are free and not slaves." He said the court had no jurisdiction on the high seas but refused to liberate the captives because the Spanish claimed

Joseph Cinqué in court, demonstrates how he was shackled aboard the Amistad

them as property, and the district court had no jurisdiction to that claim.

This was just what US District Attorney William S. Holabird, under direct pressure from the Van Buren administration, had wanted. He appealed to the judge that the president had a right to hold the captives until a definitive decision was reached. Van Buren had been under pressure from the Spanish government to turn over the *Amistad* and their captives. Although Judge Thompson's personal feelings toward slavery were unkind, he argued that the defense had not made the case that the captives had been illegally seized, and since the Constitution sanctioned slavery, "we must look at things as they are." Thompson ordered another hearing on property claims in the district court.

A foreign policy crisis in an election year was the last thing Martin Van Buren needed. The Spanish government argued José Ruiz and Pedro Montes were Spanish nationals; therefore, the ship and its cargo were Spanish property. At the same time, a domestic slave ship controversy threatened to destroy the fragile coalition keeping President Martin Van Buren in power. The Little Magician—as he was known—desperately wanted a second term, and he needed slave-state support. The effects of the financial panic of 1837 and another panic in 1838 jeopardized his reelection chances even before the *Amistad* had come ashore.

The next day, Adams received a visit from an abolitionist who carried a letter from Ellis Gray Loring, a Boston attorney favorable to the captives' cause who wanted to know Adams's opinion on the case given his decades of experience in international affairs and law. A few days later, Adams visited Loring at his office. "Mr Loring was extremely anxious to obtain my opinion as to the right of the President to deliver up the negroes, upon the demand of the Spanish Minister—Yet the time has not yet come when it would be proper for me to give an opinion for publication—Prudence would forbid my giving an opinion upon it at any time; and if I ever do, it must be with great consideration and self controul—May I walk humbly and uprightly, on this and all other occasion—flinching from no duty—obtruding no officious interposition of opinions, and prepared to meet with firmness whatever obloquy may follow the free expression of my thoughts."

While many tried to pull Adams *into* the case, there were important people pleading with him to stay out of it. His surviving son, Charles Francis, was in the middle of his own campaign for the Massachusetts State House. He begged his father not to get in any deeper with radical abolitionists. "This will be productive of results unpleasant to myself for it must greatly embarrass the political party with which I have undertaken to act." Adams listened to his son. At least for a little while.

Staying out of it did not mean ceasing to do any of his own research into the matter. Adams consulted legal books like Sir William Blackstone's *Commentaries on the Laws of England* and Matthew Bacon's *A New Abridgment of the Law*, treaties with Spain dating back to 1795, and case law of seized slave ships like the *Antelope* and the *Abby*.

In the meantime, the case of the *Amistad* captives continued winding its way through the American judicial system until the lower court ruled that the Mende should be returned to Sierra Leone. But the Van Buren administration had dug in its heels and appealed the case to the Supreme Court. The first trial took place in the Northern state of Connecticut. Abolitionists who represented the captives worried they wouldn't get the same ruling in the highest court of the land. The Supreme Court was made up almost entirely of enslavers, many from the South. Panic took hold. The *Amistad* captives needed someone with gravitas and experience to defend them before the high court. A not-so-secret weapon.

At the end of October 1840, John Quincy Adams received a couple of visitors: Lewis Tappan and a Boston abolitionist friend.

Tappan pressed Adams to join the *Amistad* defense team. Roger Baldwin was a good lawyer, but this was prime time, and they needed a well-known champion for the national stage of the Supreme Court. Adams thought they were crazy. He had seen too many winters to take on such an important case. He was in his seventies. His eyesight was fading. He had arthritis. It had been *thirty years* since he argued a case before the Supreme Court. No. The answer had to be no.

Later, Adams recorded in his diary, "They urged me so much and represented the case of those unfortunate men as so critical, it being a case of life and death, that I yielded, and told them that, if by the blessing of God my health and strength should permit, I would argue the case before the Supreme Court."

John Quincy Adams had no time to waste getting up to speed with the *Amistad* case. It was the fall of 1840, and the Supreme Court hearing was scheduled for February of 1841. The ex-president headed for New Haven, Connecticut, to meet with his co-counsel, Roger Baldwin. "He exposed to me his views of the case; the points which had been taken before the District and the Circuit Courts; and the motion to dismiss the appeal which he supposes the proper course to be taken before the Supreme Court."

Shortly after his arrival, Baldwin took Adams to visit the captives. The Mende were living in a small dormitory complex complete with an outdoor courtyard. "The three girls are in a separate house, and I did not see them—There are 36 men, confined all in one chamber perhaps 30 feet long by 20 wide—sleeping in 18 crib beds in rows two deep on both sides the length of the chamber—They are all but one young men, under 30." Many of the captives had started to learn English, including Cinqué—who had become the group's de facto leader. James Traub notes that Adams was struck, "especially by . . . Cinqué, who became the leader, who became a romantic figure in America. He was one of the most drawn figures and then photographed in the country . . . he must have been a very impressive person, and Adams was really struck. And so I think that experience made him think, I must help these people."

As the trial date drew near, Adams searched for legal precedents that would free the captives.

But many of these cases had ended badly, and Adams knew it. While he was president, the Supreme Court ruled on a mutiny aboard the Spanish slave ship, the *Antelope.* The chief justice at the time, John Marshall, ruled that international law *barred* the liberation of the *Antelope*'s "human cargo." Adams started to worry.

Just when the stakes couldn't seem higher, he received a letter from one of the captives, a Mende boy named Kale (KAH-lay): "We want you to ask the court what we have done wrong what for Americans keep us in prison. Some people say Mendi people crazy, dolts, because we no talk American language. Americans no talk Mendi. American people crazy dolts?"

Arguments before the Supreme Court started on February 22, George Washington's birthday.

Attorney General Henry Gilpin presented the case for the United States. He argued that the *Amistad* was a *Spanish* vessel carrying cargo approved by the country's authorities. Therefore, the United States was *obligated* by *treaty* to restore the ship and its cargo to the rightful owners, the Spanish government.

That way, the Spanish authorities could try them for piracy and murder.

After Gilpin's opening arguments, it was time for John Quincy and his co-counsel to make their case. Baldwin kicked off the defense by saying that the whole world was watching. "This case is not only one of deep interest in itself, as affecting the destiny of the unfortunate Africans, whom I represent, but it involves considerations deeply affecting our national character in the eyes of the whole civilized world. It presents, for the first time, the question whether the government, which was established for the promotion of JUSTICE, which was founded on the great principles of the Revolution, as proclaimed in the Declaration of Independence, can consistently with the genius of our institutions, become a party to proceedings for the enslavement of human beings cast upon our shores, and found in the condition of freemen within the territorial limits of a FREE AND SOVEREIGN STATE?"

Baldwin continued, saying the captives aboard the ship were kidnapped and forced into bondage. Why would the US government hand them *back* to their captors? "Cinque, the master spirit who guided them, had a single object in view. That object was—not piracy or robbery—but the deliverance of himself and his companions in suffering, from unlawful bondage." When he finished, Adams thought that Baldwin had done a great job laying out the *legal* argument for the defense. But where was the showmanship? They needed to break through to these justices! Show them the importance of this moment! John Quincy wrote in his diary that Baldwin had been "sound and eloquent but exceedingly mild and moderate." Adams had to bring the heat.

By the time Adams stood before the court, years of shouting down Southerners in Congress had given him an edge. A ferocity. "If any part of the article was applicable to the case it was in favor of the Africans. They were in distress, and were brought into our waters by their enemies, by those who sought, and who are still seeking, to reduce them from freedom to slavery."

Adams railed for over four hours, building his case. "If the good offices of the government are to be rendered to the proprietors of shipping in distress, they are due to the Africans only, and the United States are now bound to restore the ship to the Africans and replace the Spaniards on board as prisoners." Court adjourned for the day, deciding Adams could finish the next day. But overnight, one of the justices died! The court sat in recess for a week to mourn Justice Philip Barbour.

When arguments resumed, Adams launched back into it. He argued that the 1795 treaty with Spain did not apply in this case. They were not chattel; they were not merchandise. They were illegally enslaved. But Adams wasn't there to simply make a legal argument. He was arguing for the soul of the nation. This was bigger than case law. This was foundational. He had watched his parents, and their generation, create this nation. Now, it was up to his generation to ensure it lived up to the ideals of its founders. Adams pointed to the Declaration of Independence hung on a pillar in the court. "The moment you come, to the Declaration of Independence, that every man has a right to life and liberty, an inalienable right, this case is decided. I ask nothing more in behalf of these unfortunate men, than this Declaration."

He was speaking to a court that consisted almost entirely of slave owners or slave sympathizers. Adams called out the names of the justices he stood before decades earlier. For a moment, it was almost as if he were conjuring them from the grave. "Marshall, Cushing, Chase, Washington, Johnson, Livingston, Todd. Where are they? . . . Alas! Where is one of the very judges of the court, arbiters of life and death, before whom I commenced this anxious argument? . . . Where are they all? Gone! Gone! All Gone! Gone from the services which, in their day and generation, they faithfully rendered to their country."

Historian Richard S. Newman paraphrases: "He says, I thought the Supreme Court, like the American Republic, was dedicated to the principle of justice and whether or not it's an enslaved person struggling for justice or an American citizen struggling for justice. That's the principle that should define international law, American politics, and American jurisprudence."

When Adams wrapped, a reporter wrote, "In uttering his last sentence or two, Mr. Adams' voice almost failed him, through the force of his feelings and as he sat down, the tears started from his eyes, as they did likewise from the eyes of others." The reporter confessed that he, too, was crying, as were the "Clerk of court." As for the judges? "I did not observe the Judges, being absorbed in my own emotions, but I doubt not they were deeply affected likewise. . . . As to Mr. Adams, the nation will mourn his loss when he dies . . . God preserve him to us many years to come." Adams indeed did have more to give to his country. When he finished presenting his case, he tidied up the papers on his desk, packed them into his satchel, and walked across the street to the House of Representatives, where he got back to work.

The Supreme Court back then was faster at issuing verdicts than it is today. The court came back with its ruling just a week and a half later. But in that short time, a new president had taken office. On March 4, 1841, William Henry Harrison of Ohio was inaugurated as the ninth president of the United States. Martin Van Buren was out. Would the court case his administration set in motion be decided in his favor?

Justice Joseph Story issued the majority opinion of the court. He wrote: "They are natives of Africa, and were kidnapped there, and were unlawfully transported to Cuba, in violation of the laws and treaties of Spain, and the most solemn edicts and declarations of that Government." The court ruled 7–1 in *favor* of the captives.

Did Adams's oration tip the scales of justice in favor of the captives? Maybe. It is more likely, however, that the law was already on their side. But John Quincy Adams was a man of gravitas. He was a former president, before that a lifelong diplomat, and at the time of the decision he had been in Congress for a decade. His eight-hour speech, which spanned two days, rooted in the nation's founding principles, didn't hurt. Justice Story later wrote of Adams's argument: "Extraordinary for its power, for its bitter sarcasm, and for its dealing with topics far beyond the record and points of discussion."

Ecstasy rippled through the abolitionist communities. In the jail, however, the captives were cut off from the outside world. They were still nervously awaiting the news. Then, an abolitionist arrived with a newspaper: "The big court has come to a decision—they say that you—one and all—are free."

The captives were skeptical. They had been let down by previous rulings time and again. But Kale, the group's best reader, looked at the paper. It was true. They were going home.

The nation celebrated—not only the ruling, but Adams. He had successfully defended the founding ideals of the nation when it mattered most.

His son felt different. Charles Francis wrote to his father, "It may be very interesting to yourself and the public to be pleading in the Supreme Court, but I must admit that I do not greatly admire the anxiety it occasions to those of us who do not regard it simply as a show." That's harsh. Louisa was just glad it was over. She knew he did the right thing, but once again, he put her through a lot of anxiety and heartache.

Abolitionists raised funds through the spring and summer to send the captives back home. In November, they began their journey. Before their departure, Adams received a gift: a Bible signed by Cinqué and Kale on behalf of them all. Friends pushed Adams to make a public show of the gift. But that wasn't his style. This was a private moment between him and the people he had befriended.

"Mr Lewis Tappan has been extremely desirous of having this done by a public exhibition and ceremony, which I have repeatedly and inflexibly declined, from a clear conviction of its impropriety, and an invincible repugnance to exhibiting myself as a public raree show." John Quincy cherished the gift. Today, the Bible is on display at Peacefield. When it was all said and done, Tappan anxiously waited to receive a bill for legal services rendered. Adams never sent one.

The *Amistad* case was a victory for Cinqué and his fellow captives. Abolitionists had dealt the slavocracy a rare but decisive blow, with Adams landing the knockout punch. It was a defining moment for America's founding son. It elevated him from a failed ex-president to a national hero.

· 17 ·

ANN SPRIGG'S BOARDINGHOUSE

Late winter, 1841. A cold wind bears down on the city as William Henry Harrison walks to the steps of the US Capitol to be sworn in as the nation's ninth president. Harrison wants to project a strong image to the nation. Like Jackson, he was a war hero, having fought against several Native tribes in the country's expansion westward.

That day was cold and wet, but Harrison refused to wear an overcoat, hat, or even gloves. He wanted to distinguish himself from his aristocratic predecessor, Martin Van Buren. Harrison was a frontiersman from Ohio. A little cold wouldn't hurt him.

The Harrison administration provided new hope for the nation and John Quincy Adams. Democrats had held the reins of power for more than a decade. Now, the Whigs had taken over the House, Senate, and presidency in one fell swoop.

A week after his inauguration, President Harrison showed up at Adams's door. He told the ex-president he was welcome at the President's House anytime. "Come when you please, as often as you please, or drop me a line, for I shall at any time be happy to take your advice, and counsel, as that of a brother."

The Whig Party was formed for the sole purpose of defeating Andrew Jackson and his Democratic Party. At last, they were well-positioned to reverse what they saw as the failed banking and tariff policies of the Jackson and Van Buren administrations. But William Henry Harrison fell ill after his inauguration. First a cold. Then pneumonia. Serving just thirty-one days in office, he died on April 4, 1841. There would be no William Henry Harrison administration.

Now the man in charge was Vice President John Tyler, who could not have been more different than Harrison. Tyler was a slaveholder from Virginia. He supported John C. Calhoun during the nullification battles a decade ago. Adams did not think much of the guy either. "Tyler is a political sectarian of the Slave-driving, Virginian Jeffersonian school—Principled against all improvement—With all the interests and passions, and vices of Slavery rooted in his moral and political constitution—with talents not above mediocrity, and a spirit incapable of expansion to the dimensions of the station upon which he has been cast by the hand of Providence unseen through the apparent agency of chance." And it goes on from there. Let us pause for a second to point out that sick burn: *talents not above mediocrity*. That's why I love John Quincy Adams. Old Man Eloquent had been thrown a vicious twist of fate. Tyler's presidency threatened all his hopes of national progress. But John Quincy Adams was more cantankerous and possessed more political capital than ever.

Harrison had reserved a place of honor for Adams in the inaugural procession. But Adams had about as much interest in the dog-and-pony show of politics as Theodore Weld had for the anniversary celebrations of the AASS. As the procession passed by the windows of his home, Adams was hard at work on closing arguments in the *Amistad* trial. Joshua Leavitt, the Congregationalist minister and editor of the antislavery newspaper the *Emancipator*, was with him that day as he reviewed the case of the slave ship *Antelope*.

Leavitt had recently come to Washington to report on the petition battles and the *Amistad* trial for the *Emancipator*. Between

Adams's heroic speeches against the gag rule, Leavitt noticed, as he walked the hallways of the Capitol building, piles of antislavery petitions stacked up against the wall. Sitting in the gallery of the Supreme Court as Adams pointed to the Declaration of Independence and told a room full of enslavers and slavery sympathizers that the *Amistad* captives also had inalienable rights and were entitled to due process, the abolitionist preacher–turned–newspaper editor got the sense that if you wanted to fight the slavocracy, Washington was the place to be.

A member of the American Anti-Slavery Society executive committee since 1835, Leavitt had a front-row seat as questions of women's rights and Garrison's radicalism split the movement. He felt the impact as the AASS had its coffers drained by the financial panic. The time had come to form a third political party dedicated to antislavery that could challenge the Whigs and the Democrats. Leavitt joined with James G. Birney and helped establish the Liberty Party. With Birney as standard bearer, the Liberty Party received a paltry seven thousand votes out of a million cast. Many Northerners feared that an antislavery party would be sectional, a dangerous prospect that could lead to disunion.

But as Leavitt watched from the gallery as Adams tore into the slavocracy on the floor of the House of Representatives, he had another idea. What if the small coterie of abolitionist congressmen formed themselves into an antislavery lobby? To subvert the gag rule, they could submit resolutions and propose bills to put an antislavery spin on the issues of the day. Their floor speeches could then be published and disseminated in newspapers all over the country. This would put the issue of slavery directly before the public, which in turn might put pressure on other Northern congressmen—a better prospect than trying to get people to read the antislavery pamphlets that burned in Southern bonfires. Leavitt wanted to create a few antislavery influencers who could get the message out, the greatest of whom would be John Quincy Adams.

During the winter session of the Twenty-Seventh Congress, Leavitt harassed Whig Congressmen Joshua Giddings of Ohio, William Slade of Vermont, and Seth Gates from New York for putting the Whig Party's priorities ahead of an antislavery agenda—to the point of personally offending them. Leavitt did not know the rules of the House. He could not accept that in the real world of DC politics, you gotta play the game.

Giddings was not having it. "Must I be driven to the conclusion that you are predisposed to censure me and my abolition friends in congress?" Leavitt shot back. "I regard it as the dictate of sound wisdom to make opposition to slavery the leading object of public policy. I feel so sure I am right, that I cannot be satisfied without doing all in my power to bring people to my view." The next fall, when Congress returned for its second session, the antislavery congressman agreed to work together for the cause, on the condition Leavitt allow *them* to *school him* in the ways of Washington.

They called it the Select Committee on Slavery, but putting the plan into action was easier said than done. To take an issue like the annexation of Texas or the admission of Florida to the Union and adapt it to the antislavery agenda would add to an already heavy workload. It was difficult enough to keep up with current committee assignments, presenting petitions from constituents, and speaking and voting on the everyday business of the House. These were the days before members of Congress had a chief of staff, a press secretary, and policy people. Gates, Giddings, Slade, and the other members of the committee were overwhelmed.

They needed help. They needed what today would be considered a congressional aide or staffer. To whom could these antislavery congressmen turn to do research on these important issues? Who might have a talent for accumulating facts and data and weave it into a narrative so passionately that it could challenge the average person's coldhearted indifference toward the issue of slavery? Joshua Leavitt believed there was such a man, perhaps one man in the whole country gifted with the ability to write so powerfully and persuasively to move public opinion. His name was Theodore Dwight Weld. Weld had converted three of the Select Committee members to the abolition cause in the first place! Joshua Leavitt and Theodore Weld would be, unofficially, the first congressional staffers.

In the years since his marriage to Angelina, Theodore Weld had become a homebody. He and Angelina purchased a run-down fifty-acre farm in New Jersey at a sheriff's sale. They lived there with their two young children, Angelina's sister Sarah, and an occasional runaway slave. Although still very much involved in the abolitionist crusade, Weld spent most of his time utilizing the skills he acquired from all those years attending manual labor schools: mending fences, raising chickens, and taking care of livestock. However, when he received Leavitt's offer to come to Washington, he knew he could not refuse. "This request, coming in the shape and with the apparent earnestness that it does, impresses me with the responsibility involved in the decision . . . these men are in a position to do for the [antislavery cause] by a single speech more than our best lecturers can do in a year." Weld would be able to do what he loved, and the most appealing part was that he could do it anonymously. "The more I look at the subject the more I feel as though I *dare* not assume the responsibility of refusing to comply with such a request."

Weld arrived in Washington in late December 1841 and moved into Mrs. Sprigg's boardinghouse across from the Capitol, near the corner of First Street SE and Pennsylvania Avenue, the present location of the stairs to the Jefferson Building of the Library of Congress. Mrs. Sprigg's boardinghouse had acquired the nickname Abolition House. We do not know Ann Sprigg's views on slavery, but at the time Weld, Leavitt, Giddings, and Gates lived there, mostly free persons of color worked in the house. Which is ironic, considering Mrs. Sprigg's landlord was Duff Green, a close friend of John C. Calhoun and an ardent supporter of slavery. Weld wrote home to Angelina, "We speak on the subject of slavery with entire freedom . . . Mrs. Sprigg, our landlady, is a Virginian not a slaveholder, but hires slaves. She has eight servants all colored, 3 men, one boy and 4 women. All are free but 3 which she hires and these are buying themselves." Weld also wrote home to Angelina that no one at the boardinghouse made fun of him for adhering to a diet free of meat, dairy, and caffeine.

A few days after Weld arrived, Giddings and Leavitt took him out to attend New Year's Day observances in the city. They visited the President's House where John Tyler, a.k.a. President "talents not above mediocrity," threw the "doors of the palace" open for the annual New Year's Day Levee. Weld wrote Angelina, "Whoever pleased whether in silks or sackcloth, frocks or robes of office, went to *shake hands* with him. Leavitt, Giddings, and I went, but took care *not* to shake hands with him. An introduction to him was offered me but I refused it."

The guys quickly realized it was not their scene and decided to attend what they hoped would be a friendlier affair: "Looking with sadness and pity at the pomp and tinsel and fashion and display of magnificence, we went to pay our respects to John Quincy Adams." There, they found Old Man Eloquent himself, seated and greeting visitors. Every New Year's Day since before he was president, John Quincy and Louisa had opened their home to the Washington community. Compared to President Tyler's affair, theirs was a "plain house, plainly furnished, and themselves plainly dressed." Weld added for emphasis, "the old gentleman very plainly." When Leavitt introduced Weld to Adams, "Mr. A asked, 'Is it Mr. Theodore D. Weld?'" Weld affirmed; Adams replied, "I know you well sir by your writings." Adams, no stranger to the abolitionist scene, asked about Angelina as well. When

Weld asked about Mrs. Adams, John Quincy took the young man by the hand and walked him across the room to where she was seated surrounded by other guests.

Weld wrote Angelina, "I was glad to hear him call her '*my dear*' as I think you told me they lived unhappily together." Adams wasted no time bending the ears of his guests on all things antislavery, including a more recent slave ship mutiny on the *Creole*, which the abolition lobby had planned to be the issue on which they would begin their assault.

Giddings helped get Weld set up with a desk in a little alcove in the Library of Congress. All that was needed was an introduction to the librarians from a member of Congress. Weld took up his seat there each day between 9:00 a.m. and 3:00 p.m. He took his lunch hour in the House or Senate gallery for "relaxation."

One thing Adams and Weld had in common was their exercise habits. Weld described his in a letter to Angelina: "I walk, run, and jump about an hour every morning before breakfast. Am admirably situated for this, the Capitol square or park being directly in front of our house. It is one mile round"—the same mile on which Adams had previously timed himself to see how fast he could do a lap. "On the outside a solid pavement 20 feet wide runs all around and on the inside a gravel walk very hard and dry in all weathers. . . . A better place for exercise could not be had."

One night, Adams invited Weld and the other committee members over for dinner. Weld called it "a genuine abolition gathering and the old patriarch talked with as much energy and zeal as a Methodist at a camp meeting. Remarkable man!" Adams noted his guests that night were "all Tetotallers—Rechabites who drink no wine." Adams also made note of Weld's interesting diet: "In further improvement of which Mr Weld announced himself as a Grahamite, and ate no animal food."

Side note: Rechabite is a reference from the Old Testament book of Jeremiah about an Israelite family who drank no wine;

Grahamite was a religious movement of one Sylvester Graham. Grahamites took the temperance movement to the next step and indicated foods from which one should abstain because they were "overstimulating" like coffee, tea, all meats, etc. Graham essentially excluded all foods from the diet except for unbuttered bread made from wheat flour and water—hence Graham crackers.

The odd group of antislavery activists sparked excitement in the famously solitary old Adams. No doubt the group was excited to have Adams's attention and enthusiasm, but rather than have him a member of *their* group, he co-opted it for his own. Their plan was to use the case of the *Creole* to make a frontal assault on proslavery forces in the House, but Adams believed it would be more effective to attack the slavocracy not on the issue of slavery itself, but on First Amendment freedom of speech grounds as he had done since 1836. Adams even came up with his own pet name for the Select Committee on Slavery: the "Committee of Friends of the Right of Petition." Gathered around his dinner table on the night of January 22, he let them know the next morning "he should present some petitions that would set [the Slavocracy] in a blaze." Weld made sure not to miss it.

It was a Saturday session in the House. Adams introduced a volley of petitions that blatantly flew in the face of the gag rule and as usual, drew the ire of his Southern colleagues. The following are quoted from *The Congressional Globe.*

One was a petition from "a number of citizens of Massachusetts, stating that the Constitution of the United States guarantees to each State in the Union a Republican form of Government, and that there are thirteen States." Adams then listed the slaveholding states, "whose governments are absolutely despotic, onerous, and oppressive in its exactions on a great number of its citizens. The petitioners, therefore pray that Congress would . . . finally adopt some feasible measures by which this alarming evil may be remedied, and a Republican form of Government guaranteed to such of the States as are without it." A congressman from Maryland moved to lay the petition on the table, and so it was. But Adams was just getting started.

Next, Adams offered a resolution of the Anti-Slavery Society of Pennsylvania, "whereas it is proposed that this country shall go to war with England, for the purpose of obliging the British Government to assist in holding natives of the United States in slavery: Therefore resolved, That such war would as much exceed in unrighteousness that which was waged against this country by England in 1776, as the wrongs and privations inflicted on the slaves in some of the States in this Union exceed in magnitude the wrongs which led to the Declaration of Independence."

A little context about this petition. At the time, relations between the United States and England were at a historic low point, with many believing the two nations were on the verge of yet another war. By reading this petition, Adams intimated there was more oppression currently taking place at the hands of the United States government than colonists suffered at the hands of England before the American Revolution. Slavery, Adams contended, was an outright abdication of the principles of the Declaration of Independence.

And with that, Henry Wise had heard enough. He stood up and shouted, calling Adams to order. But Adams ignored Wise and read on until he finished the entire preamble and petition. Like a bull in a China shop, Adams plowed right through the gag. Let us pick up the coverage in *The Congressional Globe.*

> The Chair said the question had been raised before and decided that it was not in order for a member to read

the contents of a petition, without the permission of the House. He must give a brief statement of its contents.

Mr. Adams: Well, sir, I am giving a brief statement of its contents.

Mr. Wise: The question is, whether the petition is presentable at all.

Mr. Adams: [his face flushed, and much excited.] Ah! the gentleman comes to the "presentable," does he?

The Speaker: The gentleman from Massachusetts is out of order, and will take his seat.

The bickering between Adams, Wise, and the Speaker went on for a while, Adams parsing the meaning of "petition" and "resolution."

Next, Adams presented "a remonstrance from a number of citizens of Massachusetts, concluding with the declaration that they cannot conscientiously obey the provisions of the Constitution so far as to take up arms for the protection of slave-holders." That petition, too, was laid on the table.

Was that it? Nope. Adams was just getting started. He presented a petition of "41 citizens, colored seamen of the United States, stating that on visiting the island of Cuba and some of the Southern ports of the United States they are, in violation of the Constitution and without being accused of any crime but their color, subjected to grievous and unjust restrictions, and praying redress." That one as well was laid upon the table.

By this point, the proverbial table overflowed with petitions when Adams pulled the next one out of his bag. *This* was the one he warned Weld and their Committee of Friends would set the slavocracy ablaze. Adams told the Speaker that this petition, "unfortunately, was somewhat personal to himself. It came from a respectable portion of the citizens of Georgia, complaining as a great grievance that he (Mr. A.) had been appointed chairman of the Committee on Foreign Relations, and called on the House to remedy that grievance." Adams demanded to be allowed to be heard in his own defense. After all, this was an attack on a member of the House, a committee chairman no less.

Wise objected to the reception of the petition and moved to lay the question of its reception on the table. Adams charged forward. "The petition, couched in the most respectable language, and which he had reason to suppose was signed by many respectable men, charged him with being incompetent for the station which the Speaker had assigned him, and he claimed the right to defend himself."

A congressman from Georgia told Adams that he did not recognize any of the names on the petition and that it might be another hoax. Adams either did not want to hear it or may have even known that it was a hoax. He claimed the floor to defend himself. Adams, in a high-pitched voice, bellowed, "Sir, the gentleman from Massachusetts claims the right to be heard."

After a lot of debate and calls for the petition to be laid on the table with the others, the Speaker of the House said that Adams's claim of personal privilege had precedence. The petition would be read. Adams had once again worked around the gag. The *Globe* reported that the substance of the petition was that the petitioners "consider it a great grievance that the gentleman from Massachusetts should have been placed at the head of the Committee on Foreign Relations, because, although they admit him to possess patriotism, talents and all the qualifications of a statesman in the most eminent degree, yet they believe that he is possessed of a species of monomania on all subjects connected with people as dark as Mexican; and therefore he is not fit to be entrusted with the business of our relations with Mexico."

There was a debate over whether Adams indeed had privilege. Wise again moved to lay the question on the table. The motion was taken up but failed with the yeas voting 85, nays 87. As the debate over points of order dragged on, another member moved to adjourn the House for the day. At this point, many congressmen just wanted to end the whole discussion and get the hell out of there but that motion failed, 77 to 88.

Kentucky Congressman Thomas Francis Marshall addressed the question of whether the petition was a hoax. "Now, how did they know that? For one, he was more than half-way of the opinion of these petitioners, that the gentleman from Massachusetts"—of course he meant no disrespect—"was a monomaniac on a particular subject." One Congressman Sprigg, weary of the entire conversation, thought Adams needed to air his grievance before a different kind of institutional body, "as the gentleman from Massachusetts insists that he is charged with being afflicted with a certain form or description of madness, and claims the right of defending himself before this House, I can only say that I was not sent here to examine into such cases. Preferring that the usual forms of law should be observed whenever a human being is supposed to be insane." Sprigg suggested, "a commission of lunacy."

Adams was crazy, all right. He knew exactly what he was doing. He had manufactured this whole debate. His goal: Shine the national spotlight on the absurdity of the gag rule. His Southern foes had walked right into his trap. The more personal the attack, the more pointed Adams's response.

Theodore Weld sat in the gallery mesmerized by John Quincy Adams's verbal athleticism. "So the Old Nestor lifted up his voice like a trumpet; till slaveholding, slave trading, and slave breeding absolutely quailed and howled under his dissecting knife. . . . A perfect uproar like Babel would burst forth every two or three minutes as Mr. A. with his bold surgery would smite his cleaver into the very bones." One slaveholder demanded, "Mr

Adams takes on Southern congressmen on the House floor—
Old Man Eloquent, is practiced in the art of verbal jujitsu

Speaker . . . shut the mouth of that old harlequin." Weld said that in the bedlam, Adams became surrounded by Southern congressmen: "Whenever any of them broke out upon him, Mr. A. would say, 'I see where the shoe pinches, Mr. speaker, it will pinch *more* yet . . . I'll deal out to the gentlemen a diet that they'll find it hard to digest. If before I get through every slaveholder, slavetrader and slave breeder on this floor does not get materials for bitter reflection it shall be no fault of mine.'" A motion to lay the whole subject on the table was voted on, and finally passed, 94 to 92.

The spectacle Adams manufactured on the floor of the House resulted in the resignation of five Southern members from the Foreign Affairs Committee. When the Speaker of the House, John White from Kentucky, appointed another five Southern members, three of those refused to serve with Adams. It took some searching, but eventually three more Southern members took their place.

Enough was enough. Southern Whigs decided the next stunt Adams tried to pull would incur a formal censure. To avoid charges of partisanship, it would be brought by the Whig Party. John Quincy Adams was skating on thin ice.

· 18 ·

THE ACUTEST, THE ASTUTEST, THE ARCHEST ENEMY OF SOUTHERN SLAVERY THAT EVER EXISTED

On the afternoon of Monday, January 24, just days after all hell broke loose over the Georgia petition, Adams took center stage. I compare Adams here to a band playing a concert. The band takes the stage and kicks off the set list with a rocking tune, but nothing offensive or obscure. No deep cuts. On this day for Adams, it was a petition on behalf of sailmakers in New York City for a law imposing duties on imports that would allow them to carry on their business "at a reasonable profit." A petition from Ellen M. Gibbs, praying for "indemnity for spoliations on the lawful commerce of her father, by French cruisers, prior to 1800." These are examples of classic petitions.

But then, Adams reached into his catalog of hits and offered up a flurry of deep cuts. Two petitions from Dedham, Massachusetts, "one praying that no new State may be admitted into the Union whose constitution shall tolerate slavery" and one "praying the people of each State be exonerated from all obligations to assist in sustaining slavery."

Adams offered a few more just like these. But any experienced musician will tell you, once you've got the crowd up and dancing, that's when you pull out your magnum opus: "Stairway to Heaven," "Rosalita," "We Are the Champions" (at Live Aid).

Adams had a "Free Bird" sitting on his desk, and he let it rip. He presented a petition from a man named Benjamin Emerson and forty-five other "citizens of Haverhill, in the State of Massachusetts, praying Congress immediately to adopt measures peaceably to dissolve the Union of these States." The reasons for such a drastic step the petitioners listed being that "no union can be . . . permanent which does not present . . . reciprocal benefits." And because "a vast proportion of the resources of one section of the Union is annually drained to sustain the views and course of another section without any adequate return." Emerson and his Haverhill neighbors regretted, "if persisted in the present course of things [this will] certainly overwhelm the whole nation in utter destruction." Or as Lincoln would say some years into the future, "A House divided against itself cannot stand."

Adams moved the petition referred to a select committee "with instruction to the committee to report to the House the reasons why the prayer thereof should not be granted."

Treason, Southerners cried out. *Dissolve the Union?! Are you mad?!* One member from Virginia asked, "Is it in order to burn the petition in the presence of the House?" Of all the people yelling at Adams to sit down and shut up, one voice screamed louder than all the rest. Henry Wise asked, "Is it in order to move to censure any member presenting such petitions?" Adams, sitting at his desk, replied simply: "Good."

The Virginia Congressman Thomas Walker Gilmer, or as Adams liked to call him, Henry Wise's second fiddle, offered the motion. "That, in presenting for the consideration of the House a petition for the dissolution of the Union, The member from Massachusetts has justly incurred the censure of the House." Gilmer shot back at Adams, he played second fiddle to no man,

but I have been endeavoring to prevent the music of one

Who in the course of one revolving moon
Is statesman, poet, babbler and buffoon.

Some members asked themselves, *Do we really want to go down this road? Again?* A congressman objected to the resolution on the grounds that it was offered "not within the established order of business." Another moved it be laid on the table. Congressman Ward from New York had been a member the last time the House tried to censure Adams. He recalled for the gallery, "The debate that sprang up, was so violent a character that the Southern members in a body left the Hall, and it was with difficulty that they could be persuaded to return." At last, Congressman Turney moved for the House to adjourn, essentially saying, *Let's get the hell out of here before things really get nasty.* A majority agreed. The business of the day was over, but members lingered in the halls, stunned by what had transpired. Giddings recalled, "Many appeared deeply indignant . . . with knitted brows, compressed lips, and clenched fists."

That night, members of the slave states met in the Committee on Foreign Affairs room. Their dough-faced Northern allies were not invited. Thomas F. Marshall of Kentucky had been selected to prosecute the case against John Quincy Adams. Who better? He was a Whig, so Adams could not charge that there was a partisan plot against him. Marshall also happened to be the nephew of the late Chief Justice John Marshall, whose appointment to the Supreme Court was among the elder President Adams's greatest legacies. This time, the enemies of John Quincy Adams would shut him up once and for all. Silencing a former president would send a message to the other members of the ad hoc Select Committee on Slavery or anyone else who desired to take up the cause of abolition in the People's House. The Southern coalition was unified in prosecuting Adams. Would the Northern Whigs come to his defense? Not a chance. Northern politicians were not yet ready to let the nation appear divided along sectional lines.

The evening before the trial, Adams sat alone reading in his parlor. The room was dark but for the orange glow of the firelight, which provided a hint of warmth on a cold January night. There was a knock at the door. Weld and Leavitt entered.

Weld told Adams that they "were appointed a committee to wait on Mr. Adams and inform him that they and the members convened tendered him any assistance in their power." The offer struck a chord in the old man. Weld wrote to Angelina, "I . . . offered him my services to relieve him from the drudgery of gathering the requisite materials for his defense."

Adams, as if captivated by something in his line of sight, sat there silently, staring into the fireplace. His lips quivered. When he regained himself, he said that the voice of friendship was so unusual to his ears he could not express his gratitude. He thanked the men for their offer of assistance and immediately dictated "certain points to be found in the authors of which he gave them a list." He asked them to "have the books placed on his desk at the hour of meeting the next day." It was time to get to work.

Adams had been involved in countless political dustups and power plays, hard negotiations, and bitter accusations, but none were as consequential to himself and the nation he had spent his whole life serving as the one in which he was presently engaged.

The next morning, the House gallery was packed with spectators. Clio was ready as always to record the events below. Government officials blew off their duties to watch the proceedings. To kick things off, Marshall read a resolution that rocked the House: "The dissolution of the Union necessarily implies the destruction of that instrument, the overthrow of the American Republic, and the extinction of our national existence." Marshall

Adams left speechless by Leavitt and Weld's offer to help him take up his censure defense

accused Adams of "the destruction of our country and the crime of high treason." The consequence? Not just censure. Expulsion. In the eyes of the South, Adams, the seventy-five-year-old former president, was a traitor.

We need to keep in mind that Adams set all this in motion. He dared his opponents to expel him. Adams railed, "I have constituents to go to, and they will have something to say if this House expels me. Nor will it be long before the gentlemen see me here again!" Southerners heeded Adams's warning and stopped short of expelling him. Marshall's resolution added, "The House deem it an act of grace and mercy" and "only inflict upon him the severest censure." This is the moment Marshall assured the son of John and Abigail that he would be "turned over to his own conscience and the indignation of all true Americans." Everything was playing out exactly as John Quincy had hoped. And seriously? Marshall versus Adams? Not a fair fight.

Adams asked, "What is high treason? The Constitution of the United States says what high treason is, and it is not for him [Marshall] or his puny mind, to define high treason or confound it with what I have done." Adams sliced and diced Marshall, laying bare to all who were watching that the nephew inherited none of the late Chief Justice John Marshall's fertile mind and acumen. "Where did he get his law? Assuredly not from his uncle. . . . Let him go home, let him go to some law school and learn a little of the rights of citizens of these states and of the members of this House."

Once again, Adams reached for the Declaration of Independence. He asked the clerk to read the first paragraph. The clerk cleared his throat and summoned his best Hear ye! Hear ye! "*The first paragraph of the Declaration of Independence! . . . When in the course of human events, it becomes necessary for one people to dissolve the political bands which have connected them with another, and to assume among the powers of the earth, the separate and equal stations to which the Laws of Nature and of Nature's God entitle them, a decent respect to the opinions of mankind requires that they should declare the causes which impel them to the separation.*" I imagine Adams with a finger in the air, waving his arm, coaching the clerk on, "Proceed! Proceed! Down to 'the right and duty'!" The clerk obliged: *"We hold these truths to be self-evident . . . Life, Liberty, and the pursuit of Happiness. That to secure these rights, Governments are instituted among Men, deriving their just powers from the consent of the governed. That whenever any Form of Government becomes destructive of these ends, it is the Right of the People to alter or abolish it. . . . When a long train of abuses and usurpations, . . . evinces a design to reduce them under absolute Despotism, it is their Right, it is their Duty, to throw off such Government."*

Adams dropped the imaginary mic. The feedback screeched. The hall fell silent. Adams banged his fist on his desk and shouted, "Right and duty to alter and abolish it! If there is a principle sacred on earth, and established by the instrument just read, it is the right of the people to alter, to change, to destroy the government if it becomes oppressive to them. There would be no such right existing if the people had not the power, in pursuance of that right, to petition for it." The citizens of Haverhill, Massachusetts, and their fellow Northerners "for eight or ten years" had their rights trampled under the boot heel of the gag rule. "It is time for Northern people to see if they can't shake off, and it is time to present such petitions as this." Adams was sure to point out that he did not believe the time had come for disunion, but if the rights of the North continued to be imperiled, that time would come. But now it was time "to restore the right of petition."

Sensing the need to put Adams away, his opponents moved to commence with the vote. Adams demanded that he was entitled more time to prepare his defense. Citing the Sixth Amendment to the Constitution, he retorted: "In all criminal prosecutions, the accused shall enjoy the right to a speedy and public trial, by an impartial jury." Adams demanded that the proper venue for such charges was "a regular circuit court, by an impartial jury," adding, "These slaveholders are not by whom I should be judged. Their bias would make them challengeable as jurors in any court."

Thomas Marshall was not Adams's only prosecutor; his old nemesis Henry Wise took up the role of unofficial co-counsel. For most of two days, Wise launched a barrage of attacks on Adams.

If Adams was going to quote Jefferson, Wise would quote Washington. The clerk read from his farewell address, "*The unity of Government, which constitutes you one people, . . . from different causes and from different quarters, much pains will be taken, many artifices employed, to weaken, in your minds, the conviction of this truth; as this is the point in your political fortress against which batteries of internal and external enemies will be most . . . actively directed.*" Wise explained that Washington "tells us to frown upon the first dawn of every attempt to dissolve the Union. He points to the cause—the most fearful cause—that may bring about the event. That is foreign influence. That influence is at work in the very question—in this nation—at this day." Wise accused Adams of being a member of the "pro-British party" and under the spell of English abolitionists.

The Virginian ripped a page from John Quincy's old colleague John C. Calhoun's book. Echoing the conversation the two men shared twenty-two years earlier during the Missouri Crisis, Wise said, "Wherever black slavery exists, there is found an equality among the white population, but where it has no place no such equality is found. . . . Break down slavery, and you with the same blow destroy the great democratic principle of equality among men."

Wise called Adams a "fiend, the inspirer and leader of all abolition. . . . That one should so have outlived his fame! To think of the veneration, the honor, the reverence that would have been attached to every word he uttered, so that the moment he rose to speak every breath should be hushed! To think how he would have been looked upon with awe . . . the last link that bound this age to the Revolutionary Fathers!" In a final insult, Wise said, "I thank God that the gentleman . . . neither has, nor is likely to have, sufficient influence to excite a spirit of disunion throughout the land. . . . The gentleman is politically dead! Dead as Burr! Dead as Arnold! The people will look upon him with wonder, will shudder . . . and retire."

The battle raged for two long weeks. Though Adams would come home "very much exhausted," his friends said they never saw him so happy. Each morning, a few hours before the House was called to order, Weld would come to Adams's home and the two men would sketch out the contours of the day's defense. He reported to Angelina that he found Adams "as fresh and elastic as a boy. He went on for an hour, or nearly that in voice loud enough to be heard by a large audience. Wonderful man!"

Adams was enlivened by the thrill of the fight. More importantly, his cause meant something, not just for himself but for the nation he had served for the past fifty years. Ralph Waldo Emerson wrote in his diary of Adams, "He is like one of those old cardinals, who, as quick as he is chosen Pope, throws away his crutches and his crookedness, and is as straight as a boy. He is an old roué, who cannot live on slops, but must have sulphuric acid in his tea."

Even some Southern members grew weary of the proceedings and feared it was moving the House and the nation into dangerous territory. John Minor Botts, a rare Southern critic of the gag rule, argued this was hardly the first time the body had entertained resolutions that were speculated in the dissolution of the Union. Botts reminded the body a few years before that Robert Barnwell Rhett had attached a nullification amendment to a bill. Nullification, Botts warned, was not only Rhett's philosophy, "It was not only the doctrine of the gentleman from South

Carolina, but of his whole state. They held that they had a right to secede from the Union." He added, "The barrel falls to pieces the moment one stave is taken from the hoop."

Adams's trial offered the nation a 360-degree view of American history. It looked back at the principles of the nation's founding as much as it foreshadowed the coming destruction. There was no one alive better suited to mount a defense of the Declaration of Independence than John Quincy Adams. After all, he was America's founding son. What was perhaps most stark about the affair was that, almost two decades before the Civil War, Americans were forced to reckon with slavery and its consequences.

As the proceedings of the House were reported daily in the newspapers, Adams received death threats. One, Adams included in his defense: "I produced the anonymous Letter from Jackson N.C. 20 Jany 1842, threatening me with assassination; and the engraved portrait of me, with the mark of a rifle ball on the forehead, with the motto to stop the music of John Quincy Adams 6th. President of the United States who in the space of one revolving moon Is statesman, poet, babbler and buffoon—These were Gilmer's own words excepting the word fiddler which his echo changed to babbler." But for every threat, Adams received a note of support. "Stand your ground like a man and a Christian, and the North will sustain you." "Go on, Sir. The hearts of free men are with you." "Old Man, there is reverence round thy name." "God bless thee and preserve thee!"

As the trial dragged on, it began to wear Adams down. "The pressure upon my mind, in the preparation for my defence is so great that for several successive nights I have had little sleep . . . I am in the midst of that fiery ordeal, and day and night are absorbed in the struggle to avert my ruin.—God send me a good deliverance!"

Adams withstood the onslaught. Weld described the battle for Angelina, saying that Southern members "have resorted to every artifice and device to put him down. They have resorted to threats, sound and fury, questions of order to tire him out . . . harangues, invectives and accusations against him, etc. But all in vain. The Old Nestor has cast all their counsels headlong, turned all their guns against themselves, and smitten the whole host with dismay and discomfiture."

The old man had worn them down. Gilmer offered to withdraw his motion if Adams withdrew the controversial petition. Adams might as well have replied, *Hell no!* He wrote, "If I withdrew the petition I would consider myself as having sacrificed the right of habeas corpus; as having sacrificed trial by jury; as having sacrificed the sacred confidence of the post office; as having sacrificed freedom of the press; as having sacrificed every element of liberty that was enjoyed by my fellow citizens."

On February 5, in the middle of an attack against Marshall, another member, Romulus M. Saunders from North Carolina, "started up a point of order" that Adams "had no right to discuss the subject of Slavery." The Speaker ruled against Saunders: "He appealed and demanded the yeas and nays which were refused, and the decision of the speaker sustained 97 to 25." For the first time, the gag rule had been defeated. Adams wrote in his diary, "I saw my cause was gained and Marshall was sprawling in his own compost—I came home scarcely able to crawl up to my chamber, but with the sound of Io triumphe! ringing in my ear."

The next day, after two weeks of trial, Marshall moved to table the censure resolution, never to be taken up again. Adams had yet again defeated the slavocracy. Weld wrote, "This is the first victory over the slaveholders *in a body* ever yet achieved since the foundation of the *government,* and from this time their downfall *takes its date.*"

After the vote, Thomas Marshall was overheard telling another congressman, "I would rather die a thousand deaths than again encounter that old man." It would be Marshall's last session in

Congress. Henry Wise, too, had had enough of tangling with Adams. On the campaign trail years later, Wise touted his many tussles with Adams as a badge of honor. He proclaimed, "The acutest, the astutest, the archest enemy of Southern slavery that ever existed. I mean the 'Old Man Eloquent,' John Quincy Adams."

This is the point in our story where we part ways with Theodore and Angelina. For it seems that in the next few years, just as the antislavery faction began to gather political momentum, Theodore Weld was nowhere to be found. "Where is Theodore Weld?" asked the abolitionist poet John Greenleaf Whittier in an 1847 letter to Weld's old patron Lewis Tappan. Tappan replied, "He is in a ditch opposite his house doing the work any Irishman could do for 75 cents a day. His wife is suckling fools and chronicling small beer." The harsh retort is typical of the embittered Tappan, but he was correct. In the years since the aiding of John Quincy Adams in Washington, Weld had become disillusioned with the antislavery movement and the church as well. The Welds were more concerned with matters of hearth and home. Angelina was beset with health issues and the couple had been unhappy with the options available for their children's education. Theodore and Angelina decided to start the Weld Institute on their Belleville, New Jersey, farm. Many of their old antislavery friends like Gerrit Smith, James G. Birney, and Henry B. Stanton sent their children to be educated at the feet of the man who converted them to the cause of abolition.

19

LET JUSTICE BE DONE, THOUGH THE HEAVENS FALL!

In January 1842, Charles Dickens made a historic visit to the United States. The arrival of the famed author of *The Pickwick Papers* and *Oliver Twist* set Boston ablaze like nothing since Lafayette's 1824 tour. Charles Francis wrote to his mother, "Society here is in a state of ferment at the appearance of Mr Dickens the celebrated Boz. He is lionized at a rate beyond the imagination of a moderate man to conceive." Charles Francis admitted he had not been hip to the greatest writer of the age, but warned his parents about the sensation that was headed for Washington.

Following his victories in the *Amistad* case and censure trial in the House of Representatives, John Quincy Adams had become a bit of a sensation himself. It is notable that it was Dickens who was determined to meet Old Man Eloquent in the flesh. After three letters of introduction on behalf of the celebrated Boz from New York businessman Charles A. Davis went unanswered, Dickens called on Adams at his home. Not finding him there, New York Senator Nathaniel Tallmadge escorted the author on the floor of the House of Representatives where Dickens and Adams finally met.

A couple of days later, Dickens and his wife, Catherine, lunched with John Quincy and Louisa at their home. Adams recorded in his diary, "They are so beset with civilities, and kind attentions, that they have not a moment of time to spare, and it was only by snatching an hour from other engagements that they could see us at all." Adams noted, "Dickens's fame has been acquired, by sundry novels and popular tales published in England under the name of Boz—republished in this country in many newspapers, and more universally read perhaps than any other writer who ever put pen to paper." The two men fascinated each other. They had dinner three times during Dickens's short visit to the capital city, including at a reception at the President's House for famed American writer Washington Irving. Before his departure, Dickens asked John Quincy Adams for *his* autograph.

Dickens's hatred for slavery only added to his admiration for John Quincy. He recorded an account of Adams and his recent trial before the House in his travel journal, *American Notes.* "It was but a week, since an aged, grey-haired man, a lasting honour to the land that gave him birth, who has done good service to his country, as his forefathers did, and who will be remembered scores upon scores of years after the worms bred in its corruption are but so many grains of dust—it was but a week, since this old man had stood for days upon his trial before this very body, charged with having dared to assert the infamy of that traffic, which has for its accursed merchandize men and women, and their unborn children."

The glaring hypocrisy between the ideals Jefferson outlined in the Declaration of Independence and the reality of the oppression of Southern slavery screamed forth to Dickens just as it had to Benjamin Lundy, Theodore Weld, and John Quincy Adams. Dickens continued, "Yes. And publicly exhibited in the same city all the while; to strangers not with shame, but pride; is the Unanimous Declaration of The Thirteen States of America, which solemnly declares that All men are created Equal; and are endowed by their Creator with the Inalienable Rights of Life, Liberty, and the Pursuit of Happiness!"

John Quincy Adams had become a national treasure. Once an unpopular one-term president, he was now a champion of freedom of speech and defender of the Constitution. Biographer James Traub commented, "Adams's nobility was almost suicidal. What's extraordinary is that at the end of his career, he finds a cause which is perfectly suited to his solitude. And it's precisely because he is so solitary and heroic that finally, at the end of his life, he's hero worshipped."

Adams enjoyed his newfound celebrity, but with his health beginning to deteriorate, he declined most offers for speaking engagements—that is, until he received an offer he could not refuse. The Cincinnati Astronomical Society invited Adams to lay the cornerstone for a new observatory. Congress never funded John Quincy's dream of "Lighthouses in the Sky." The march of scientific progress vindicated Adams as universities and astronomical societies across the country made their own investments in telescopes.

The trip was Adams's first and only visit to the West. Along the way, he stopped in Buffalo, where he was celebrated by fellow congressman and future president Millard Fillmore. He visited a barbershop in Cleveland and spent the afternoon shaking hands with hundreds of people who gathered to catch a glimpse of America's founding son. While there, Adams received an invitation to a celebration in his honor at the town hall in nearby Akron. He gave a short speech and shook the hands of everyone in attendance. As for the ladies, Adams offered more than a handshake. "Among the women, a very pretty one, as I took her hand kissed me on the cheek. I returned the salute on the lip and kissed every woman that followed; at which some made faces, but none refused."

Adams arrived in Columbus, Ohio, and was escorted by two German military companies, which included a band playing martial music. Adams met huge crowds at stops in Jefferson and Springfield, Ohio. He rode in an "elegant open barouche" and entered the city of Dayton in a "triumphal procession" where a "dense mass of population" swarmed him on all sides. When he finally arrived in Cincinnati, he was greeted by a banner that read, "JOHN QUINCY ADAMS, DEFENDER OF THE RIGHTS OF MAN."

The morning of the cornerstone laying, Adams arose at 4:00 a.m. He barely had time to put the finishing touches on his address when he was called on by a swarm of visitors. At 10:00 a.m., a massive crowd assembled in the street in front of the Henry House Hotel. From the crowd, a procession consisting of Astronomical Society members took shape. Adams stepped out of his hotel to cheers and huzzahs. He climbed into an open barouche accompanied by Professor Mitchel, president of the Astronomical Society.

Behind Adams's barouche was a parade of carriages, military companies, and marching bands. As the procession set out, a light rain started to fall. It quickly turned into a torrential downpour. But the cortège paused only briefly to cover the barouche and continued its way. The road before him was "a sea of mud." The horses struggled and nearly lost their footing as they ascended the steep hill to where the cornerstone was to be laid.

Crowds who braved the cold November downpour were not discouraged. They had come to see and hear Old Man Eloquent. Adams looked out at the soaked mass of humanity from the platform. When he took his speech out of his overcoat, it was soaked. A soggy, illegible piece of paper was all that remained of his speech, a bunch of black smudges on the page. The event organizers agreed it would be best for Adams to hold off on his speech and give it the next day inside a local church.

After leaving Cincinnati, Adams gave a little stump speech in Maysville, Kentucky, for his old friend, the once and future presidential candidate Henry Clay. Clearing the air for posterity all these years later, Adams stated in no uncertain terms "that the charges of corrupt bargaining which had been trumped up against him and me were utterly without foundation." In Pittsburgh, the last stop on Adams's Western tour, factories closed for the day. Newspapers announced his arrival.

It was a journey filled with huzzahs, three cheers, and torchlight parades, all in honor of John Quincy Adams. Each handshake and every kiss on the cheek put a face to the names on those thousands of petitions Adams had offered over the years. Everywhere he went he was met by the gratitude of fellow citizens, who shared his belief that slavery was a blot on the American character, and a contradiction to the Declaration of Independence. In a nation divided between the forces of despotism and freedom, the man standing in the breach was John Quincy Adams.

John Quincy Adams was riding high. *Then,* the midterm elections of 1842 happened. His party took one of the largest electoral drubbings in American history; their forty-two-seat Whig majority became a sixty-seat deficit. Democrats now held a massive majority. After redistricting, Adams narrowly won his race by less than four hundred votes. Adams, Giddings, and their abolitionist allies all but lost hope of ever overturning the gag rule. One year later, Old Man Eloquent made his final stand.

In its earliest incarnations, the gag rule had to be reintroduced with the beginning of each session of Congress. This loophole, if you will, made the hours before the rules of the House were introduced and voted on an opportunity to let a few antislavery petitions slip by. For the slavocracy, the Pinckney gag, the Patton gag, and the Atherton gag were all temporary fixes to silence any mention of slavery. In 1840, the gag rule became a standing rule of the House. From that point on, at the beginning of each congressional session, the gag would automatically go into effect as part of the existing rules of the House. However, it was not impenetrable. The gag rule had shown signs of weakening after Adams fought off the Southern attempt to censure him and after Joshua Giddings, himself being censured, was reelected by his constituents in a landslide.

In December of 1843, Adams lost a vote to rescind the gag rule by just four votes. In that vote, Adams gained the support of all Northern Whigs and Democrats. Even Henry Wise voted to repeal the measure. Wise told the court reporter, "Henceforth, and forever, he ceased to contend in that war which was being carried on in the House by certain men against the South." Why did Adams's old nemesis flip-flop on the gag? Some speculate that Wise was up for a diplomatic appointment, and he needed Northern votes in the Senate. I like to think that Adams's perseverance wore him down.

At seventy-six years old, Adams was pretty worn down himself. Still susceptible to bouts of depression, at one point Adams told Giddings he had hoped to live to see the gag rule repealed but no longer believed it would be the case.

Adams refused to give up: for the thousands of petitioners across the North, many of whom he had recently met on his Western tour; for men, like Giddings, who remained in the fight with him; for the memory of Benjamin Lundy, who had not lived to see victory in the *Amistad* case or Adams vindicate himself in the 1842 censure trial. He told Giddings there was "but one cause for public men . . . *to do their duty*." If he had air in his lungs and could feel his heartbeat in his chest, John Quincy Adams would continue to do his.

Adams lost the vote to repeal the gag rule but won a vote for the formation of a special committee on the rules, to which the Speaker of the House appointed him chair. The release of the committee's report in January of 1844 unleashed a new offensive against Adams by the slavocracy. This time James Dellet, a congressman from Alabama, led the attack.

Dellet used Adams's own words as ammo against him. He pulled a quote from a speech Adams gave on his Western tour to a group of free Black men and women. Dellet, quoting Adams, read to the House, "We know that the day of your redemption must come. The time and manner of its coming we know not: It may come in peace, or it may come in blood; but *whether in peace or in blood,* let it come."

Repeating the quote for effect, Dellet told the body that this was the true agenda of anti-gag activists: the end of slavery through bloodshed. Adams shouted from his seat, "I say now, let it come."

Dellet repeated himself, feeling vindicated: "Though it cost the blood of thousands of white men." Adams again shouted from his seat, "Let it come! Let justice be done though the heavens fall!" John Quincy's outburst shook the chamber and horrified the slaveholders.

America's founding son had reached the end of his patience. He shuddered in 1820, when he prophesied a violent dissolution of the Union, but all he had experienced in the nearly twenty-five years since proved to him that the South would never, ever, voluntarily or otherwise, give up being the enslavers. On the issue of slavery, John Quincy Adams had become a nullifier.

· 20 ·

THIS IS THE END OF EARTH

February 28, 1844
The Potomac River

Glasses clanked. Champagne spilled. President John Tyler and his four hundred guests sang songs, exchanged toasts, and got drunk below the deck of the new crown jewel of the United States Navy, the USS *Princeton*. All afternoon the dignitaries had been treated to round after round of cannon fire from the ship's state-of-the-art armament, which included twelve carronades and two large fourteen-inch cannons capable of firing 225-pound cannonballs. But the showstopper was the "Peacemaker," a twelve-inch wrought-iron cannon with a fifteen-foot barrel.

As the ship passed George Washington's Mount Vernon home, a partygoer suggested one more blast in honor of the Father of the Country. Trying to shrug off the likely inebriated fellow, Captain Robert F. Stockton responded, "No more guns tonight." But the captain could only endure so many *Aw, c'mon, mans* and acceded to the request. The president tarried below as Stockton, Secretary of State Abel P. Upshur, Secretary of the Navy Thomas Gilmer (you'll recall, Henry Wise's second fiddle), and several others went up on deck for the tribute.

Moments later, there was a loud blast. At first, the revelers downstairs cheered. But seconds later, they heard shrieks of horror above their heads. The "Peacemaker" had exploded, killing Upshur, Gilmer, the president's Black servant Henry, and four others. Nine were injured, including Stockton and Missouri Senator Thomas Hart Benton. John Quincy and Louisa had declined an invitation from Stockton to attend. Adams had toured the *Princeton* a week earlier as part of a congressional delegation.

It was one of the most gruesome tragedies to befall the nation up to that point. Shock gave way to grief in the city of Washington. Horrific events that seem to come from out of nowhere spark ruminations about mortality for us all. Adams attended a memorial service in the Hall of the House of Representatives in which the chaplain of the Senate preached from the book of Revelations, 20:11. Adams pondered the awesomeness of the passage: "The throne of God—The Sea—Death—Hell—Books of Account, A book of life, Judgement for eternity according to their works . . . discourse was impressive and edifying, but hardly adequate to the occasion."

More appropriate was the evening service Adams attended at St. John's Church. The Reverend Frapley of Philadelphia preached from Amos 4:12, "Prepare to meet thy God." Deeply affected, Adams wrote, "It behooved me perhaps more than any other person present, to lay to heart." It had been two decades since Adams wandered through the graveyard of his elders on the eve of the 1824 presidential election. Back then he speculated about "moldering" in the dust of his ancestors. What would be said of him? John Quincy knew he was close to death. He could feel it in his bones as he rose in the morning. He could feel it in his crooked gait as he walked around the Capitol, aided by his cane. He felt it in his palsied hands that could barely hold the quill pen when writing in his diary at night. What of his time on this earth? What would be written of him in the book of life? What would be his judgment for eternity? When he crossed over, would the Creator of all greet him with a hearty "well done, my good and faithful servant"?

Less than a week later, the sting of death was met by the prick of doom when President Tyler nominated John C. Calhoun to replace Upshur. It was Tyler's third secretary of state in four years. Adams knew his old nemesis would stop at nothing to complete the annexation of Texas. Adams later confessed, "John C. Calhoun and South Carolina are in the ascendant. . . . The prospect is deathlike."

Abolitionists Lewis Tappan and Joshua Leavitt saw the tragedy of the USS *Princeton* as a divine act of retribution against the slavocracy, one they hoped would at least temporarily forestall the annexation of Texas. Tappan knew what they were up against and admitted "there is no knowing what the Satanic designs of wicked men may achieve."

A ray of hope appeared on December 3, 1844, as the Twenty-Eighth Congress took its place for the second session. John Quincy Adams offered a resolution to rescind the twenty-fifth standing rule of the House. The time had come. After getting so close over the last couple of years, the votes might finally be there to assign the gag rule to the dustbin of history.

This time, it was Jacob Thompson of Mississippi who moved to lay the resolution on the table. Adams and Joshua Giddings shouted in unison, "Call the yeas and nays!" Jacob Thompson's motion to lay on the table failed, 81 yeas, nays 104. But before the vote on Adams's motion could be taken, the president's son and personal secretary, John Tyler Jr., appeared at the bar of the House with his father's annual message to Congress. Thompson rose to demand the president's message certainly takes precedence over any other motion—especially one he was trying to squash. But not today. This day, fortune shone on the founding son. The yeas and nays were called and the gag rule went down to defeat, 108 to 80. At long last, the gag rule fell. Afterward, Adams wrote in his diary, "Blessed ever be the name of God!"

John Quincy achieved one of the greatest political accomplishments in congressional history.

The election of 1844 turned on the issue of Texas. A mere two weeks into his term as secretary of state, Calhoun signed a treaty for the annexation of Texas. In fact, one had been sitting on his desk when he arrived at the State Department. Upshur had finalized a negotiated treaty with the Republic of Texas on February 27, one day prior to his fateful cruise on the Potomac. The treaty stipulated Texas become part of the Union as a slave state. The secretary of state sent the treaty over to the Senate, along with the copy of a letter he wrote to the British minister to the United States, Richard Pakenham, in which he extolled the virtues of slavery. The British foreign minister, Lord Aberdeen, wished to see an independent Texas free of enslaved persons. The letter was not only an admonition to Great Britain to stop meddling with Mexico regarding Texas, but also a clear statement that the United States was sick and tired of abolitionist finger-wagging from across the pond. Calhoun informed Pakenham, wherever emancipation had occurred, the African race "had been invariably sunk into vice and pauperism . . . insanity, and idiocy—to a degree without example."

In the near term, Calhoun's "Texas Bombshell," as Thomas Hart Benton called the letter, sunk the chances for Senate ratification. But it forced all the presidential candidates to come out publicly for, or against, annexation. Whig candidate Henry Clay and Martin Van Buren, at the time the leading Democratic candidate, squirmed as they tried to come up with a stance that would please all constituencies. In the end, both men came out against immediate annexation and both men saw their candidacies sunk.

In the final days of his presidency, under intense pressure from John C. Calhoun, and over the objections of John Quincy Adams, John Tyler annexed Texas. The election came down to the wire, but Henry Clay lost, again—this time to the Democratic dark horse candidate, James K. Polk. Polk, who, you may recall, was *the slaveholder in the chair*, who first gagged Adams back in 1836. Now Polk was president and inheritor of the massive new state of Texas.

The Mexican government saw Tyler's annexation of Texas as an act of aggression, which also reignited the long-simmering feud between the old warriors Adams and Andrew Jackson. This final round of the Adams-versus-Jackson grudge match is a bit complicated, so let me break it down.

First, you need to understand that Andrew Jackson had lived a rough life, and he was getting old. It reminds me of that Indiana Jones quote, "It's not the years, it's the mileage." Jackson's memory on Texas became foggy with age. Jackson biographer David S. Brown points out, "As he got older, he seemed to think that Texas had been part of the United States in 1819, when the United States signed the [Adams-Onís Treaty] with Spain that did give us Florida, but did not give us Texas. So Jackson and a few others would refer not to the annexation of Texas, as in 'We want Texas annexed.' They would refer to it as the re-annexation."

This takes us back to the Monroe administration, back to the beginning of our story when John Quincy was secretary of state and negotiated the Adams-Onís Treaty. Now, some twenty-plus years later, Jackson said that Texas would have been part of the deal if it were not for the underhanded dealings of President Monroe and his lackey Adams, who always hated slavery. You must understand that, for Jackson, he considered the annexation of all new Southern states part of a domino effect that *he* started. Texas was simply the next domino to fall.

In a speech in Boston, Adams attacked Jackson and the annexation of Texas. He spoke of Jackson's ingratitude. "I defended him against his enemies in [Monroe's cabinet], defended him against remonstrances of ministers of Spain and of Great Britain, and here and in Europe, Congress and throughout the nation, for what I could and did not approve."

Jackson's allies responded by attacking Adams's entire career. A longtime Pennsylvania politician and Jackson supporter, Charles Ingersoll, said of Adams, "He gave away half of the North American continent, lest Braintree should suffer or complain. All of our present troubles in Texas and Oregon are bitter fruits of Mr. Adams' generosity—an attribute of which he is seldom accused. . . . The navigation of the Mississippi would not be an American possession if Mr. Adams could have swapped it for codfish. Grocers will make packing paper of his speeches, lectures, letters, and interminable diaries." Charles Ingersoll really missed the mark on Adams's legacy. Who remembers Charles Ingersoll anyway?

When Jackson read what his friend said about Adams, he thought it was hilarious. "It is the severest castigation and withering sarcasm I ever read . . . I would not be surprised to hear that he was stricken down by a paralytic stroke." Things were getting heated. But Jackson's wish to watch Adams die would go unfulfilled.

On a warm June evening in 1845, Andrew Jackson lay on his deathbed . . . his heart slowly failing. He fumbled for his glasses. When he put them on, he could see the tearful faces of family, friends, and the people he enslaved who had come to see him off to the next world. Before he passed, he said to those gathered: "Do not cry; I hope to meet you all in Heaven—yes, All in heaven, white and black. . . . My conversation is for you all. Christ has no respect to color. I am in God and God is in me. He dwelleth in me and I dwell in him."

Old Hickory shut his eyes and never opened them again. He was seventy-eight years old, older than the country he had not long ago led as president. America mourned the death of Andrew Jackson. Even old enemies and Northerners set aside the malice they once felt for him. Well, except for one. Adams wrote, "Jackson was a hero, a murderer, an adulterer, and a profoundly pious presbyterian, who in the last days of his life belied and slandered me before the world." In other words, Adams was like, *F that guy. I don't care if he's dead.*

Polk was not only interested in Texas and California; he also aimed to secure control of the Oregon Territory for the United States. The Democratic Party included possession of Oregon up to Russian Alaska, at latitude 54°40', in their 1844 platform. Their rallying cry, "54°40' or fight!" was a signal for Northern Democrats that Manifest Destiny was not solely for the proslavery faction. The goal aligned with what Adams had long sought—to establish the United States as a continental nation stretching from the Atlantic to the Pacific. As secretary of state, Adams negotiated with Spain to relinquish its claim to the Oregon Territory as part of the Transcontinental Treaty in 1819. He also negotiated a joint occupation agreement with Great Britain the following year and renewed it in 1827. Adams always believed that the United States was entitled to all of Oregon. In what would be one of his final extended speeches in Congress, Adams had the clerk read from the book of Genesis and the second Psalm as he argued that when God decreed man to "be fruitful and multiply" and "replenish the earth, and subdue it" and "have dominion over the fish of the sea, and over the fowl of the air, and over every living thing moveth on earth" that was the foundation of the United States' territorial rights to Oregon. The difference between Adams's support for Oregon and opposition to Texas was simple: slavery.

The long-standing agreement between the United States and Britain stipulated that either nation could terminate the joint occupation agreement within one year after giving notice. In April of 1846, Congress passed a notice of termination. After earlier rebuffing offers from the Tyler and Polk administrations for Oregon, Britain agreed to terms to cede Oregon to the United States at the forty-ninth parallel. There was no appetite for either country to go to war over Oregon.

Shortly after Polk concluded peace with Great Britain, war broke out with Mexico, the result of a territorial dispute following the annexation of Texas after Polk ordered Zachary Taylor's troops beyond the Nueces River. By early August, Polk asked Congress for an appropriation to the tune of $2 million to negotiate peace and purchase two Mexican territories. The territories in question compose present-day California, Nevada, and Utah, as well as parts of Wyoming, Colorado, New Mexico, and Arizona.

Adams opposed the war. On this he was in agreement with John C. Calhoun, who had returned to his seat in the Senate. Polk defied the Constitution when he instigated hostilities with Mexico prior to coming to Congress for a formal declaration of war. Adams and Calhoun knew that the Constitution gave Congress the power to declare war. When the vote finally came, John Quincy Adams voted against the "unrighteous war."

Adams was not surprised when Polk requested $2 million. Then a young Democratic congressman from Pennsylvania, David Wilmot offered an amendment that surprised everyone.

David Wilmot's amendment stated "that as an express and fundamental condition to the acquisition of any territory from the Republic of Mexico . . . neither slavery nor involuntary servitude shall ever exist in any part of said territory, except for crime, whereof the party shall first be duly convicted." What made the Wilmot Proviso so earth-shattering was that Wilmot was a Northern congressman voting against his Southern-dominated party. In the amendment, Wilmot used the exact same language Thomas Jefferson used for the Northwest Ordinance in 1787. In a speech he made after presenting the proviso, Wilmot declared, "Whatever territory might be acquired, he declared himself opposed, now and forever, to the extension of this 'peculiar institution' that belongs to the South." Adams agreed with Wilmot's amendment "with my whole heart."

In the frenzied floor fight that followed, a fellow Democrat from Indiana tried to substitute Wilmot's amendment for one that would extend the line of the Missouri Compromise, 36°30', to any new territory, but it was defeated. The Wilmot Proviso passed the House and might have passed the Senate had time in the session not expired due to the clock in the House of Representatives being eight minutes faster than the one in the Senate. Dead for now, the Wilmot Proviso would be resurrected in the years to come. The measure deepened the growing sectional divide between North and South, bringing the nation one step closer to Adams's long-predicted "war between the two severed portions of the Union." There was little doubt that the United States would defeat Mexico and claim the territory. The question was, would the new territory be slave or free?

In late 1846, Adams collapsed while on a walk with a friend in Boston. His doctor told him he'd had a stroke. By the spring of the next year, he had recovered enough to return to his seat in Congress. Aware of how little time he had left, he wrote in his diary, "I date my decease, and consider myself for every useful purpose to myself or to my fellow creatures dead; and hence I call this and what I may write hereafter a posthumous Memoir." From that day on, Adams rarely wrote in his journal, and when he did, it was by dictation to his granddaughter, Louisa Catherine. His entries became less thoughtful, personal, and political analysis and more a recitation of the events of the day.

John Quincy still managed to write a few letters. He wrote one note to Charles Francis in early December 1847. The two had a public rift over Adams's support for Robert Winthrop for House

Speaker. Winthrop was a conservative Whig and Charles had recently become a conscience Whig, a member of the antislavery faction of the party. His father's unpredictable political exploits were an embarrassment. John Quincy did not mean to harm his son. He knew his remaining days on Earth were few. He was so proud of the man Charles had become. With what control he had left of a pen, he wrote these lines: "From the time when the creator established the relation of father to son, between men on earth no more truehearted, faithful and affectionate son than you have been to me ever existed." Adams wrote again to his son on January 1, 1848, "for all the blessings which you have been and still are to me" and closed the letter "have a stout heart and a clear conscience and never despair." These were the last words John Quincy Adams wrote to his surviving son.

Months after his stroke, Adams received a standing ovation when he entered the hall to once again take his seat in the House of Representatives. Adams was eighty years old and in failing health but could not be kept away from Congress. No longer a force of nature, Adams railed against the Mexican war with all remaining energy.

On Friday, February 18, 1848, John Quincy Adams attended a party for Whig congressmen at the E Street home of Washington mayor Colonel William W. Seaton. Adams is reported to have looked well, although one person reported that John Quincy confided he did not expect to survive the congressional session.

Seated on a couch as he greeted his fellow Whig members of Congress, Adams likely met a young first-term Illinois congressman, Abraham Lincoln. The two men had something in common: They had both fiercely denounced war with Mexico.

On February 21, Adams shouted an emphatic, "No!" on a vote to suspend the rules of order so that the House could offer resolutions honoring several generals for their service in the recent Mexican campaign. Henry B. Stanton, in the chamber as a reporter, looked over and noticed Adams's hands trembling. His right arm was moving on his desk, and he seemed to be trying to speak. Attempting to stand up, Adams appeared to reach for the corner of his desk for support, but unable to get a firm grasp, toppled over. A group of nearby congressmen caught him and gently lowered him to the ground. A collective gasp rang out on the House floor. Lawmakers jumped to their feet. Cries of "Mr. Adams is dying! Adams is dying!" echoed through the chamber. Two men brought over a couch and Adams was carried into the Speaker's chamber. Adams was out of it, but not yet unconscious. He was overheard whispering, "This is the end of earth, but I am composed."

Friends and foes gathered to pay their respects. When he heard the news, Henry Clay rushed over from the Senate. He sat next to Adams crying as he held his hand.

A group of lawmakers rushed to Adams's home to tell Louisa what happened. She thought he had only fainted, but by the time she arrived at the Capitol, John Quincy was barely conscious. He did not recognize his partner of fifty years. Overcome with grief, Louisa was allowed a few private hours with her husband, but as his breathing became shallower, doctors and members of Congress shuffled her away. She was furious. She wanted to be the one to close his eyes. "I was *forced* to leave him without even the privilege of indulging the feelings, which all hold sacred at such moments." A knife twisted in her broken heart—strangers stood between her and her dying husband.

On February 23 at 7:15 p.m., John Quincy Adams died in the United States Capitol. A reporter who managed to squeeze into the tiny Speaker's chamber reported Adams's passing this way. "The pallor of death is upon his face, and he has ceased to struggle with nature; his is passing away as gently as a babe sinks into slumber. He dies in the harness—he dies in the service of his

The end of Earth

country—he dies in the Capitol itself, and almost upon the birthday of Washington, it is a fit end to a career so glorious."

Upon hearing of his father's collapse in the Capitol, Charles Francis left Boston, hoping to be with his father—his mentor—his hero, one more time. He did not make it to Washington until the morning of the twenty-fifth. When he finally arrived at the Capitol's Common Room where his father's body lay in state, John Quincy's only surviving son was given time to be alone with his father.

It is remarkable John Quincy Adams died in the hall where he had spent the last seventeen years of his life serving the country he loved. The young boy who had witnessed the Battle of Bunker Hill and saw the flash of cannon fire, heard the boom, and smelled the smoke, died on another field of battle: the greatest war waged against slavery in the nation's history up to that point, making straight the way for the next generation of abolitionists to carry on the fight.

Over the course of his long life, Adams had made many enemies. He listed them in the pages of his diary. He nursed old wounds and plotted his revenge. So, it is a little ironic that John C. Calhoun was one of the pallbearers who carried his casket to the congressional cemetery. I can only imagine how Adams would have recorded that scene. Another irony of American history is that the young congressman from Illinois, Abraham Lincoln, a member of the funeral committee, watched as the train carrying John Quincy Adams's body left Washington for Quincy one last time. People gathered along the tracks for hundreds of miles to see the train pass.

The last entry in Louisa Catherine Adams's diary is dated March 18, 1849. The short passage speaks to her heartbreak over the loss of her husband. "Thy fiat has gone forth, O Lord my God: and I am left a helpless Widow to morn his loss which nothing on this dreary earth can supply—Les Soupirs étouffe le Chagrin! Les larmes soulage le Coeur!!! (Sighs Smother Grief! Tears soothe the heart!)" She would survive three more years and died in Washington on May 15, 1852. Today, Louisa Catherine Adams is entombed beside her husband, John Quincy; his mother, Abigail; and his father, John, in the basement crypt at United First Parish Church in Quincy, Massachusetts.

Of all the great tributes offered at the time of his passing, perhaps Philip Hone best captured the essence of what the nation meant to the man and the man meant to the nation. "He died, as he must have wished to die, breathing his last in the capitol, stricken down by the angel of death on the field of his civil glory, employed in the service of the people, in the people's Senate house, standing by the constitution at the side of its alter, and administering in the temple of liberty the rites which he had assisted in establishing."

Adams brought the issue of slavery out of the darkness and into the light of the center of politics in the United States—the People's House. John Quincy Adams preserved and protected the American democracy established by the founding generation—his father's generation. John Quincy fought a different revolution, because as hard as it is to create a democracy, it takes the long-suffering skill of perseverance to uphold it. As the man standing in the breach, Adams passed the aspirations of the Declaration of Independence on to the next generation. With one hand reaching back to the founding and the other reaching forward toward the Civil War, John Quincy Adams is a bridge and perhaps the best representation of America's tortured adolescence. John Quincy Adams may not have been an extraordinary president like Washington and Lincoln, but he is our most extraordinary ex-president. A maverick. A public servant. An American hero.

END OF ACT THREE

EPILOGUE

In 1836, John Quincy Adams knew he was engaged in his final crusade. One month after he was gagged and suggested the Congress possessed the necessary war powers to interfere with slavery in the states where it existed, he wrote, "This is a cause I am entering at the last stage of my life and with the certainty that I cannot advance in it far; my career must close, leaving the cause at the threshold. To open the way for others is all that I can do. The cause is good and great." For almost twelve more years, Adams showed "the way" and carved a path for the next generation to follow.

In February 1848, as Adams lay in the Capitol on the brink of death, down the other end of Pennsylvania Avenue, Polk prepared to send the Treaty of Guadalupe Hidalgo to the Senate for ratification. The United States demanded Mexico cede 55 percent of its territory. Since the nation's inception, Americans had been an unstoppable force, pushing westward and plowing through any obstacles that stood in the way of continental dominance. Once again, Congress was left to answer the question—will this land be slave, or will it be free?

The stage was set for a fiery clash that would make the Missouri Compromise look like child's play. It was a cruel twist of fate that John Quincy Adams left this earth at the exact moment the country needed him most. Who would take up the struggle for freedom Adams for so long carried alone?

By 1848, Charles Francis Adams had come a long way from his days as an aspiring politician embarrassed by his father's abolitionist exploits. In 1844, as a member of the Massachusetts legislature, Charles worked to advance resolutions against Texas annexation. John Quincy was proud of his son, but could foresee a rocky road ahead. "My heart aches at the prospect of the dangers that await and already beset him. May the God of Justice be his guide and guard—and the God of Mercy protect him."

Charles Francis did what he could to advance the cause of freedom, which included standing for vice president alongside Martin Van Buren on the Free-Soil Party ticket in 1848.

When the Civil War John Quincy Adams had long predicted finally came, Abraham Lincoln was thrust into the crucible of history and forced to grapple with questions abolitionists of the 1830s and 1840s left unanswered. Mainly, "How and When to free the enslaved?" Lincoln bore the weight of these questions as he navigated the treacherous waters of a nation in tumult.

It should be no surprise that when Lincoln asked William Henry Seward to serve as secretary of state, Seward asked Charles Francis Adams to serve as ambassador to England. George Washington once said of the thirty-year-old diplomat John Quincy Adams, "I give it as my decided opinion that Mr. Adams is the most valuable character we have abroad." Diplomacy was like a family business for the Adamses. It was in their blood.

In September of 1862, Charles Francis, in London, received a letter from Secretary of State Seward in which he wrote, "The President has issued a Proclamation, in which he gives notice that Slavery will be no longer recognized in any State which shall be found in armed rebellion on the first of January next." The Emancipation Proclamation would go into effect on January 1, 1863. Lincoln had come to the same conclusion that John Quincy

Adams had in his speech on the Tomahawk resolutions in 1836. The Constitution granted Congress and the executive branch the ability to end slavery through constitutionally granted war powers.

We tread on unsteady ground when we attempt to draw parallels between the past and the present. If moments and events do not repeat, perhaps people do.

Back when the Avett Brothers was just three of us and we traveled from town to town in a Chevy conversion van, we met new people every day, many of whom reminded us of the folks we knew back home. We mused, "*There are only so many molds.*"

I was reminded of that refrain again and again as I worked on this book.

Ask yourself, as I have many times, who today reminds you of John C. Calhoun, Henry Wise, Thomas Marshall?

Do we have in our midst a Benjamin Lundy? A man willing to walk from one end of the continent to the other, on faith, in the name of a righteous cause?

Who is our Theodore Weld? A skilled orator and writer, who seeks not his own celebrity, but justice for the oppressed?

Is there among us today an Angelina Grimké? A woman so bold as to refuse to yield as the glass shatters around her, torches flare, and a mob closes in from all directions?

And what about John Quincy Adams? Egotistical to the extreme. Flawed. A difficult husband and overbearing father. Yet with enough vulnerability and humility to work through it all in the pages of his diary. A man of great perseverance. A public servant who is willing to put duty, principle, and country before all else. John Quincy Adams reminds us that change happens when good people have the courage to make good trouble in the face of long odds, violent mobs, and apathetic cynicism. During the tumultuous period between the era of the founding fathers and the Civil War, John Quincy Adams was the man standing in the breach. He may not have been an extraordinary president like Washington or Lincoln, but I believe he is our most extraordinary ex-president and the nation's greatest public servant. He held the promise of the Declaration of Independence in one hand and, in the other, what we have come to understand as Lincoln's "new birth of freedom . . . that government of the people, by the people, and for the people, shall not perish from the earth."

ACKNOWLEDGMENTS

I owe a deep debt of gratitude to the many individuals who made this book possible.

First, my heartfelt thanks to Sara Martin and the dedicated, knowledgeable team working with the Adams papers at the Massachusetts Historical Society. I encourage every reader of this book to visit Masshist.org and immerse themselves, as I did, in John Quincy Adams's diary on primarysourcecoop.org—a truly invaluable gift to us all.

I am profoundly thankful to Gwen Fries for her meticulous fact-checking and her remarkable skill in organizing the notes section. Her unparalleled expertise on John Quincy Adams and his papers has greatly enriched this book.

Thank you to my agent, Matt Carlini, whose belief in my ability to write a book about John Quincy Adams gave me the courage to begin this journey. I am also incredibly grateful to my supportive and endlessly encouraging editor, Sarah Reïd.

A special thanks to Maximillian Potter for reading an early draft and guiding me through what felt like a graduate-level creative writing course over the past few years. Your input has been invaluable.

To Alexis Coe, James Bradley, Chris DeRose, and Michael Tackett—thank you for sharing your wisdom and experiences in writing history. Your advice left me inspired and helped make this book stronger. I am extremely grateful for my podcast producing partner, James Morrison, who was the first to help me organize and articulate my thoughts about John Quincy Adams. Finally, my gratitude goes to Garrett Morlan for his brilliant illustrations, which brought both Adams and his era vividly to life.

To the entire Avett band and crew family, thank you for tolerating my ability to somehow bring John Quincy Adams into every conversation. To my busmates, thank you for being good sports about the inconveniences of me taking over our small communal space for writing and research.

Thank you to my dear friend and fellow *Road to Now* cohost, Dr. Ben Sawyer. I am grateful for you and the over three hundred hours we've spent together talking history with so many fascinating and knowledgeable guests.

Most importantly, thank you to Melanie, Hallie, and Sam for giving my life meaning and filling it with love.

NOTES

AUTHOR'S NOTE

"on trial for censure": *The Congressional Globe*, vol. 11, 27th Cong., 2nd sess., 1842, 169–70 CG or 185–86 UNT, ed. Francis P. Blair, Sr., and John C. Rives (Washington, DC), University of North Texas Libraries, UNT Digital Library, crediting UNT Libraries Government Documents Department, https://digital.library.unt.edu/ark:/67531/metadc29279.

INTRODUCTION

"The captious disputations": *Vermont Phœnix* (Brattleboro), June 28, 1839. Chronicling America: Historic American Newspapers, Library of Congress.

The petition read: *The Congressional Globe*, vol. 11, 168.

"Threatened never to return": *The Congressional Globe*, vol. 11, 168.

He confessed to his diary: John Quincy Adams Digital Diary, December 3, 1828, ed. Neal E. Millikan and others, www.primarysourecoop.org/jqa/.

Kentucky Congressman Thomas Marshall: Biographical Directory of the United States Congress, 1774–2005, rev. edn. (Washington, DC: 2005), bioguide.congress.gov.

"Merit expulsion": *The Congressional Globe*, vol. 11, 169–170.

William H. Freehling points out: William W. Freehling, *The Road to Disunion*, vol. 1 (New York: Oxford University Press, 2007), 144, 146–149. Freehling provides a great analysis of the narrow margin between the age of Adams and the age of Jefferson. For an in-depth discussion of how Southerners shaped American domestic and foreign policy in the antebellum period, see Matthew Karp's *This Vast Southern Empire: Slaveholders at the Helm of American Foreign Policy* (Cambridge, MA: Harvard University Press, 2016).

"Angel upon Earth": John Quincy Adams Digital Diary, February 11, 1820.

A promise he made to God: Merton Lynn Dillon, *Benjamin Lundy and the Struggle for Negro Freedom* (Urbana, Ill.: University of Illinois Press, 1966, Ann Arbor: University Microfilms International, 1986), 7.

Long and bloody road to emancipation: *Letters of Theodore Dwight Weld, Angelina Grimke Weld and Sarah Grimke*, vol. 2, 913.

Upon Adams's death in 1848: Phillip Hone, *The Diary of Philip Hone, 1828–1851* (New York: Arno Press, 1970), 840.

CHAPTER 1

"Plan for sending a Colony of Free People": John Quincy Adams Digital Diary, September 12, 1817; October 11, 1817. Adams learns from Elias Boudinot Caldwell, a clerk of the Supreme Court, that the man from the steamship who approached him regarding the ACS was "Mr. Mills." Adams has no other reference to him in his diaries.

He recognized the son: John Quincy Adams Digital Diary, September 12, 1817.

The term *White House*: "How did the White House get its name?" White House Historical Association, https://whitehousehistory.org/questions/how-did-the-white-house-get-its-name.

"The Northwest Territory": Northwest Ordinance (1787) | National Archives, https://www.archives.gov/milestone-document/northwest-ordinance.

Aversion to enslaved labor: John Quincy Adams Digital Diary, September 20, 1817.

John Quincy Adams walked to his office: John Quincy Adams Digital Diary, September 22, 1817.

The slavery issue was ever present: Samuel Flagg Bemis, *John Quincy Adams and the Foundations of American Foreign Policy* (New York: A. A. Knopf, 1949), 255–257.

President Monroe and some: John Quincy Adams Digital Diary, March 12, 1819.

The House Speaker: Eric Burin, *Slavery and the Peculiar Solution: A History of the American Colonization Society* (University Press of Florida, 2016), 11; Merrill D. Peterson, *The Great Triumvirate: Webster, Clay, and Calhoun* (New York: Oxford University Press, 1989), 284.

He told his cabinet: Tim McGrath, *James Monroe: A Life* (New York: Dutton, 2020), 200.

The American Colonization Society: William W. Freehling, *The Road to Disunion*, 147–148.

gained many adherents: William Lee Miller, *Arguing About Slavery: The Great Battle in the United States Congress* (New York: Vintage Books, 1998), 72.

James Tallmadge placed: William W. Freehling, *The Road to Disunion*, 144, 146–149. Freehling provides a great analysis of the narrow margin between the age of Adams and the age of Jefferson.

James K. Polk's war: For an in-depth discussion of how Southerners shaped American domestic and foreign policy in the antebellum period, see Matthew Karp's *This Vast Southern Empire: Slaveholders at the Helm of American Foreign Policy* (Cambridge, MA: Harvard University Press, 2016).

The slavocracy: According to the Oxford English Dictionary, the first known use of the term *slavocracy* dates to 1839 in the Antislavery Journal the *Emancipator*.

"I have no business": Rufus King quote as quoted in William W. Freehling, *The Road to Disunion*, 148.

Big Cotton: Sean Wilentz, *The Rise of American Democracy: Jefferson to Lincoln* (New York: W. W. Norton, 2009), 220.

The Era of Good Feelings: *Columbian Centinel*, July 12, 1817. In a July 27, 1817, letter to Thomas Jefferson, James Monroe expressed a renewed affection for the Union from the crowds he visited in the Northeast, for which see *The Papers of Thomas Jefferson*, Retirement Series, vol. 11, ed. J. Jefferson Looney (Princeton: Princeton University Press, 2014), 568–570.

Monroe declared: James Monroe, First Inaugural Address (speech, Washington, DC, March 4, 1817), Avalon Project, https://avalon.law.yale.edu/19th_century/monroe1.asp.

"These Cabinet Councils": John Quincy Adams Digital Diary, January 9, 1818.

Throughout his tenure: *Heel* is the term given to the villain in professional wrestling. "William Harris Crawford, 1772–1834," Biographical Directory of the United States Congress.

He noted: John Quincy Adams Digital Diary, January 6, 1818.

He attended Yale: "John Caldwell Calhoun, 1782–1850," Biographical Directory of the United States Congress.

"Calhoun thinks": John Quincy Adams Digital Diary, January 6, 1818.

"Rapid nor rich": William Wirt, *The Letters of the British Spy* (Chapel Hill: University of North Carolina Press, 1970), 174.

Adams confided to his diary: John Quincy Adams Digital Diary, January 9, 1818.

James Traub described President James Monroe: James Traub, *John Quincy Adams: Militant Spirit,* 235.

As late as the 1820s: James Traub, *John Quincy Adams: Militant Spirit,* 235. Note here also that in addition to Washington and Monroe serving in the Continental Army and then going on to the presidency many historians would argue that Andrew Jackson also served in the Revolutionary War, albeit as a boy soldier, aged thirteen. Though he wasn't officially in the army, he did see action at the Battle of Hanging Rock as part of the militia and was captured by the British.

The results were sectional: John Robert Van Atta, *Wolf by the Ears: The Missouri Crisis, 1819–1821* (Baltimore: Johns Hopkins University Press, 2015), 75.

Five free-state senators: William W. Freehling, *The Road to Disunion,* 23.

He was determined: William W. Freehling, *The Road to Disunion,* 152.

The contentious issue of slavery's expansion: John Robert Van Atta, *Wolf by the Ears,* 75–78.

James Barbour intoned: James Barbour quote "little speck" in Annals of Congress, 16 Cong., 1st Session., 107–108.

Crawford's toast: John Quincy Adams Digital Diary, July 5, 1819.

"The attempt to introduce": John Quincy Adams Digital Diary, July 5, 1819.

CHAPTER 2

What he lacked in education: Merton Lynn Dillon, *Benjamin Lundy and the Struggle for Negro Freedom,* 1, 6–7; Benjamin Earle, comp., *The Life, Travels, and Opinions of Benjamin Lundy; Including His Journeys to Texas and Mexico, with a Sketch of Contemporary Events, and a Notice of the Revolution in Hayti,* compiled under the direction and on behalf of his children by Thomas Earle (Philadelphia: W. D. Parrish, 1847; reprinted New York: Negro Universities Press, 1969), 13–14.

The Lundy family: Benjamin Earle, *The Life, Travels, and Opinions of Benjamin Lundy,* 13.

Printed in Philadelphia: "Benjamin Lay," *The Dictionary of National Biography,* www.oxforddnb.com.

A collection of biographical anecdotes: Benjamin Rush, *Essays, Literary, Moral &Amp; Philosophical by Benjamin Rush, M.D. and Professor of the Institutes of Medicine and Clinical Practice in the University of Pennsylvania* (Philadelphia: Thomas & Samuel F. Bradford, 1798), 305–311.

Lay stood up and shouted: Celia Caust-Ellenbogen, "Fearless and Fiery," *Swarthmore Bulletin* 115, no. 2 (Winter 2018), https://www.swarthmore.edu/bulletin/archive/winter-2018-issue-ii-volume-cxv/fearless-and-fiery.html. For more on Benjamin Lay, see Markus Rediker, *The Fearless Benjamin Lay* (Boston: Beacon Press, 2017).

"Had some concern for the future": Benjamin Earle, *The Life, Travels, and Opinions of Benjamin Lundy,* 14–15.

The two men learned: Merton Lynn Dillon, *Benjamin Lundy and the Struggle for Negro Freedom*, 5, 8. Benjamin Stanton (1793–1861) was the uncle of Edwin McMasters Stanton (1814–1869) through Edwin's father, David Edwin Stanton (1788–1828). He is not to be confused with Ohio Congressman Benjamin Stanton who lived from 1809–1872.

Lundy's heart broke: Benjamin Earle, *The Life, Travels, and Opinions of Benjamin Lundy*, 15.

He made a vow to God: Merton Lynn Dillon, *Benjamin Lundy and the Struggle for Negro Freedom*, 6–7.

"I had then a loving wife": Merton Lynn Dillon, *Benjamin Lundy and the Struggle for Negro Freedom*, 9; Benjamin Earle, *The Life, Travels, and Opinions of Benjamin Lundy*, 15–16.

A big thinker: Merton Lynn Dillon, *Benjamin Lundy and the Struggle for Negro Freedom*, 18.

Inspired by the revolution: Kevin R. C. Gutzman, *The Jeffersonians: The Visionary Presidencies of Jefferson, Madison, and Monroe* (New York: St. Martin's Griffin, 2024), 84.

The Act Prohibiting the Importation of Slaves: "An Act to Prohibit the Importation of Slaves into Any Port or Place Within the Jurisdiction of the U.S. from and After Jan. 1, 1808," March 2, 1807, RG11: General Records of the United States Government, National Archives Building, Washington, DC.

These men worked: Merton Lynn Dillon, *Benjamin Lundy and the Struggle for Negro Freedom*, 13, 15, 16–17.

Osborn printed Lundy's appeal: Benjamin Earle, *The Life, Travels, and Opinions of Benjamin Lundy*, 16, 18.

Lundy wrote: Benjamin Earle, *The Life, Travels, and Opinions of Benjamin Lundy*, 18.

His saddle business: Benjamin Earle, *The Life, Travels, and Opinions of Benjamin Lundy*, 18.

When he returned to Mount Pleasant: Merton Lynn Dillon, *Benjamin Lundy and the Struggle for Negro Freedom*, 32–35.

CHAPTER 3

Turmoil in the manufacturing sector: Sean Wilentz, *The Rise of American Democracy*, 206.

American cotton prices: Sean Wilentz, *The Rise of American Democracy*, 206.

John C. Calhoun told Adams: John Quincy Adams Digital Diary, May 22, 1820.

A growing sense of unease: Merton Lynn Dillon, *Benjamin Lundy and the Struggle for Negro Freedom*, 36–42.

"There are several Subjects": John Quincy Adams Digital Diary, January 2, 1820.

This included chartering: Ben McNitt, *A House Divided: Slavery and American Politics from the Constitution to the Civil War* (Lanham: Stackpole Books, 2021), 127–128.

"If we should unfortunately fail": Briscoe G. Baldwin, *Preamble and Resolutions Offered by Mr. Baldwin, to the House of Delegates on the Missouri Question* (Richmond: Thomas Ritchie, 1819).

He considered three possibilities: John Quincy Adams Digital Diary, January 8, 1820.

"Good Feelings": "Jesse Burgess Thomas, 1777–1853" and "James Barbour, 1775–1842," Biographical Directory of the United States Congress.

"Star of the West": David S. Heidler and Jeanne T. Heidler, *Henry Clay: The Essential American* (New York: Random House, 2010), 9–10.

James Traub writes that, in Ghent: James Traub, *John Quincy Adams: Militant Spirit*, 191.

There was not a Westerner: Tim McGrath, *James Monroe: A Life*, 381.

Adams wrote of Clay: John Quincy Adams Digital Diary, February 13, 1820.

Clay confessed to Adams: John Quincy Adams Digital Diary, February 13, 1820.

Adams commented in his diary: John Quincy Adams Digital Diary, February 13, 1820.

Clay's game of keep-away: John Quincy Adams Digital Diary, March 3, 1820; David S. Heidler and Jeanne T. Heidler, *Henry Clay*, 146–148.

Adams biographer Samuel Flagg: Samuel Flagg Bemis, *John Quincy Adams and the Foundations of American Foreign Policy*, 416, 422–423.

He confided to himself: John Quincy Adams Digital Diary, March 3, 1820.

"It is a contemplation": John Quincy Adams Digital Diary, March 3, 1820.

"The Slave men": John Quincy Adams Digital Diary, January 16, 1820.

"The great Slave-holders": John Quincy Adams Digital Diary, February 11, 1820.

"Here a single question": John Quincy Adams Digital Diary, February 11, 1820.

"Slave-holders": John Quincy Adams Digital Diary, February 11, 1820.

The Missouri Crisis: John Quincy Adams Digital Diary, February 24, 1820.

Calhoun replied that the South: John Quincy Adams Digital Diary, February 24, 1820.

The result would be: John Quincy Adams Digital Diary, February 24, 1820.

Adams continued in his diary that night: John Quincy Adams Digital Diary, February 24, 1820.

CHAPTER 4

Monroe posed two questions: John Quincy Adams Digital Diary, March 3, 1820.

Calhoun, Crawford, and Wirt: If you want to understand why Adams was so frustrated with Crawford, Calhoun, Wirt, and Secretary Thompson, see Article IV, Section Three, Clause Two of the Constitution. "The Congress shall have Power to dispose of and make all needful Rules and Regulations respecting the Territory or other Property belonging to the United States; and nothing in this Constitution shall be so construed as to Prejudice any Claims of the United States, or of any particular State."

Adams argued: For more on this first act of foreign aid on the part of the United States Congress, see Caitlin Fitz, *Our Sister Republics: The United States in an Age of American Revolutions* (New York: W. W. Norton, 2016).

"If the Union must be dissolved": John Quincy Adams Digital Diary, March 3, 1820.

The "wolf": *The Papers of Thomas Jefferson*, Retirement Series, vol. 16, ed. J. Jefferson Looney et al. (Princeton: Princeton University Press, 2019), 92.

CHAPTER 5

Lundy rebutted the argument: Merton Lynn Dillon, *Benjamin Lundy and the Struggle for Negro Freedom*, 36–39.

He argued against the idea: M. Andrew Holowchak, "A 'Cretinous' Construal of Jefferson's 'Diffusion Argument,'" December 6, 2022, Blog, https://www.abbevilleinstitute.org/a-cretinous-construal-of-jeffersons-diffusion-argument/.

"My bed, at night": Merton Lynn Dillon, *Benjamin Lundy and the Struggle for Negro Freedom*, 37, 39–40; Benjamin Earle, *The Life, Travels, and Opinions of Benjamin Lundy*, 19.

On a brisk Sunday morning: John Quincy Adams Digital Diary, November 12, 1820.

Nullification is a theory: John Quincy Adams Digital Diary, November 12, 1820.

Adams believed: John Quincy Adams Digital Diary, November 24, 1820; Virginia Resolutions, December 21, 1798, *The Papers of James Madison*, vol. 17, ed. David B. Mattern (Charlottesville: University Press of Virginia, 1991), 185–191; Resolutions Adopted by the Kentucky General Assembly, November 10, 1798, *The Papers of Thomas Jefferson*, vol. 30, ed. Barbara B. Oberg (Princeton: Princeton University Press, 2003), 550–556.

Adams said that the article: John Quincy Adams Digital Diary, November 29, 1820.

Baldwin's response: Samuel Flagg Bemis, *John Quincy Adams and the Foundations of American Foreign Policy*, 422.

An appetite for a war: David S. Heidler and Jeanne T. Heidler, *Henry Clay*, 150–152.

"There must be": John Quincy Adams Digital Diary, February 28, 1821.

Lincoln said of his times: "Speech of Hon. Abraham Lincoln at Ottawa, August 30, 1858," Northern Illinois Digital Library, https://digital.lib.niu.edu/islandora/object/niu-lincoln%3A38360.

The newspaper's motto: Merton Lynn Dillon, *Benjamin Lundy and the Struggle for Negro Freedom*, 45–46.

Lundy announced his intention: *The Philanthropist, a Weekly Journal*, VI (Mount Pleasant, Ohio), June 2, 1821.

"I had begun the work": Benjamin Earle, *The Life, Travels, and Opinions of Benjamin Lundy*, 20.

***Genius of Universal Emancipation*:** Benjamin Earle, *The Life, Travels, and Opinions of Benjamin Lundy*, 20; Merton Lynn Dillon, *Benjamin Lundy and the Struggle for Negro Freedom*, 46.

He was accompanied by Isaiah Osborn: Merton Lynn Dillon, *Benjamin Lundy and the Struggle for Negro Freedom*, 47–48.

In 1822, Charleston: John Lofton, *Denmark Vesey's Revolt: The Slave Plot That Lit a Fuse to Fort Sumter* (Kent, Ohio: The Kent State University Press, 1983), 38.

Historians believe Denmark Vesey: John Lofton, *Denmark Vesey's Revolt*, 10–11, 28.

A Black man told investigators: William W. Freehling, *Prelude to Civil War: The Nullification Controversy in South Carolina 1818–1836* (New York: Harper & Row, 1966), 54.

Incarceration seems tame: John Lofton, *Denmark Vesey's Revolt*, 132–133.

One informant told: Sean Wilentz, *The Rise of American Democracy*, 238.

"Nine thousand slaves": Sean Wilentz, *The Rise of American Democracy*, 239.

One co-conspirator confessed: Sean Wilentz, *The Rise of American Democracy*, 239.

The purpose of the law: William W. Freehling, *Prelude to Civil War*, 113–115.

"Where is this to land us?": Philip M. Hamer. "Great Britain, the United States, and the Negro Seamen Acts, 1822–1848," *Journal of Southern History* 1, no. 1 (February 1935): 3–28, https://doi.org/10.2307/2191749.

South Carolina: Fred Kaplan, *John Quincy Adams: American Visionary* (New York: Harper Perennial, 2015), Kindle, 635.

"Acts of fire and blood": Merton Lynn Dillon, *Benjamin Lundy and the Struggle for Negro Freedom*, 51.

The conspiracy also included: Merton Lynn Dillon, *Benjamin Lundy and the Struggle for Negro Freedom*, 52.

It's a little ironic: Melinda Wenner Moyer, "People Drawn to Conspiracy Theories Have a Cluster of Psychological Features," *Scientific American*, March 1, 2019, https://www.scientificamerican.com/article/people-drawn-to-conspiracy-theories-share-a-cluster-of-psychological-features/.

In the summer of 1823: Merton Lynn Dillon, *Benjamin Lundy and the Struggle for Negro Freedom*, 83–84.

The committee also suggested: Merton Lynn Dillon, *Benjamin Lundy and the Struggle for Negro Freedom*, 79, 81–82.

The convention rejected: Merton Lynn Dillon, *Benjamin Lundy and the Struggle for Negro Freedom*, 84–85.

As a token of their appreciation: Merton Lynn Dillon, *Benjamin Lundy and the Struggle for Negro Freedom*, 84–85.

CHAPTER 6

In the words of James Traub: "The Corrupt Bargain," *Founding Son: John Quincy's America.* Podcast audio, April 14, 2023. https://www.iheart.com/podcast/1119-founding-son-john-quincys-111619900/.

His father admonished: John Adams to John Quincy Adams, April 23, 1794, *Adams Family Correspondence*, vol. 10, ed. Margaret A. Hogan, C. James Taylor, et al. (Cambridge, MA: Harvard University Press, 2011), 150–153.

Andrew Jackson was born: "Andrew Jackson, 1767–1845," Biographical Directory of the United States Congress.

Andrew's mother: Jon Meacham, *American Lion: Andrew Jackson in the White House* (New York: Random House, 2009), 8–9.

After the war, Jackson: Jon Meacham, *American Lion*, 11–13, 25–26.

After four days of fighting: Robert V. Remini, *The Battle of New Orleans: Andrew Jackson and America's First Military Victory* (New York: Penguin Books, 2014), 124–136.

Jackson remarked: *The Papers of Andrew Jackson*, vol. 3, ed. Harold D. Moser, David R. Hoth, et al. (Knoxville: University of Tennessee Press, 1991), 258.

In December 1817: Monroe to Jackson, December 28, 1817, as quoted in Jon Meacham, *American Lion*, 36.

"The whole conduct of General Jackson": John Quincy Adams Digital Diary, July 17, 1818, and July 20, 1818.

Clay denounced Jackson: Annals of Congress,15th Cong., 2nd sess., 631–674; Epes Sargent, *The Life and Public Services of Henry Clay* (New York: C. M. Saxton, Barker & Co, 1860), 83; *Papers of Andrew Jackson*, vol. 4, 267–269.

The celebration was not initially her idea: *Diary and Autobiographical Writings of Louisa Catherine Adams*, Judith S. Graham, Beth Luey, et al. (Cambridge, MA: Belknap, 2013), 680–688. Louisa's diary entry detailing the events of the party, January 8, 1824, is the last entry in her diary until November 6, 1835. The years in between were turbulent and her lack of writing underscores the pain she experienced throughout the intervening years.

In addition to wooing Jackson: Catherine Allgor, *Parlor Politics: In Which the Ladies of Washington Help Build a City and a Government* (Charlottesville: University of Virginia Press, 2000), 172–184.

Louisa wrote in her diary: Samuel Flagg Bemis, *John Quincy Adams and the Union* (New York: A. A. Knopf, 1956), 15.

Jackson received the endorsement: Samuel Flagg Bemis, *John Quincy Adams and the Union*, 14.

"I have no desire": Samuel Flagg Bemis, *John Quincy Adams and the Union*, 14.

On the other hand, Adams believed: Samuel Flagg Bemis, *John Quincy Adams and the Union*, 15–16; John Quincy Adams Digital Diary, December 14, 1825.

Adams believed Crawford: Samuel Flagg Bemis, *John Quincy Adams and the Union*, 16.

When the president refused to yield: Samuel Flagg Bemis, *John Quincy Adams and the Union*, 16.

To men like John Quincy Adams: Samuel Flagg Bemis, *John Quincy Adams and the Union*, 14.

Adams wanted to be president: Louisa Catherine Adams to George Washington Adams, December 12, 1823 (MHS: Adams Papers).

John Quincy told McDuffie: John Quincy Adams Digital Diary, May 24, 1824.

He found them: John Quincy Adams Digital Diary, "Day" July 1824. Adams often included an entry at the end of the month he called the "Day" entry that acted as a summary of the past month's routines and mood.

The end of what he called: John Quincy Adams Digital Diary, August 28, 1824.
John Quincy commented: John Quincy Adams Digital Diary, September 8, 1824.
"Pass another century": John Quincy Adams Digital Diary, September 20, 1824.
"To suffer without feeling": John Quincy Adam Digital Diary, May 8, 1824.
"I took leave of my father": John Quincy Adams Digital Diary, September 24, 1824.
Adams joined Lafayette: John Quincy Adams Digital Diary, October 4, 1824.
The House scheduled the vote: John Quincy Adams Digital Diary, January 17, 1825.
Henry Clay despised Andrew Jackson: David S. Heidler and Jeanne T. Heidler, *Henry Clay*, 179.
About Clay supporting Adams: John Quincy Adams Digital Diary, December 17, 1824.
Clay told Adams: John Quincy Adams Digital Diary, January 1, 1825.
After their second meeting, Adams wrote: John Quincy Adams Digital Diary January 29, 1825.
"I received this morning": John Quincy Adams Digital Diary January 29, 1825.
When he opened his eyes: Samuel Flagg Bemis, *John Quincy Adams and the Union*, 46.
Adams wrote: John Quincy Adams Digital Diary, February 9, 1825.
When Jackson got to Adams: Jon Meacham, *American Lion*, 45.
Jackson wrote to a friend: Andrew Jackson to William Berkley Lewis, February 14, 1825 (DLC: Andrew Jackson Papers, 1775–1874), http://hdl.loc.gov/loc.mss/maj.06160_0233_0233; Annals of Congress,15th Cong., 2nd sess., 631–674; Epes Sargent, *The Life and Public Services of Henry Clay*, 83; *Papers of Andrew Jackson*, vol. 4, 267–269.

CHAPTER 7

***The Genius of Universal Emancipation* as the:** Quoted in Merton Lynn Dillon, *Benjamin Lundy and the Struggle for Negro Freedom*, 114.
Convinced them to: Merton Lynn Dillon, *Benjamin Lundy and the Struggle for Negro Freedom*, 90–92.
To rebut the accusations: Merton Lynn Dillon, *Benjamin Lundy and the Struggle for Negro Freedom*, 94.
According to the Haitian government: Merton Lynn Dillon, *Benjamin Lundy and the Struggle for Negro Freedom*, 95.
Lundy had an idea: Manisha Sinha, *The Slave's Cause: A History of Abolition* (New Haven: Yale University Press, 2017), 178.
Lundy was on a mission: Merton Lynn Dillon, *Benjamin Lundy and the Struggle for Negro Freedom*, 100.
So he sought: Merton Lynn Dillon, *Benjamin Lundy and the Struggle for Negro Freedom*, 100–101.
"I persuaded the captain": Benjamin Earle, *The Life, Travels, and Opinions of Benjamin Lundy*, 24.
When the authorities allowed Lundy: Benjamin Earle, *The Life, Travels, and Opinions of Benjamin Lundy*, 24.
Lundy's sister would later write: Benjamin Earle, *The Life, Travels, and Opinions of Benjamin Lundy*, 309.
With the death of Esther: Merton Lynn Dillon, *Benjamin Lundy and the Struggle for Negro Freedom*, 102.
According to historian Calvin Schermerhorn: Calvin Schermerhorn, *The Business of Slavery and the Rise of American Capitalism, 1815–1860* (New Haven: Yale University Press, 2015), 60.

Newspaper tagged as being: Quoted in Calvin Schermerhorn, *The Business of Slavery*, 33.
The *Decatur*: Calvin Schermerhorn, *The Business of Slavery*, 34–39, 61.
Woolfolk allegedly shouted: Merton Lynn Dillon, *Benjamin Lundy and the Struggle for Negro Freedom*, 118.
In early January 1827: Merton Lynn Dillon, *Benjamin Lundy and the Struggle for Negro Freedom*, 119.
Lundy testified: Benjamin Earle, *The Life, Travels, and Opinions of Benjamin Lundy*, 208.
Woolfolk was charged: Merton Lynn Dillon, *Benjamin Lundy and the Struggle for Negro Freedom*, 120.
The petition requested that Congress: Annals of Congress, 1 Cong., 2 Sess., 1239–1241.
Would it not light: Annals of Congress, 1 Cong., 2 Sess., 1242; "James Jackson, 1757–1806," Biographical Directory of the United States Congress.
When Lundy sent the memorial: Merton Lynn Dillon, *Benjamin Lundy and the Struggle for Negro Freedom*, 124.
"Of sundry citizens of Baltimore": Register of Debates, 19 Cong., 2 Sess., 1099–1101.
"Taxation without Representation": Annals of Congress, 1 Cong., 2 Sess., 1247.
McDuffie began by saying: Register of Debates, 19 Cong., 2 Sess., 1099.
But the people of Maryland: Register of Debates, 19 Cong., 2 Sess., 1100.
Virginia Congressman Alfred H. Powell: Register of Debates, 19 Cong., 2 Sess., 1100; "Alfred H. Powell, 1781–1831," Biographical Directory of the United States Congress.
Barney told his colleagues: Register of Debates, 19 Cong., 2 Sess., 1100–1101.
The exception was Charles Miner: "Charles Miner, 1780–1865," Biographical Directory of the United States Congress.
The paper printed Charles's column: Dave Janoski, "Charles Miner Played a Major Role in Shaping of Local, National History," *Times Leader*, January 23, 2000, https://www.timesleader.com/archive/974040/charles-miner-played-a-major-role-in-shaping-of-local-national-history.
Miner at best imitated: Dave Janoski, "Charles Miner Played a Major Role in Shaping of Local, National History."
Lundy also convinced: Merton Lynn Dillon, *Benjamin Lundy and the Struggle for Negro Freedom*, 125; Minutes of the twentieth session of the American Convention for Promoting the Abolition of Slavery, and Improving the Condition of the African Race: convened at Philadelphia, on the second of October (Baltimore: Benjamin Lundy, 1827), https://www.loc.gov/item/91898197/.
According to the great historian: Richard S. Newman, *The Transformation of American Abolitionism: Fighting Slavery in the Early Republic* (Chapel Hill: University of North Carolina Press, 2002), 152.
In Boston: Merton Lynn Dillon, *Benjamin Lundy and the Struggle for Negro Freedom*, 131.
Too much antislavery agitation: Merton Lynn Dillon, *Benjamin Lundy and the Struggle for Negro Freedom*, 132.
Garrison had been aware: Merton Lynn Dillon, *Benjamin Lundy and the Struggle for Negro Freedom*, 132; "William Lloyd Garrison," *Dictionary of American Biography*, vol. 7 (New York: Charles Scribner's Sons, 1937), 168–172.
The older man told the younger: Wendell Phillips Garrison, *William Lloyd Garrison, 1805–1879; The Story of His Life Told by His Children*, vol. 1 (New York: Century Co., 1885), 93.

CHAPTER 8

Having secured his election: Robert Elder, *Calhoun: American Heretic* (New York: Basic Books, 2021), 217.

Adams recorded: John Quincy Adams Digital Diary, July 15, 1818.

Calhoun expressed: John Caldwell Calhoun to Andrew Jackson, March 30, 1823 (Andrew Jackson Papers, Library of Congress).

Jackson and Calhoun: Robert Elder, *Calhoun: American Heretic*, 217.

John Quincy bid: John Quincy Adams Digital Diary, March 4, 1825.

According to reporters: *Daily National Intelligencer*, Washington, DC, March 5, 1825.

It was to be: John Quincy Adams, "First Annual Message," December 6, 1825, Miller Center, https://millercenter.org/the-presidency/presidential-speeches/december-6-1825-first-annual-message.

"General Jackson we were": *Gettysburg Republican Compiler*, March 16, 1825.

While foreign nations: John Quincy Adams, "First Annual Message."

"When I view": Andrew Jackson to John Branch, March 3, 1826, *Papers of Andrew Jackson*, vol. 6, 142–143.

As historian Lindsay: "Andrew Jackson Strikes Back," *Founding Son: John Quincy's America.* Podcast audio, April 14, 2023, https://www.iheart.com/podcast/1119-founding-son-john-quincys-111619900/.

In October of 1825: Robert Coleman Foster to Andrew Jackson, [October 14, 1825], *Papers of Andrew Jackson*, vol. 6, 111–113.

And that system: James M. Bradley, *Martin Van Buren: America's First Politician* (New York: Oxford University Press, 2024), 247.

New York City Mayor: *Diary of Phillip Hone*, vol. 2 (New York: Dodd and Mean and Company, 1927), 840.

It was the fiftieth: John Quincy Adams Digital Diary, July 6, 1826.

The tavern keeper: John Quincy Adams Digital Diary, July 9, 1826.

Upon learning about: John Quincy Adams Digital Diary, July 9, 1826.

Putting his father's affairs: John Quincy Adams Digital Diary, July 14, 1826.

Calhoun's transformation: John Quincy Adams Digital Diary, November 21, 1826.

Adams declined: John Quincy Adams Digital Diary, December 11, 1826.

After his release: John Quincy Adams Digital Diary, May 15, 1828.

The ACS eventually: For more of Abdul Rahman Ibrahima's extraordinary life, read Terry Alford, *Prince Among Slaves* (New York: Oxford University Press, 2007).

Adams wrote in his diary: John Quincy Adams Digital Diary, January 10, 1832.

Johnson, a lawyer: Lindsay M. Chervinsky, Callie Hopkins, "The Enslaved Household of President John Quincy Adams," WHHA (en-US). Accessed July 29, 2025, https://www.whitehousehistory.org/the-enslaved-household-of-john-quincy-adams.

On February 23: John Quincy Adams Digital Diary, February 23, 1828, February 24, 1828.

How should a mortal's: *Horace, Odes and Carmen Saeculare of Horace,* John Conington, trans. (London: George Bell and Sons, 1882), Book I, Ode 4.

Notably, Mary signed: Lindsay M. Chervinsky, Callie Hopkins, "The Enslaved Household of President John Quincy Adams," WHHA (en-US). Accessed July 29, 2025, https://www.whitehousehistory.org/the-enslaved-household-of-john-quincy-adams.

What America needed: *Richmond Enquirer*, December 28, 1827, https://www.virginiachronicle.com/?a=d&d=RE18271228.1.4.

The truth was that: For more on Louisa's early life—and Czar Alexander I's infatuation—see *Diary and Autobiographical Writings of Louisa Catherine Adams*, vols.

1–2 (1778–1815, 1819–1849), eds. Judith S. Graham, Beth Luey, Margaret A. Hogan, and C. James Taylor, 2013.

One Louisa Adams biographer: "Andrew Jackson Strikes Back," *Founding Son: John Quincy's America.*

"Prospects whether of public": John Quincy Adams Digital Diary, April 10, 1828.

It was a worthy: John Quincy Adams Digital Diary, July 1, 1828.

It was much too little: John Quincy Adams Digital Diary, July 4, 1828.

For the rest of his days: Paul F. Boller Jr., *Presidential Campaigns: From George Washington to George W. Bush* (New York: Oxford University Press, 2004), 46.

Adams complained: John Quincy Adams Digital Diary, "Day" July 1827.

It looked as though: John Quincy Adams Digital Diary, December 3, 1828.

Like his father before him: John Quincy Adams Digital Diary, March 3, 1829.

Washington socialite Margaret: Quoted in Sean Wilentz, *The Rise of American Democracy,* 313; Louisa Thomas, *Louisa: The Extraordinary Life of Mrs. Adams* (New York: Penguin Books, 2017), 379.

"I write this": Charles Francis Adams to Louisa Catherine Adams, April 4, 1829. Adams Papers, Massachusetts Historical Society.

He wrote in his diary: John Quincy Adams Digital Diary, "Day" March 1829.

Neither project was: John Quincy Adams Digital Diary, April 6, 1829, April 27, 1829.

It is hard to believe: John Quincy Adams Digital Diary, April 27, 1829.

John Quincy lamented: John Quincy Adams Digital Diary, May 2, 1829.

In his "pockets": Fred Kaplan, *John Quincy Adams: American Visionary* (New York: HarperPerennial, 2015), 417.

Charles, circumspect, blamed: Martin B. Duberman, *Charles Francis Adams, 1807–1886* (Stanford, CA: Stanford University Press, 1968), 33.

"Oh this agony": Louisa Thomas, *Louisa,* 166; Margaret A. Hogan, and C. James Taylor, *A Traveled First Lady: Writings of Louisa Catherine Adams* (Cambridge, MA: The Belknap Press of Harvard University Press, 2014), 201.

There a choir sang: John Quincy Adams Digital Diary, September 17, 1830.

"No person could be": John Quincy Adams Digital Diary, September 18, 1830.

He wished: John Quincy Adams Digital Diary, September 25, 1830.

A seat in Congress: John Quincy Adams Digital Diary, November 7, 1830.

"The grave of my": *Founding Son: John Quincy's America.*

After leaving the vice: Louisa Catherine Adams to Charles Francis Adams, January 24, 1830, as quoted in Jon Meacham, *American Lion,* 116.

CHAPTER 9

As the 1820s: Sean Wilentz, *The Rise of American Democracy,* 265.

From the Burned-Over: Anne C. Loveland, "Evangelicalism and 'Immediate Emancipation' in American Antislavery Thought," *Journal of Southern History* 32, no. 2 (1966): 172–188, https://doi.org/10.2307/2204556.

He was sick: Gilbert Hobbes Barnes, *The Anti-Slavery Impulse: 1830–1844* (New York: Harcourt, Brace & World, 1964), 9.

Finney believed excitement: Quoted in Gilbert Hobbes Barnes, *The Anti-Slavery Impulse,* 11.

The young woman: Quoted in Gilbert Hobbes Barnes, *The Anti-Slavery Impulse,* 34.

At manual labor school: Lawrence Thomas Lesick, *The Lane Rebels: Evangelicalism and Antislavery in Antebellum America* (Metuchen, NJ: Scarecrow Press, 1980), 72.

Weld posed five questions: Theodore Weld to John Quincy Adams, November 23, 1832, Adams Papers, Massachusetts Historical Society.

"I believe Exercise": John Quincy Adams to Theodore Weld, December 5, 1832, Adams Papers, Massachusetts Historical Society.

Walker claimed he attended: For the mystery surrounding David Walker's birth, see Peter P. Hinks, *To Awaken My Afflicted Brethren: David Walker and the Problem of Antebellum Slave Resistance* (University Park, PA: Pennsylvania State University Press, 1997), 11–13. For David Walker's involvement in the Denmark Vesey Conspiracy, see 30–32.

Newman describes Walker: "Don't Mess with Texas," *Founding Son: John Quincy's America.* Podcast audio, April 19, 2023, https://www.iheart.com/podcast/1119-founding-son-john-quincys-111619900/.

Walker exhorted free: David Walker, *Walker's Appeal, in Four Articles: Together with a Preamble, to the Coloured Citizens of the World, but in Particular, and Very Expressly, to Those of the United States of America, Written in Boston, State of Massachusetts, September 28, 1829* (Boston, 1830), 18.

While Walker respected Lundy: Quoted in Peter P. Hinks, *To Awaken My Afflicted Brethren,* 130.

Walker "indulges himself": Benjamin Earle, *The Life, Travels, and Opinions of Benjamin Lundy,* 238.

An atmospheric aberration: This section adapted and quoted from Bob Crawford and James Morrison, *Founding Son,* Episode Three.

"While laboring": *The Confessions of Nat Turner, the Leader of the Late Insurrection in Southampton* (Baltimore: T. R. Gray, 1831), 10.

They went house: *The Confessions of Nat Turner, the Leader of the Late Insurrection in Southampton* (Baltimore: T. R. Gray, 1831), 13.

"I presented fifteen": *Founding Son,* Episode Three; John Quincy Adams Digital Diary, December 12, 1831.

"It may aggravate": John Quincy Adams Digital Diary, January 10, 1831.

He noted sparingly: John Quincy Adams Digital Diary, February 13, 1831.

Upper Canada: Nikki Taylor, "Reconsidering the 'Forced' Exodus of 1829: Free Black Emigration from Cincinnati, Ohio to Wilberforce, Canada," *Journal of African American History* 87 (2002): 283–302, https://doi.org/10.2307/1562479.

Many risked the 377-mile: Nikki Taylor, "Reconsidering the 'Forced' Exodus of 1829."

In January 1832: Manisha Sinha, *The Slave's Cause,* 207–208.

He had noted: Merton Lynn Dillon, *Benjamin Lundy and the Struggle for Negro Freedom,* 171.

They even elected: Nikki Taylor, "Reconsidering the 'Forced' Exodus of 1829," 294.

From what Lundy could: Merton Lynn Dillon, *Benjamin Lundy and the Struggle for Negro Freedom,* 172.

And while he continued: Merton Lynn Dillon, *Benjamin Lundy and the Struggle for Negro Freedom,* 173–175; Benjamin Earle, *The Life, Travels, and Opinions of Benjamin Lundy,* 233.

As usual, Lundy sought: Merton Lynn Dillon, *Benjamin Lundy and the Struggle for Negro Freedom,* 174.

"The worst travelling": Merton Lynn Dillon, *Benjamin Lundy and the Struggle for Negro Freedom,* 180–181.

He dressed "rough": Merton Lynn Dillon, *Benjamin Lundy and the Struggle for Negro Freedom,* 180–181.

Awakened by a violent: Marcia J. Heringo Mason, *Remember the Distance That Divides Us: The Family Letters of Philadelphia Quaker Abolitionist and Michigan Pioneer Elizabeth Margaret Chandler, 1830–1842* (East Lansing: Michigan State University Press, 2004), 135–137.

In response to: Marcia J. Heringo Mason, *Remember the Distance That Divides Us*, 135–137.

Lundy petitioned: Merton Lynn Dillon, *Benjamin Lundy and the Struggle for Negro Freedom*, 182.

CHAPTER 10

"I asked him": John Quincy Adams Digital Diary, January 10, 1832.

Is the Constitution: To understand the roots of nullification and the origin of the Kentucky and Virginia Resolutions and Thomas Jefferson and James Madison's role in crafting them, see Sean Wilentz, *The Rise of American Democracy*, 79–80.

"They'd get very drunk": "Our Federal Union: It Must Be Preserved," *Founding Son: John Quincy's America*. Podcast audio, April 19, 2023, https://www.iheart.com/podcast/1119-founding-son-john-quincys-111619900/.

When they both: Jon Meacham, *American Lion*, 135–136.

Locking eyes with Jackson: Quoted from Robert Elder, *Calhoun: American Heretic*, 262–263. Elder sourced from Martin Van Buren, *The Autobiography of Martin Van Buren*, 416; and the great historian Robert V. Remini, *Andrew Jackson and the Course of American Freedom*, 235–236.

If they had: Parts of this section are adapted from Bob Crawford and James Morrison, "Our Federal Union: It Must Be Preserved," *Founding Son: John Quincy's America*.

Jackson made the: Andrew Jackson's Proclamation to South Carolina, December 10, 1832, U.S. Congress, U.S. Statutes at Large, vol. 11, 771–781.

"[The] Civil War's": "Our Federal Union: It Must Be Preserved," *Founding Son: John Quincy's America*.

But it was just: Andrew Jackson to Andrew J. Crawford, May 1, 1833, *Papers of Andrew Jackson*, vol. XI, 284–285.

Reflecting on their: John Quincy Adams Digital Diary, September 5, 1831.

A Southern congressman: *Register of Debates*, 22 Cong., 2 Sess., 1609–1617.

Andrew Jackson's fourth: Andrew Jackson, Fourth Annual Message to Congress, December 4, 1832 (National Archives).

Adams believed: John Quincy Adams, *Minority Report for the Committee of Manufactures* (Boston: John H. Eastburn, February 28, 1833).

As he lay: John Quincy Adams Digital Diary, March 2, 1833.

"I do not know": *Diary of Charles Francis Adams*, vol. 5, eds. Aïda DiPace Donald and David Donald (Cambridge, MA: The Belknap Press of Harvard University Press, 1964), 143–144.

"Do not hesitate": Louisa Catherine Adams to John Adams II, July 31, 1834, Adams Papers, Massachusetts Historical Society.

John Quincy would go: John Quincy Adams Digital Diary, October 18, 1834.

"I feel the duty": John Quincy Adams Digital Diary, October 19, 1834.

The evening must: John Quincy Adams Digital Diary, October 20, 1834.

With a heavy heart: John Quincy Adams Digital Diary, October 22, 1834.

"May God, in his": John Quincy Adams Digital Diary, October 23, 1834.

Her son Charles: *Diary of Charles Francis Adams*, vol. 5, 409–410.

At least for the time: *Diary of Charles Francis Adams*, vol. 2, 144.

CHAPTER 11

"Tis yet a babe": J. L. Tracy to Theodore Dwight Weld, November 24, 1831, *Letters of Theodore Dwight Weld, Angelina Grimke Weld and Sarah Grimke*, vol. 1 (Massachusetts: Gloucester, 1965), 56–58.

Now it appeared: Lawrence Thomas Lesick, *The Lane Rebels*, 28–29.

Among the students: William Lee Miller, *Arguing About Slavery*, 87.

"They have given": Lawrence Thomas Lesick, *The Lane Rebels*, 78–79.

He grew up: Gilbert Hobbes Barnes, *The Anti-Slavery Impulse*, 67.

Fifty years later: Quoted in Lawrence Thomas Lesick, *The Lane Rebels*, 81.

"I believe its doctrines": Quoted in Lawrence Thomas Lesick, *The Lane Rebels*, 81.

"God has committed": *Letters of Theodore Dwight Weld, Angelina Grimke Weld and Sarah Grimke*, vol. 1, 120.

Hall criticized the: Quoted in Lawrence Thomas Lesick, *The Lane Rebels*, 91.

Why "should not students": Lawrence Thomas Lesick, *The Lane Rebels*, 92.

Weld refused: Weld to Tappan, March 18, 1834, *Letters of Theodore Dwight Weld: Angelina Grimke Weld and Sarah Grimke*, vol. 1, 132–135.

But on campuses: Gilbert Hobbes Barnes, *The Anti-Slavery Impulse*, 71. See also footnote 15, 228–229.

The trustees gagged: William Lee Miller, *Arguing About Slavery*, 91.

In other words: Gilbert Hobbes Barnes, *The Anti-Slavery Impulse*, 71.

"This is the name": William Lee Miller, *Arguing About Slavery*, 91–92.

CHAPTER 12

"The theory of the rights": John Quincy Adams Digital Diary, August 11, 1835.

Authorities executed ten: *Lancaster Herald and Examiner* (Lancaster), August 6, 1835, Newspaper Archive.com, https://newspaperarchive.com/Other-Articles-Aug-06-1835-3907055.

Black men hiding: "Riot in Philadelphia," *Newburyport Herald*, July 17, 1835. Accessed at Newspaperarchive.com.

Silence would be: John Quincy Adams Digital Diary, February 24, 1820.

Local politicians: John Quincy Adams Digital Diary, August 18, 1835; Samuel Flagg Bemis, *John Quincy Adams and the Union*, 334.

In what became known: *Richmond Enquirer* (Richmond), August, 28, 1835. Accessed at Newspaperarchive.com.

At the conclusion: Gilbert Hobbes Barnes, *The Anti-Slavery Impulse*, 81.

Weld did admit: Gilbert Hobbes Barnes, *The Anti-Slavery Impulse*, 80, 82.

Stanton stood up: Gilbert Hobbes Barnes, *The Anti-Slavery Impulse*, 80, 82.

The Ohio State: Gilbert Hobbes Barnes, *The Anti-Slavery Impulse*, 82–83.

Between 1837 and 1838: "The Gag Rule," National Archives, https://www.archives.gov/exhibits/treasures_of_congress/text.html.

Borden, flustered, caved: John Quincy Adams Digital Diary, December 18, 1835.

Adams confessed: John Quincy Adams Digital Diary, December 19, 1835.

"Will you introduce": Register of Debates, 24 Cong., 1 Sess., 2002.

"The language of cutting": Benjamin Earle, *The Life, Travels, and Opinions of Benjamin Lundy*, 284.

In just a few short years: Benjamin Earle, *The Life, Travels, and Opinions of Benjamin Lundy*, 285.

CHAPTER 13

The Battle of the Alamo: Bob Crawford and James Morrison, "Don't Mess with Texas," *Founding Son: John Quincy's America.* Podcast audio. April 27, 2023, https://www.iheart.com/podcast/1119-founding-son-john-quincys-111619900/episode/founding-son-episode-4-dont-113949678/.

The Mexican Army was happy: William B. Travis, "To the People of Texas and All Americans in the World, 24 February 1836," Texas State Library and Archives.

During Benjamin Lundy's: Merton Lynn Dillon, *Benjamin Lundy and the Struggle for Negro Freedom,* "Cholera," 191; "time in Monclova," 192–193; "land grant," 203–206.

Benjamin Lundy wrote: Merton Lynn Dillon, *Benjamin Lundy and the Struggle for Negro Freedom,* 213.

"There can be *no doubt*": Merton Lynn Dillon, *Benjamin Lundy and the Struggle for Negro Freedom,* 227–228; Benjamin Lundy to John Quincy Adams, May 9, 1836, Adams Papers, Massachusetts Historical Society.

Lundy candidly expressed: Lundy to Adams, June 25, 1836, Adams Papers, Massachusetts Historical Society.

According to Richard S. Newman: "Don't Mess with Texas," *Founding Son: John Quincy's America.*

"The peculiar institution": Register of Debates, 24 Cong., 1 Sess., 2184–2185.

"Sleep the sleep of death": Register of Debates, 24 Cong., 1 Sess., 2036.

Congressman Henry Wise: Register of Debates, 23 Cong., 2 Sess., 1399.

The three resolutions: William Lee Miller, *Arguing About Slavery,* 205.

The first resolution read: Register of Debates, 24 Cong., 1 Sess., 4031. This section has been condensed for the ease of the reader, but I encourage everyone to read the Register of Debates from May 18–26, 1836.

"Am I gagged": Register of Debates, 4029–4030.

His objections fell: Register of Debates, 4053.

But Adams was quick: Register of Debates, 4036–4038.

"In your relations": Register of Debates, 4038.

"Suppose Congress were called": Register of Debates, 4040.

James Traub points out: James Traub, *John Quincy Adams: Militant Spirit,* 438.

"The war now raging": Register of Debates, 24 Cong., 1 Sess., 4041.

"Do not you": Register of Debates, 24 Cong., 1 Sess., 4041.

Adams then spun: Register of Debates, 4044.

"The eyes of *millions*": Quoted in James Traub, *John Quincy Adams: Militant Spirit,* 455.

"I gave them a full": John Quincy Adams Digital Diary, July 9, 1836.

"I had free conversation": John Quincy Adams Digital Diary, July 11, 1836.

She must have known: Louisa Thomas, *Louisa,* 181.

CHAPTER 14

His friend and: Quoted in Gilbert Hobbes Barnes, *The Anti-Slavery Impulse,* 84–85.

A local man: Quoted in Gilbert Hobbes Barnes, *The Anti-Slavery Impulse,* 85.

He did not know it: Quoted in Gilbert Hobbes Barnes, *The Anti-Slavery Impulse,* 86.

As William Lloyd Garrison put it: Gilbert Hobbes Barnes, *The Anti-Slavery Impulse,* 104–105. Garrison is quoted on page 103.

William Lee Miller points out: William Lee Miller, *Arguing About Slavery,* 314–316.

With a tone: Angelina Grimke, *Appeal to the Christian Women of the South* (New York: American Anti-Slavery Society, 1836), 2, 9.

She tells her audience: Angelina Grimke, *Appeal to the Christian Women of the South* (New York: American Anti-Slavery Society, 1836), 15.

In 1837, Weld wrote: Theodore Weld, *The Bible Against Slavery* (New York: American Anti-Slavery Society, 1837).

Weld and his colleagues: Gilbert Hobbes Barnes, *The Anti-Slavery Impulse*, 132–135.

Antislavery petitions: Gilbert Hobbes Barnes, *The Anti-Slavery Impulse*, 135–136.

Maybe not: Register of Debates, 24 Cong., 2 Sess., 1587.

Polk replied: Register of Debates, 24 Cong., 2 Sess., 1587.

Another congressman suggested: Register of Debates, 1588.

The only name: Register of Debates, 1589; William Lee Miller, *Arguing About Slavery*, 228–230.

Thompson "resolved": Register of Debates, 24 Cong., 2 Sess., 1590.

Adams stood up: Register of Debates, 1594–1595.

"If the house": Register of Debates, 1595–1596.

"Where, in the land": Register of Debates, 1596.

"I am glad the gentleman": Register of Debates, 1675–1676; William Lee Miller, *Arguing About Slavery*, 252.

"If a member of that": Register of Debates, 24 Cong., 2 Sess., 1679.

"If you once admit": Register of Debates, 1676.

And another that denied: Register of Debates, 1733.

"Van Buren's personal": John Quincy Adams Digital Diary, April 13, 1836, and November 11, 1836.

Martin Van Buren did not: James M. Bradley, *Martin Van Buren*, 319.

The populist wave: James M. Bradley, *Martin Van Buren*, 326–327.

Some nights: John Quincy Adams Digital Diary, May 3, 1837.

The ad then requests: John Quincy Adams Digital Diary, October 23, 1837.

"Were there in the House": John Quincy Adams Digital Diary, November 1, 1837.

When asked why: John Quincy Adams Digital Diary, October 28, 1837.

Her owner would: John Quincy Adams Digital Diary, November 2, 1837.

Adams went home: John Quincy Adams Digital Diary, November 13, 1837.

Adams wrote a check: John Quincy Adams Digital Diary, November 2, 1837.

John Quincy assuredly could relate: John Quincy Adams Digital Diary, September 1, 1837.

"My own family": John Quincy Adams Digital Diary, November 22, 1837; Louis Filler, *The Crusade Against Slavery: 1830–1860* (New York: Harper, 1960), 80; Kevin C. Julius, *The Abolitionist Decade, 1829–1838* (Jefferson, NC: McFarland & Co., 2004), 216.

Adams agreed to write: John Quincy Adams Digital Diary, November 22, 1837.

Before concluding, Lundy warned: Benjamin Lundy to John Quincy Adams, March 26, 1838, Adams Papers, Massachusetts Historical Society.

To the dismay of Adams: Abraham Lincoln, "Lyceum Address," January 27, 1838, *The Collected Works of Abraham Lincoln*, vol. 1, Roy P. Basler, ed. (New Brunswick: Rutgers University Press, 1953–1955), 108–115.

A letter of congratulations: John Quincy Adams to Samuel Webb and William H. Scott, January 19, 1838, Letterbook copy, Adams Papers, Massachusetts Historical Society.

A newspaper later reported: *Washington Globe*, June 11, 1838.

"Those voices without": Samuel Webb, *History of Pennsylvania Hall* (Philadelphia: Marrihew & Gunn, 1838), 123–124.

Garrison would later write: Quoted from Ken Finkel, "The Wedding That Ignited Philadelphia," *The Philly History Blog,* March 14, 2013, https://blog.phillyhistory.org/index.php/2013/05/the-wedding-that-ignited-philadelphia/.
Angelina stiffened her spine: Samuel Webb, *History of Pennsylvania Hall,* 124.
Sugar neither grown: Ken Finkel, "The Wedding That Ignited Philadelphia."
Reports of a mingling: *Washington Globe,* June 11, 1838.
A report from Philadelphia: *Richmond Enquirer,* May 22, 1838.
According to one newspaper: *Richmond Enquirer,* May 22, 1838.
The charred remains: Samuel Webb, *History of Pennsylvania Hall,* 168.
Adams recorded in his diary: John Quincy Adams Digital Diary, May 19, 1838.

CHAPTER 15

One petitioner suggested: Marie B. Hecht, *John Quincy Adams: A Personal History of an Independent Man* (Newtown, CT: American Political Biography Press, 1972), 555–556.
In a moment of weakness: Quoted in Samuel Flagg Bemis, *John Quincy Adams and the Union,* 361–362.
Never "a nation": Quoted in Samuel Flagg Bemis, *John Quincy Adams and the Union,* 362.
Chairman Howard was ready: Quoted in Samuel Flagg Bemis, *John Quincy Adams and the Union,* 368.
"Was this from a son": Quoted in Leonard Falkner, *The President Who Wouldn't Retire* (Coward-McCann, 1967), 195.
Like Captain America: Bob Crawford and James Morrison, "Don't Mess with Texas," *Founding Son: John Quincy's America.* Podcast audio, April 27, 2023, https://www.iheart.com/podcast/1119-founding-son-john-quincys-111619900/episode/founding-son-episode-4-dont-113949678/.
He himself believed: John Quincy Adams Digital Diary, December 13, 1837.
Lundy signed off: Benjamin Lundy to John Quincy Adams, February 2, 1839, Adams Papers, Massachusetts Historical Society.
Published in the *National Intelligencer*: *Daily National Intelligencer* (Washington, DC), April 23, 1839, and May 21, 1839.
The slavocracy had corrupted: *The Voice of Freedom* (Brandon, VT), June 15, 1839.
He never recovered: Benjamin Earle, *The Life, Travels, and Opinions of Benjamin Lundy,* 304–305.
On September 16, Adams wrote: John Quincy Adams Digital Diary, September 16, 1839.
A monumental indictment of slavery: Theodore Weld, *American Slavery as It Is: Testimony of a Thousand Witnesses* (New York: American Anti-Slavery Society, 1839), 1.
It also moved John Quincy: John Quincy Adams Digital Diary, July 23, 1839.

CHAPTER 16

He was chained: Parts of this chapter are adapted from Bob Crawford and James Morrison, "Amistad," *Founding Son: John Quincy's America.* Podcast audio, April 14, 2023, https://www.iheart.com/podcast/1119-founding-son-john-quincys-111619900/episode/founding-son-episode-5-amistad-114410097/.
Overnight, it became a national sensation: Marcus Rediker, *The Amistad Rebellion: An Atlantic Odyssey of Slavery and Freedom* (New York: Penguin Books, 2013), 1–2.
People were talking about the *Amistad*: Marcus Rediker, *The Amistad Rebellion,* 99.
The roughly fifty *Amistad* captives: Marcus Rediker, *The Amistad Rebellion,* 99.

Jay noted that the queen: "Documents Relating to the Africans Taken in the Amistad," *The American and Foreign Anti-Slavery Reporter,* December 1840.

He could not help but write: Samuel Flagg Bemis, *John Quincy Adams and the Union,* 394.

"I fear they will be": John Quincy Adams Digital Diary, September 26, 1839.

Which meant they were slaves: James Traub, *John Quincy Adams: Militant Spirit,* 468.

Adams visited Loring at his office: John Quincy Adams Digital Diary, September 26, 1839.

At least for a little while: *Diary of Charles Francis Adams,* vol. 13, Adams Papers, Massachusetts Historical Society.

Adams consulted legal books: John Quincy Adams Digital Diary, October 2, 1839.

Adams recorded in his diary: John Quincy Adams Digital Diary, October 27, 1840.

"He exposed to me": John Quincy Adams Digital Diary, November 17, 1840; James Traub, *John Quincy Adams: Militant Spirit,* 453.

"The three girls": John Quincy Adams Digital Diary, November 17, 1840.

James Traub notes: "Amistad," *Founding Son: John Quincy's America,* Podcast audio.

He received a letter: Kale to John Quincy Adams, January 4, 1841, Adams Papers, Massachusetts Historical Society.

John Quincy wrote in his diary: John Quincy Adams Digital Diary, February 22, 1841.

"Marshall, Cushing, Chase": *Argument of John Quincy Adams, Before the Supreme Court of the United States in the Case of the United States, Appellants, vs. Cinque, and Others, Africans, Captured in the Schooner Amistad, by Lieut. Gedney, Delivered on the 24th of February and 1st of March, 1841* (New York: S. W. Benedict, 1841).

Richard S. Newman paraphrases: "Amistad," *Founding Son: John Quincy's America.*

"I did not observe the Judges": *Brandon Vermont Telegraph* (Brandon), March 17, 1841.

The court ruled 7–1: Supreme Court of the United States, *United States v. The Amistad,* 40 U.S. 15 Pet. 518. 1841. https://www.loc.gov/item/usrep040518/.

She knew he did the right thing: Charles Francis Adams to John Quincy Adams, March 16, 1841, Adams Papers, Massachusetts Historical Society.

Adams never sent one: John Quincy Adams Digital Diary, November 19, 1841.

CHAPTER 17

"Come when you please": Quoted from James Traub, *John Quincy Adams: Militant Spirit,* 483.

Adams was more cantankerous: John Quincy Adams Digital Diary, April 4, 1841.

A better prospect than: See chapter XVIII of Gilbert Hobbes Barnes, *The Anti-Slavery Impulse* and chapter 33 of William Lee Miller, *Arguing About Slavery.*

He could not accept: "Joshua Reed Giddings, 1795–1864," "William Slade, 1786–1859," and "Seth Merrill Gates, 1800–1877," Biographical Directory of the United States Congress.

Leavitt shot back: Gilbert Hobbes Barnes, *The Anti-Slavery Impulse,* 178–179.

"The more I look at the subject": Theodore Weld to Lewis Tappan, December 14, 1841, *Letters of Theodore Dwight Weld, Angelina Grimke Weld and Sarah Grimke,* vol. 2, 879–882.

Weld also wrote home: "Ann Sprigg," *Bytes of History* blog, 2010, http://bytesofhistory.com/Collections/UGRR/Sprigg_Ann/Sprigg_Ann-Biography.html.

Weld wrote Angelina: Quoted in William Lee Miller, *Arguing About Slavery,* 407.

I was glad: *Letters of Theodore Dwight Weld, Angelina Grimke Weld and Sarah Grimke,* vol. 2, 886.

He took his lunch hour: *Letters of Theodore Dwight Weld, Angelina Grimke Weld and Sarah Grimke,* vol. 2, 889.

Adams also made note: John Quincy Adams Digital Diary, January 8, 1842.

Graham essentially excluded: Jan Whitaker, "Dining with the Grahamites," *Restaurant-ing Through History* blog, 2016, https://restaurant-ingthroughhistory.com/2016/03/06/dining-with-the-grahamites/.

Adams even came up with: Samuel Flagg Bemis, *John Quincy Adams and the Union*, 424.

Weld made sure not to miss it: *Letters of Theodore Dwight Weld, Angelina Grimke Weld and Sarah Grimke*, vol. 2, 899.

Adams, in a high-pitched voice: *The Congressional Globe*, vol. 11, 158.

Congressman Sprigg: *The Congressional Globe*, vol. 11, 159.

Weld said that in the bedlam: *Letters of Theodore Dwight Weld, Angelina Grimke Weld and Sarah Grimke*, vol. 2, 900.

A motion to lay: *The Congressional Globe*, vol. 11, 159.

CHAPTER 18

As Lincoln would say: Samuel Flagg Bemis, *John Quincy Adams and the Union*, 427 see footnotes.

Offered the motion: *The Congressional Globe*, vol. 11, 168.

Giddings recalled: William Lee Miller, *Arguing About Slavery*, 431.

It was time to get to work: William Lee Miller, *Arguing About Slavery*, 432–433.

In the eyes of the South: *The Congressional Globe*, vol. 11, 169–170.

Not a fair fight: *The Congressional Globe*, vol. 11, 180.

"What is high treason": Leonard Falkner, *The President Who Wouldn't Retire*, 252.

"Restore the right of petition": Leonard Falkner, *The President Who Wouldn't Retire*, 253.

Wise accused Adams: William Lee Miller, *Arguing About Slavery*, 438.

In a final insult, Wise said: Leonard Falkner, *The President Who Wouldn't Retire*, 255.

He found Adams: *Letters of Theodore Dwight Weld, Angelina Grimke Weld and Sarah Grimke*, vol. 2, 905.

Emerson wrote in his diary of Adams: Ralph Waldo Emerson, *Journals*, vol. 6, eds. Edward W. Emerson and Waldo E. Forbes (Boston and New York, 1909–1914), 349–350.

"The barrel falls to pieces": *The Congressional Globe*, vol. 11, 198.

Adams included in his defense: John Quincy Adams Digital Diary, February 3, 1842.

Adams received a note of support: Samuel Flagg Bemis, *John Quincy Adams and the Union*, 438.

"The pressure upon my mind": John Quincy Adams Digital Diary, January 31, 1842.

Weld described the battle for Angelina: *Letters of Theodore Dwight Weld, Angelina Grimke Weld and Sarah Grimke*, vol. 2, 911.

Adams wrote in his diary: John Quincy Adams Digital Diary February 5, 1842.

Weld wrote: *Letters of Theodore Dwight Weld, Angelina Grimke Weld and Sarah Grimke*, vol. 2, 913.

He proclaimed: Traub, 493, 436.

Tappan replied: Robert Henry Abzug and Theodore Dwight Weld, *Passionate Liberator* (New York: Oxford University Press, 1980), 245.

CHAPTER 19

Dickens and Adams finally met: "Dickens the 'Literary Monster' Comes to D.C.," Beehive, Massachusetts Historical Society, 2023, www.masshist.org/beehiveblog/2023/11/dickens-the-literary-monster-comes-to-d-c/.

Adams noted: John Quincy Adams Digital Diary, March 13, 1842.

Dickens continued: Charles Dickens, *American Notes* (New York: Penguin Classics, 2001), 132.

"He's hero worshipped": Bob Crawford, *Founding Son: John Quincy's America*, "The Last of Earth." Podcast audio, https://www.iheart.com/podcast/1119-founding-son-john-quincys-111619900/episode/founding-son-episode-6-the-114879367/.

He stopped in Buffalo: John Quincy Adams Digital Diary, October 29, 1843.

"Among the women": John Quincy Adams Digital Diary, November 2, 1843.

He rode in: John Quincy Adams Digital Diary, November 6, 1843.

The event organizers agreed: John Quincy Adams Digital Diary, November 9, 1843.

Adams stated: John Quincy Adams Digital Diary, November 14, 1843.

Adams's perseverance wore him down: James Traub, *John Quincy Adams: Militant Spirit*, 507.

If he had air: William Lee Miller, *Arguing About Slavery*, 469.

Adams again shouted: William Lee Miller, *Arguing About Slavery*, 469.

CHAPTER 20

But the showstopper: Edward Crapol, *John Tyler: The Accidental President* (Chapel Hill: University of North Carolina Press, 2006), 207–209; "Princeton I (Screw Steamer)," *Dictionary of American Naval Fighting Ships*, Navy Department, Naval History and Heritage Command.

Adams had toured: John Quincy Adams Digital Diary, February 20, 1844.

Deeply affected, Adams wrote: John Quincy Adams Digital Diary, March 3, 1844.

Adams later confessed: John Quincy Adams Digital Diary, December 20, 1844.

Tappan knew what they: Edward Crapol, *John Tyler*, 210.

The gage rule fell: *The Congressional Globe*, vol. 14, 7.

Adams wrote in his diary: John Quincy Adams Digital Diary, December 3, 1844.

Calhoun informed Pakenham: *The Works of John C. Calhoun*, vol. 5: *Reports and Public Letters of John C. Calhoun*, ed. Richard K. Crallé (New York: D. Appleton and Co., 1859), 333–339.

Both men came out against: Sean Wilentz, *The Rise of American Democracy*, 567–569.

Jackson biographer David S. Brown: Bob Crawford, "The Last of Earth," *Founding Son: John Quincy's America*. Podcast audio, https://www.iheart.com/podcast/1119-founding-son-john-quincys-111619900/episode/founding-son-episode-6-the-114879367/.

He spoke of Jackson's ingratitude: "The Last of Earth," *Founding Son: John Quincy's America*.

"He gave away half": "The Last of Earth," *Founding Son: John Quincy's America*.

"It is the severest castigation": *Correspondence of Andrew Jackson*, vol. 6, 344–345.

He said to those gathered: This scene and quote are borrowed from Jon Meacham, *American Lion*, chapter 34.

"Jackson was a hero": John Quincy Adams Digital Diary, June 18, 1845.

The territories in question: Chris DeRose, *Congressman Lincoln: The Making of America's Greatest President*, 57.

"Unrighteous war": John Quincy Adams Digital Diary, May 11, 1846.

"Whatever territory might be acquired": *The Congressional Globe*, vol. 15, 1214.

The Wilmot Proviso passed: David M. Potter and Don E. Fehrenbacher, *The Impending Crisis: America Before the Civil War: 1848–1861* (New York: Harper & Row, 1976), 20–22.

His entries became: John Quincy Adams Digital Diary, March 14, 1847.

"From the time": John Quincy Adams to Charles Francis Adams, December 7, 1847, Adams Papers, Massachusetts Historical Society.

They were the last words: John Quincy Adams to Charles Francis Adams, January 1, 1848.

Adams is reported: Chris DeRose, *Congressman Lincoln: The Making of America's Greatest President*, 157.

He was overheard whispering: James Traub, *John Quincy Adams: Militant Spirit*, 525–527. There is debate as to whether Adams said "last of earth" or "end of earth," but "I am content" or "I am composed." I will not go over every example but a few for illustration. Faulkner records his last words, "They heard him whisper, 'This is the last of earth.' A silence, then 'I am content.'" In Traub's book on page 306, like Bemis, he favors Adams's last words as described by John G. Palfrey who wrote to Charles Francis, "Dr. Payton [*sic*] tells me he [JQA] has just said: 'This is the end of earth, but I am composed [*sic*].'" A reporter from the *National Intelligencer* who was in the house at the time recorded the same but omitted the word "but." Bemis, *John Quincy Adams and the Union*, 536.

"I was *forced* to leave": Louisa Catherine Adams to Harriet Boyd, April 8, 1848, Tanner Family Papers, Wisconsin Historical Society.

"He dies in the harness": *Cambridge Chronicle*, March 2, 1848.

When he finally arrived: "'He has been the great landmark of my life': Charles Francis Adams on John Quincy Adams's Death and Legacy," Beehive, Massachusetts Historical Society, 2018.

People gathered along the tracks: Samuel Flagg Bemis, *John Quincy Adams and the Union*, 540.

"Thy fiat has gone forth": *Diary and Autobiographical Writings of Louisa Catherine Adams*, 770.

"He died, as he must": *Diary of Philip Hone*, 341.

EPILOGUE

For almost twelve more years: John Quincy Adams Digital Diary, June 19, 1836.

John Quincy was proud: John Quincy Adams Digital Diary, February 23, 1844.

George Washington once said: George Washington to John Adams, February 20, 1797, Adams Papers, Massachusetts Historical Society.

A letter from Secretary: Charles Francis Adams, October 4, 1862, diary entry, Adams Papers, Massachusetts Historical Society.

INDEX

Illustrations are indicated by *italic* page references.

ABOUT THE AUTHOR

Best known as the bassist for the Avett Brothers, **Bob Crawford** brings decades of musicality to his historical work, infusing it with rhythm, urgency, and heart. He is the host of *American History Hotline* on iHeartRadio and cohost of *The Road to Now* on SiriusXM's POTUS channel, where he engages public figures and scholars in conversations that connect the past to the present. Crawford also serves as comanaging partner of the Press On Fund, a nonprofit dedicated to advancing pediatric cancer research. Whether on stage, on air, or on the page, Crawford invites audiences to reckon with America's unfinished story—and to find courage in those who speak truth to power.